# INCOGNEGRO

VERTIGO
DC COMICS

WRITTEN BY MAT JOHNSON

ART BY WARREN PLEECE

# INCOGNEGRO

LETTERED BY CLEM ROBINS

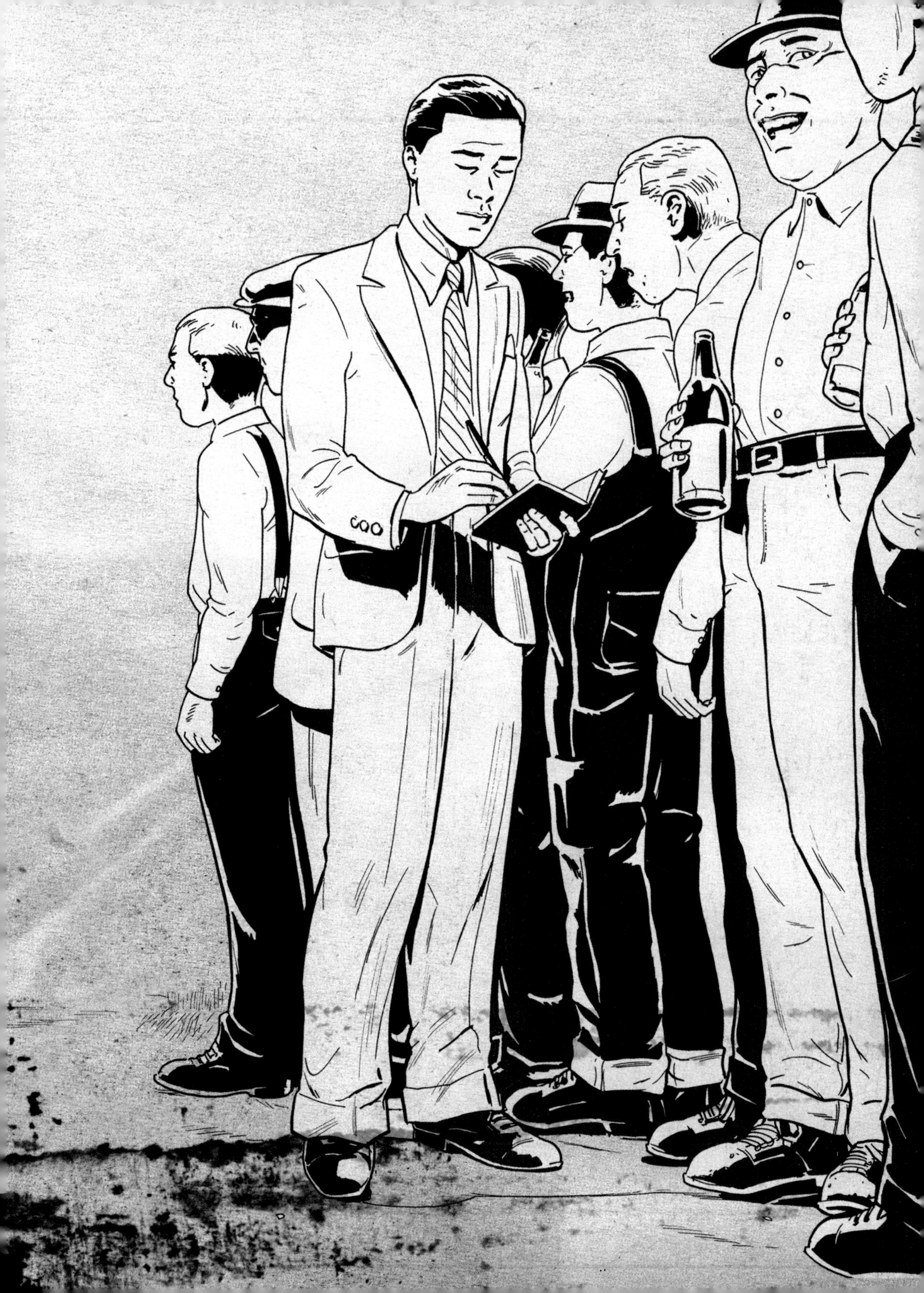

# Author's Note

I grew up a black boy who looked white. This was in a predominantly African-American neighborhood, during the height of the Black Power era, so I stood out a bit. My mom even got me a dashiki so I could fit in with the other kids, but the contrast between the colorful African garb and my nearly blond, straight brown hair just made things worse. Along with my cousin (half black/half Jewish) I started fantasizing about living in another time, another situation, where my ethnic appearance would be an asset instead of a burden. We would "go Incognegro," we told ourselves as we ran around, pretending to be race spies in the war against white supremacy.

I forgot my "Incognegro" dreams until college, when I read about Walter White, the former head of the NAACP. White was an African-American even paler than I was. In the early 20th century, White went undercover, posing as a white man in the deep south to investigate lynchings. It was as if my little childhood fantasy had come to life. From then on, the idea continued to gestate. I started feeling that what once seemed silly was turning into something I had to write about.

The birth of my twins in 2005, one of whom is brown-skinned with black Afro hair, the other with the palest of pink skins and more European curly hair, brought the rest of the story home to me. Two people with the exact same ethnic lineage destined to be viewed differently only because of genetic randomness. From there, the story found itself.

*And now it finds you.*

**— Mat Johnson**

**Karen Berger** Sr. VP-Executive Editor **Jonathan Vankin** Editor **Mark Doyle** Assistant Editor **Louis Prandi** Art Director
**Paul Levitz** President & Publisher **Georg Brewer** VP-Design & DC Direct Creative **Richard Bruning** Sr. VP-Creative Director
**Patrick Caldon** Exec. VP-Finance & Operations **Chris Caramalis** VP-Finance **John Cunningham** VP-Marketing
**Terri Cunningham** VP-Managing Editor **Alison Gill** VP-Manufacturing **David Hyde** VP-Publicity
**Hank Kanalz** VP-General Manager, WildStorm **Jim Lee** Editorial Director-WildStorm **Paula Lowitt** Sr. VP-Business & Legal Affairs
**MaryEllen McLaughlin** VP-Advertising & Custom Publishing **John Nee** Sr. VP-Business Development
**Gregory Noveck** Sr. VP-Creative Affairs **Sue Pohja** VP-Book Trade Sales **Steve Rotterdam** Sr. VP-Sales & Marketing
**Cheryl Rubin** Sr. VP-Brand Management **Jeff Trojan** VP-Business Development, DC Direct **Bob Wayne** VP-Sales
Cover photograph by **Stephen John Phillips**

INCOGNEGRO Published by DC Comics, 1700 Broadway, New York, NY 10019.  Printed in Canada. First Printing. DC Comics, a Warner Bros. Entertainment Company.
ISBN: 1-4012-1097-X ISBN 13: 978-1-4012-1097-7

# PART I

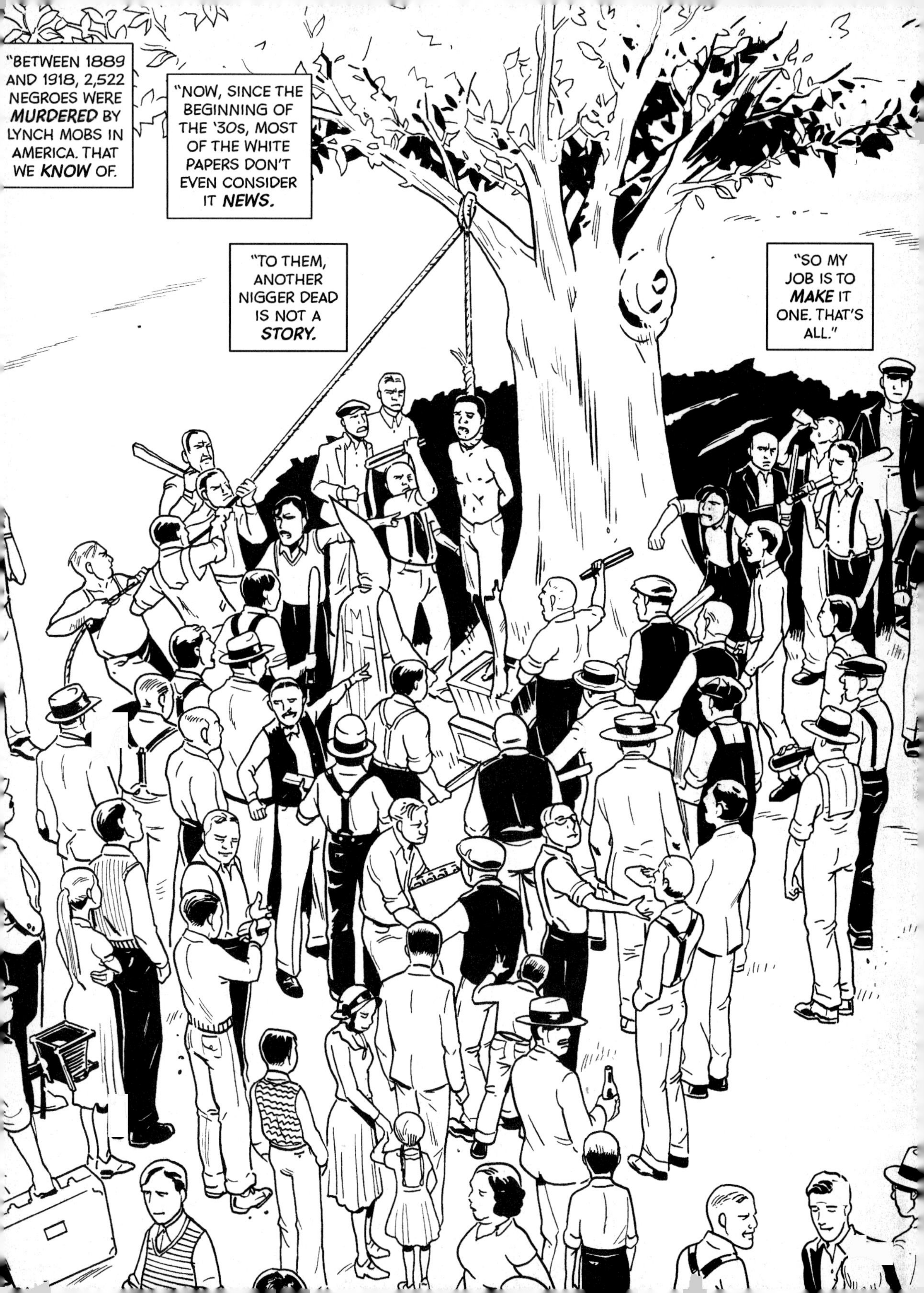
"BETWEEN 1889 AND 1918, 2,522 NEGROES WERE MURDERED BY LYNCH MOBS IN AMERICA. THAT WE KNOW OF.
"NOW, SINCE THE BEGINNING OF THE '30s, MOST OF THE WHITE PAPERS DON'T EVEN CONSIDER IT NEWS.
"TO THEM, ANOTHER NIGGER DEAD IS NOT A STORY.
"SO MY JOB IS TO MAKE IT ONE. THAT'S ALL."

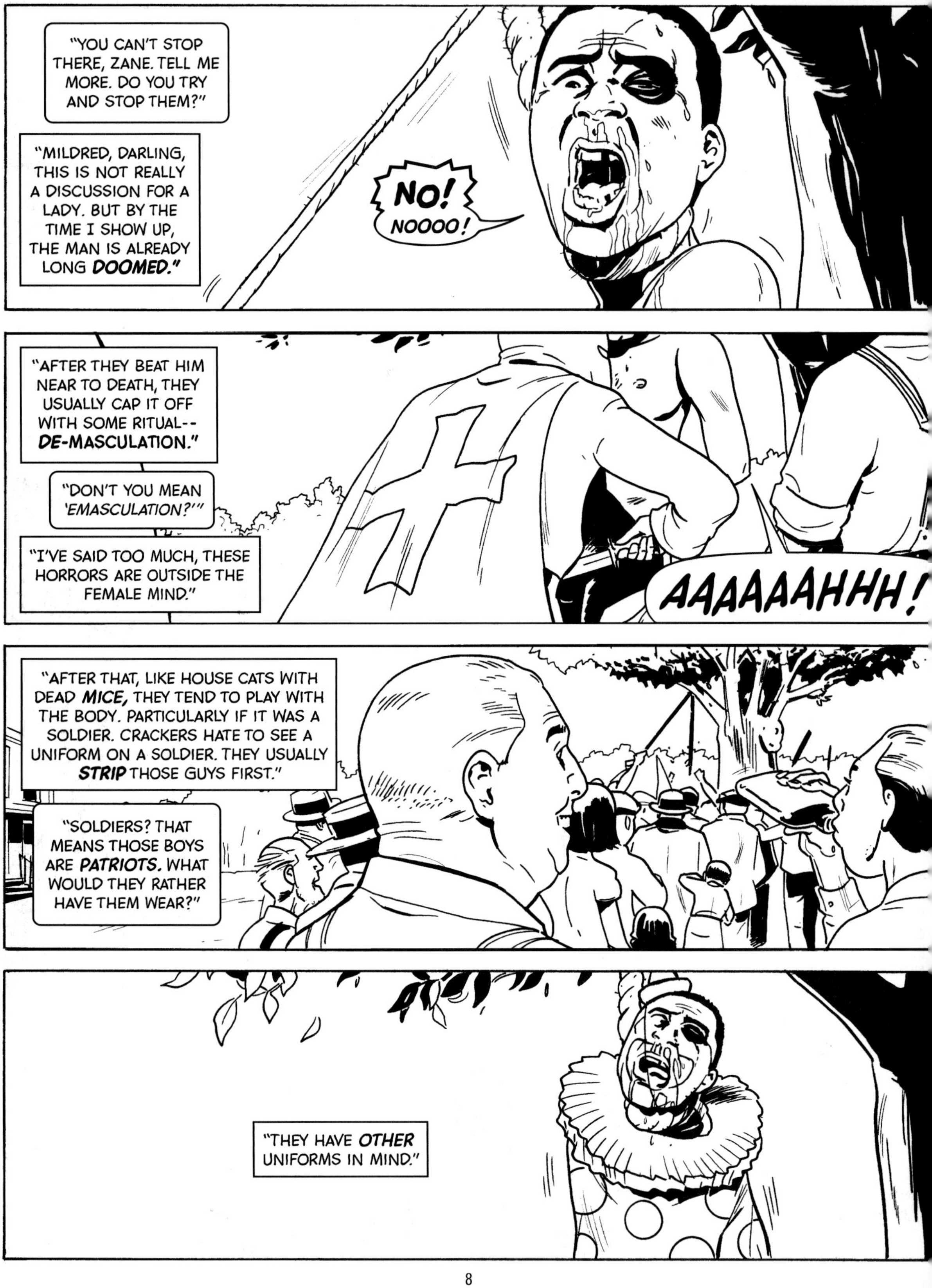
"YOU CAN'T STOP THERE, ZANE. TELL ME MORE. DO YOU TRY AND STOP THEM?"
"MILDRED, DARLING, THIS IS NOT REALLY A DISCUSSION FOR A LADY. BUT BY THE TIME I SHOW UP, THE MAN IS ALREADY LONG DOOMED."
NO! NOOOO!
"AFTER THEY BEAT HIM NEAR TO DEATH, THEY USUALLY CAP IT OFF WITH SOME RITUAL-- DE-MASCULATION."
"DON'T YOU MEAN 'EMASCULATION?'"
"I'VE SAID TOO MUCH, THESE HORRORS ARE OUTSIDE THE FEMALE MIND."
AAAAAAHHH!
"AFTER THAT, LIKE HOUSE CATS WITH DEAD MICE, THEY TEND TO PLAY WITH THE BODY. PARTICULARLY IF IT WAS A SOLDIER. CRACKERS HATE TO SEE A UNIFORM ON A SOLDIER. THEY USUALLY STRIP THOSE GUYS FIRST."
"SOLDIERS? THAT MEANS THOSE BOYS ARE PATRIOTS. WHAT WOULD THEY RATHER HAVE THEM WEAR?"
"THEY HAVE OTHER UNIFORMS IN MIND."

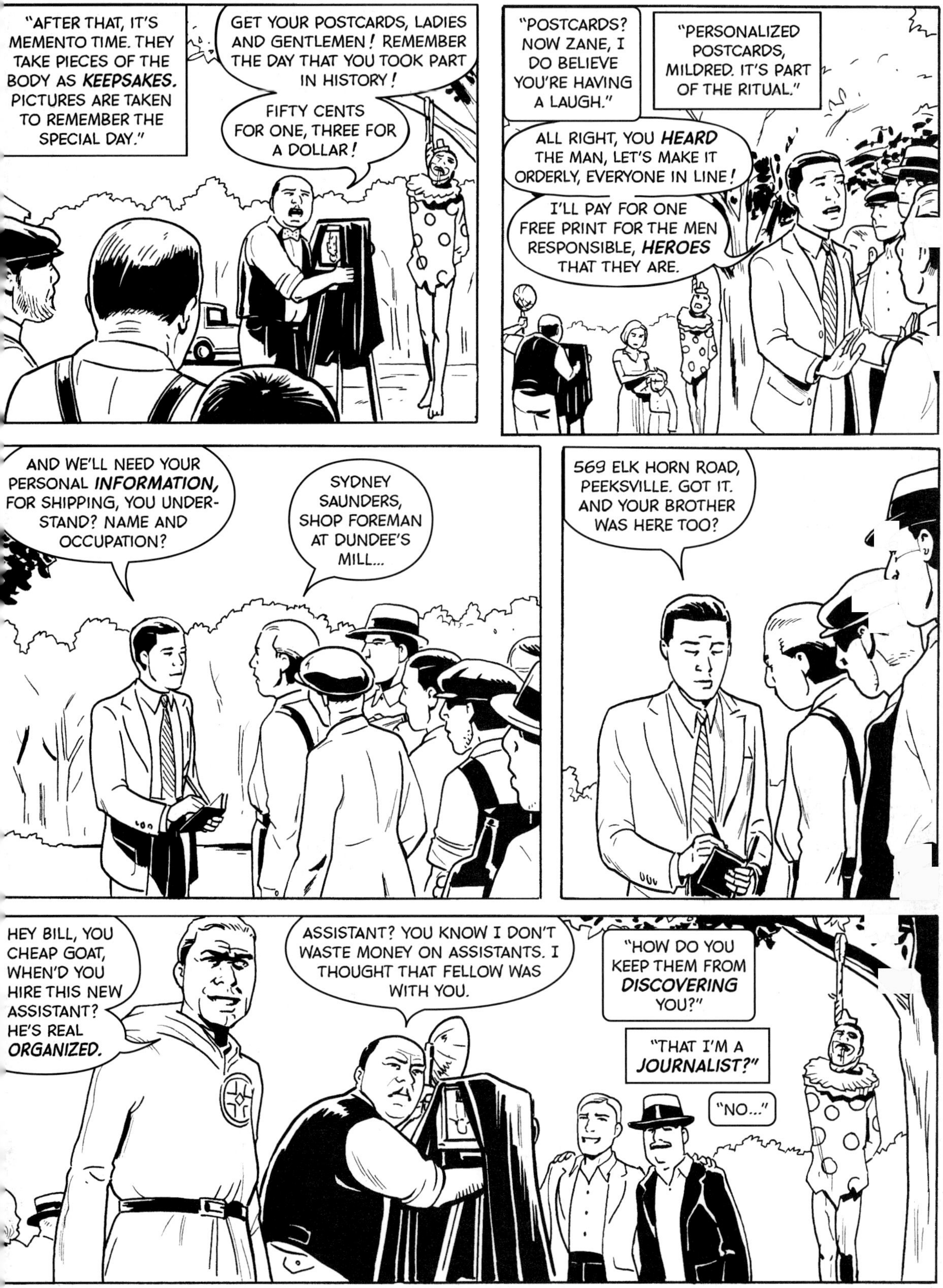
"AFTER THAT, IT'S MEMENTO TIME. THEY TAKE PIECES OF THE BODY AS KEEPSAKES. PICTURES ARE TAKEN TO REMEMBER THE SPECIAL DAY."
GET YOUR POSTCARDS, LADIES AND GENTLEMEN! REMEMBER THE DAY THAT YOU TOOK PART IN HISTORY!
FIFTY CENTS FOR ONE, THREE FOR A DOLLAR!
"POSTCARDS? NOW ZANE, I DO BELIEVE YOU'RE HAVING A LAUGH."
"PERSONALIZED POSTCARDS, MILDRED. IT'S PART OF THE RITUAL."
ALL RIGHT, YOU HEARD THE MAN, LET'S MAKE IT ORDERLY, EVERYONE IN LINE!
I'LL PAY FOR ONE FREE PRINT FOR THE MEN RESPONSIBLE, HEROES THAT THEY ARE.
AND WE'LL NEED YOUR PERSONAL INFORMATION, FOR SHIPPING, YOU UNDERSTAND? NAME AND OCCUPATION?
SYDNEY SAUNDERS, SHOP FOREMAN AT DUNDEE'S MILL...
569 ELK HORN ROAD, PEEKSVILLE. GOT IT. AND YOUR BROTHER WAS HERE TOO?
HEY BILL, YOU CHEAP GOAT, WHEN'D YOU HIRE THIS NEW ASSISTANT? HE'S REAL ORGANIZED.
ASSISTANT? YOU KNOW I DON'T WASTE MONEY ON ASSISTANTS. I THOUGHT THAT FELLOW WAS WITH YOU.
"HOW DO YOU KEEP THEM FROM DISCOVERING YOU?"
"THAT I'M A JOURNALIST?"
"NO..."

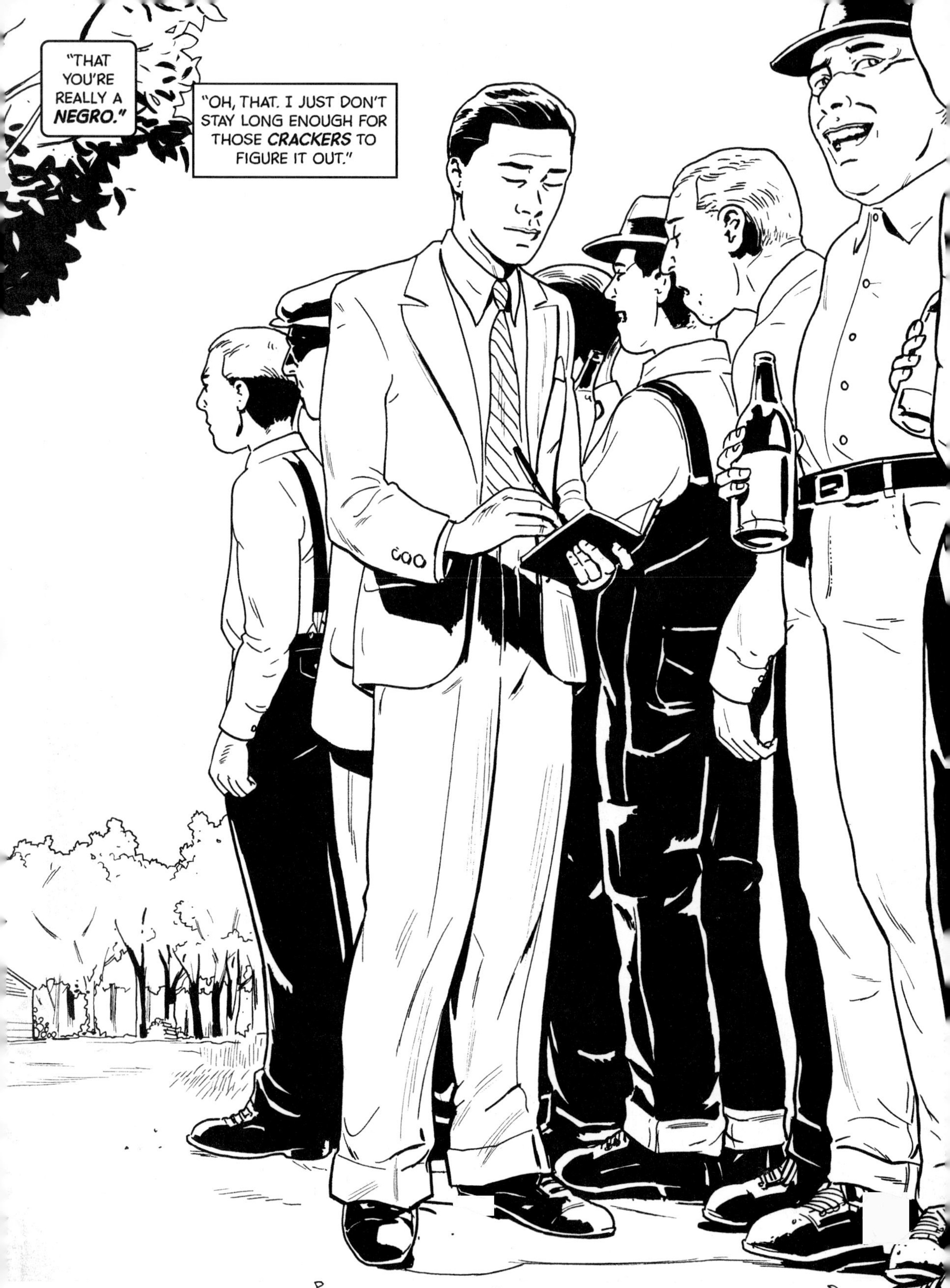
"THAT YOU'RE REALLY A NEGRO."
"OH, THAT. I JUST DON'T STAY LONG ENOUGH FOR THOSE CRACKERS TO FIGURE IT OUT."

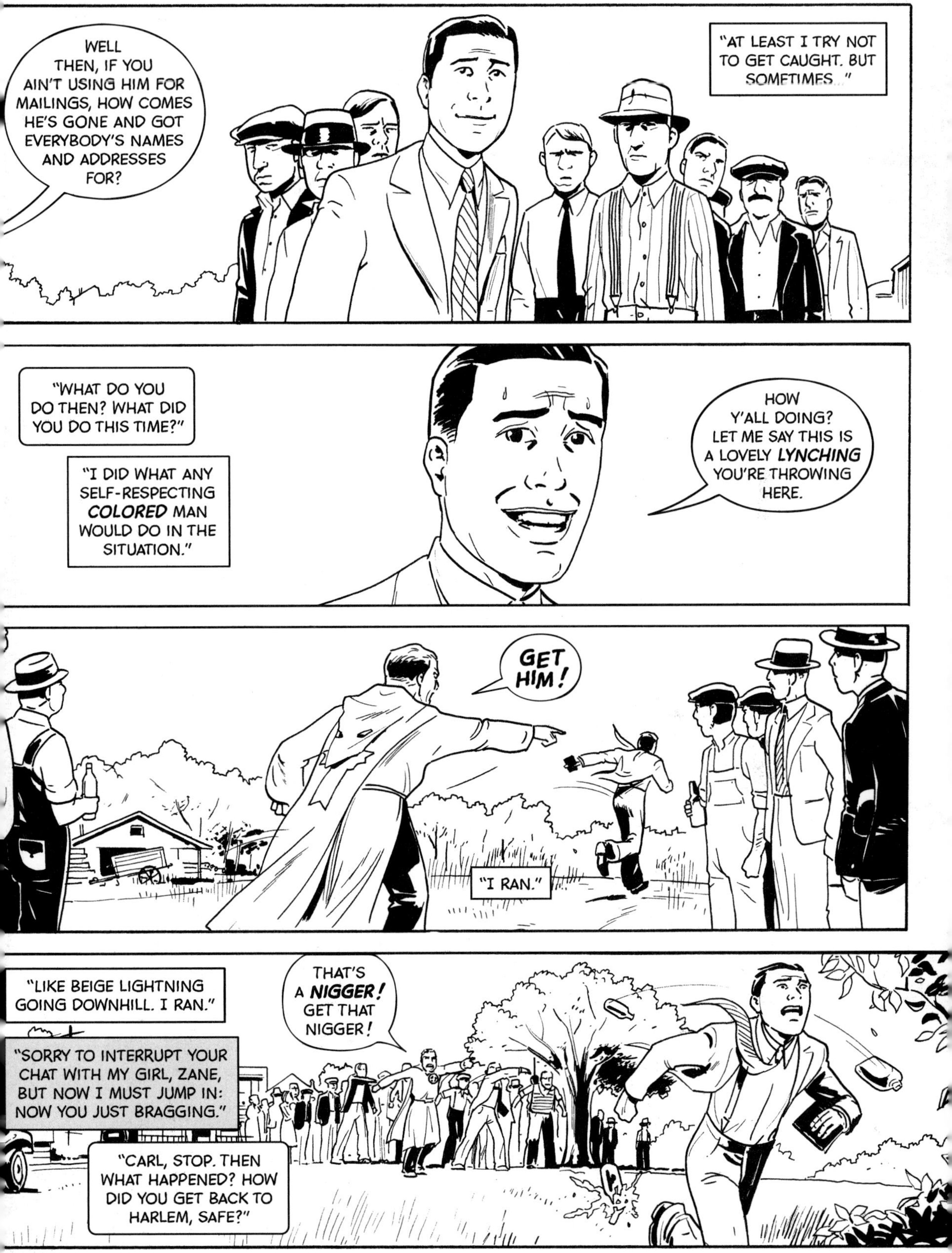
WELL THEN, IF YOU AIN'T USING HIM FOR MAILINGS, HOW COMES HE'S GONE AND GOT EVERYBODY'S NAMES AND ADDRESSES FOR?
"AT LEAST I TRY NOT TO GET CAUGHT. BUT SOMETIMES..."
"WHAT DO YOU DO THEN? WHAT DID YOU DO THIS TIME?"
"I DID WHAT ANY SELF-RESPECTING COLORED MAN WOULD DO IN THE SITUATION."
HOW Y'ALL DOING? LET ME SAY THIS IS A LOVELY LYNCHING YOU'RE THROWING HERE.
GET HIM!
"I RAN."
"LIKE BEIGE LIGHTNING GOING DOWNHILL. I RAN."
THAT'S A NIGGER! GET THAT NIGGER!
"SORRY TO INTERRUPT YOUR CHAT WITH MY GIRL, ZANE, BUT NOW I MUST JUMP IN: NOW YOU JUST BRAGGING."
"CARL, STOP. THEN WHAT HAPPENED? HOW DID YOU GET BACK TO HARLEM, SAFE?"

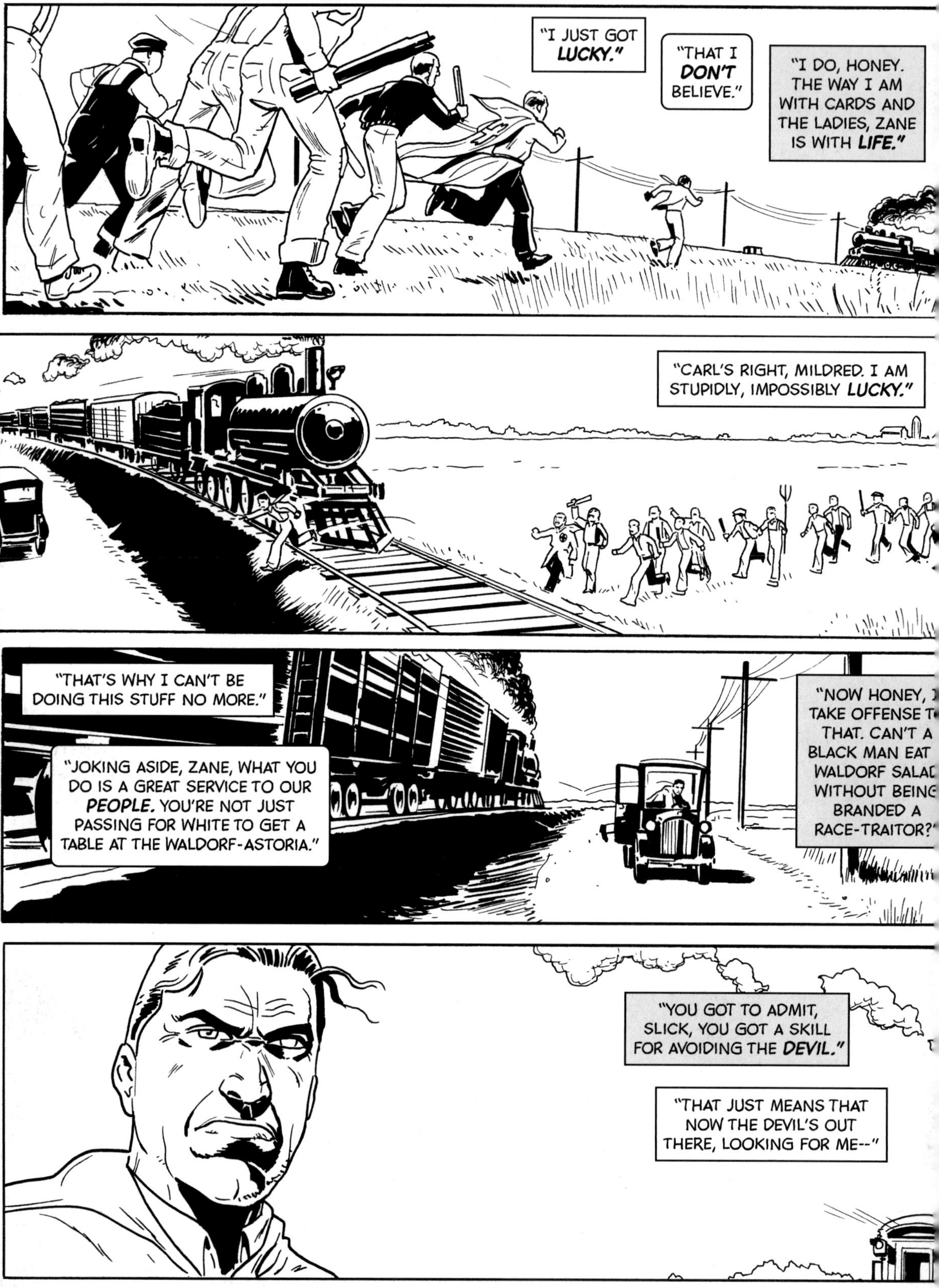
"I JUST GOT LUCKY."
"THAT I DON'T BELIEVE."
"I DO, HONEY. THE WAY I AM WITH CARDS AND THE LADIES, ZANE IS WITH LIFE."
"CARL'S RIGHT, MILDRED. I AM STUPIDLY, IMPOSSIBLY LUCKY."
"THAT'S WHY I CAN'T BE DOING THIS STUFF NO MORE."
"JOKING ASIDE, ZANE, WHAT YOU DO IS A GREAT SERVICE TO OUR PEOPLE. YOU'RE NOT JUST PASSING FOR WHITE TO GET A TABLE AT THE WALDORF-ASTORIA."
"NOW HONEY, I TAKE OFFENSE TO THAT. CAN'T A BLACK MAN EAT WALDORF SALAD WITHOUT BEING BRANDED A RACE-TRAITOR?"
"YOU GOT TO ADMIT, SLICK, YOU GOT A SKILL FOR AVOIDING THE DEVIL."
"THAT JUST MEANS THAT NOW THE DEVIL'S OUT THERE, LOOKING FOR ME--"

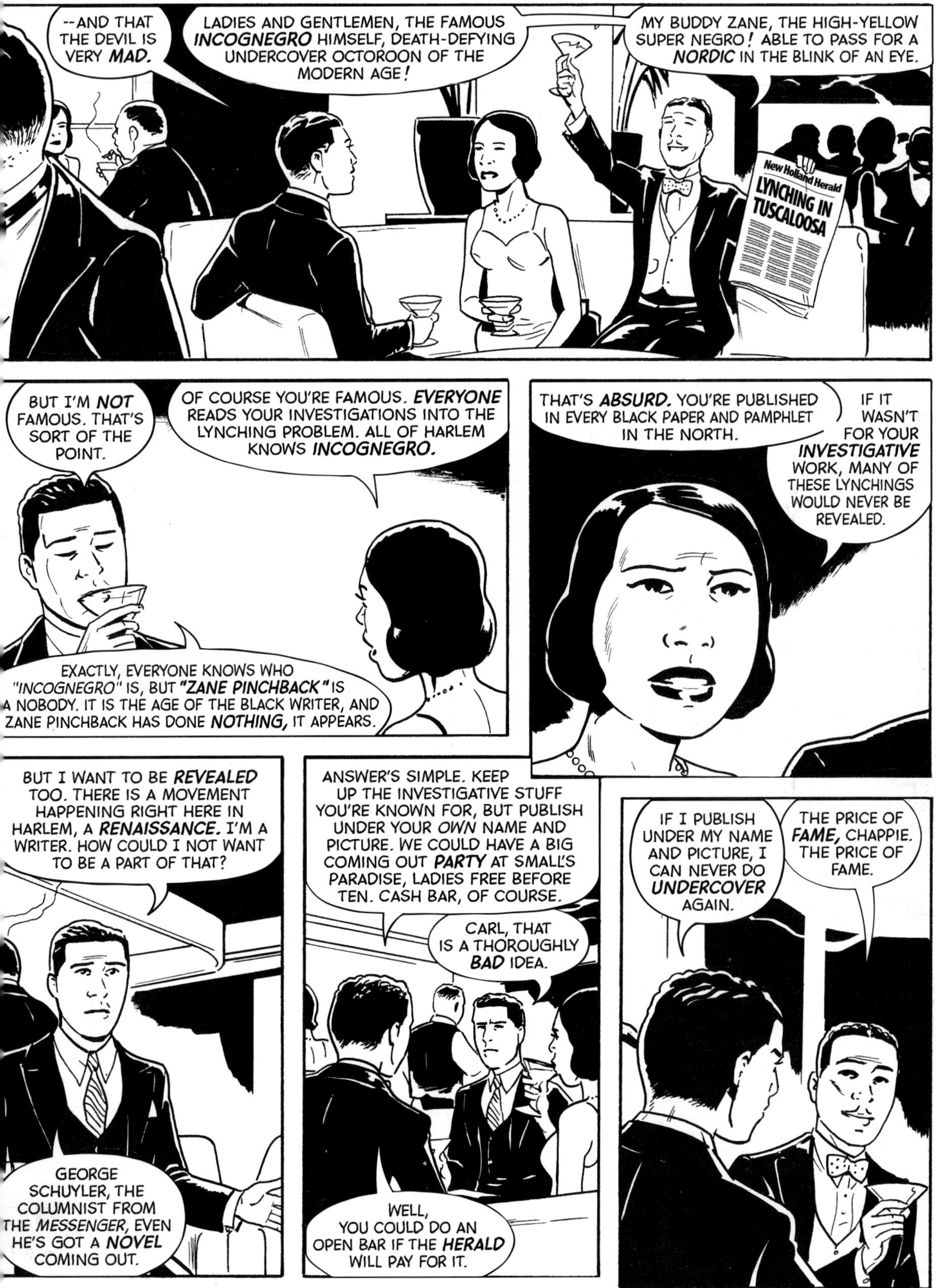
--AND THAT THE DEVIL IS VERY MAD.
LADIES AND GENTLEMEN, THE FAMOUS INCOGNEGRO HIMSELF, DEATH-DEFYING UNDERCOVER OCTOROON OF THE MODERN AGE!
MY BUDDY ZANE, THE HIGH-YELLOW SUPER NEGRO! ABLE TO PASS FOR A NORDIC IN THE BLINK OF AN EYE.
New Holland Herald
LYNCHING IN TUSCALOOSA
BUT I'M NOT FAMOUS. THAT'S SORT OF THE POINT.
OF COURSE YOU'RE FAMOUS. EVERYONE READS YOUR INVESTIGATIONS INTO THE LYNCHING PROBLEM. ALL OF HARLEM KNOWS INCOGNEGRO.
EXACTLY, EVERYONE KNOWS WHO "INCOGNEGRO" IS, BUT "ZANE PINCHBACK" IS A NOBODY. IT IS THE AGE OF THE BLACK WRITER, AND ZANE PINCHBACK HAS DONE NOTHING, IT APPEARS.
THAT'S ABSURD. YOU'RE PUBLISHED IN EVERY BLACK PAPER AND PAMPHLET IN THE NORTH.
IF IT WASN'T FOR YOUR INVESTIGATIVE WORK, MANY OF THESE LYNCHINGS WOULD NEVER BE REVEALED.
BUT I WANT TO BE REVEALED TOO. THERE IS A MOVEMENT HAPPENING RIGHT HERE IN HARLEM, A RENAISSANCE. I'M A WRITER. HOW COULD I NOT WANT TO BE A PART OF THAT?
GEORGE SCHUYLER, THE COLUMNIST FROM THE MESSENGER, EVEN HE'S GOT A NOVEL COMING OUT.
ANSWER'S SIMPLE. KEEP UP THE INVESTIGATIVE STUFF YOU'RE KNOWN FOR, BUT PUBLISH UNDER YOUR OWN NAME AND PICTURE. WE COULD HAVE A BIG COMING OUT PARTY AT SMALL'S PARADISE, LADIES FREE BEFORE TEN. CASH BAR, OF COURSE.
CARL, THAT IS A THOROUGHLY BAD IDEA.
WELL, YOU COULD DO AN OPEN BAR IF THE HERALD WILL PAY FOR IT.
IF I PUBLISH UNDER MY NAME AND PICTURE, I CAN NEVER DO UNDERCOVER AGAIN.
THE PRICE OF FAME, CHAPPIE. THE PRICE OF FAME.

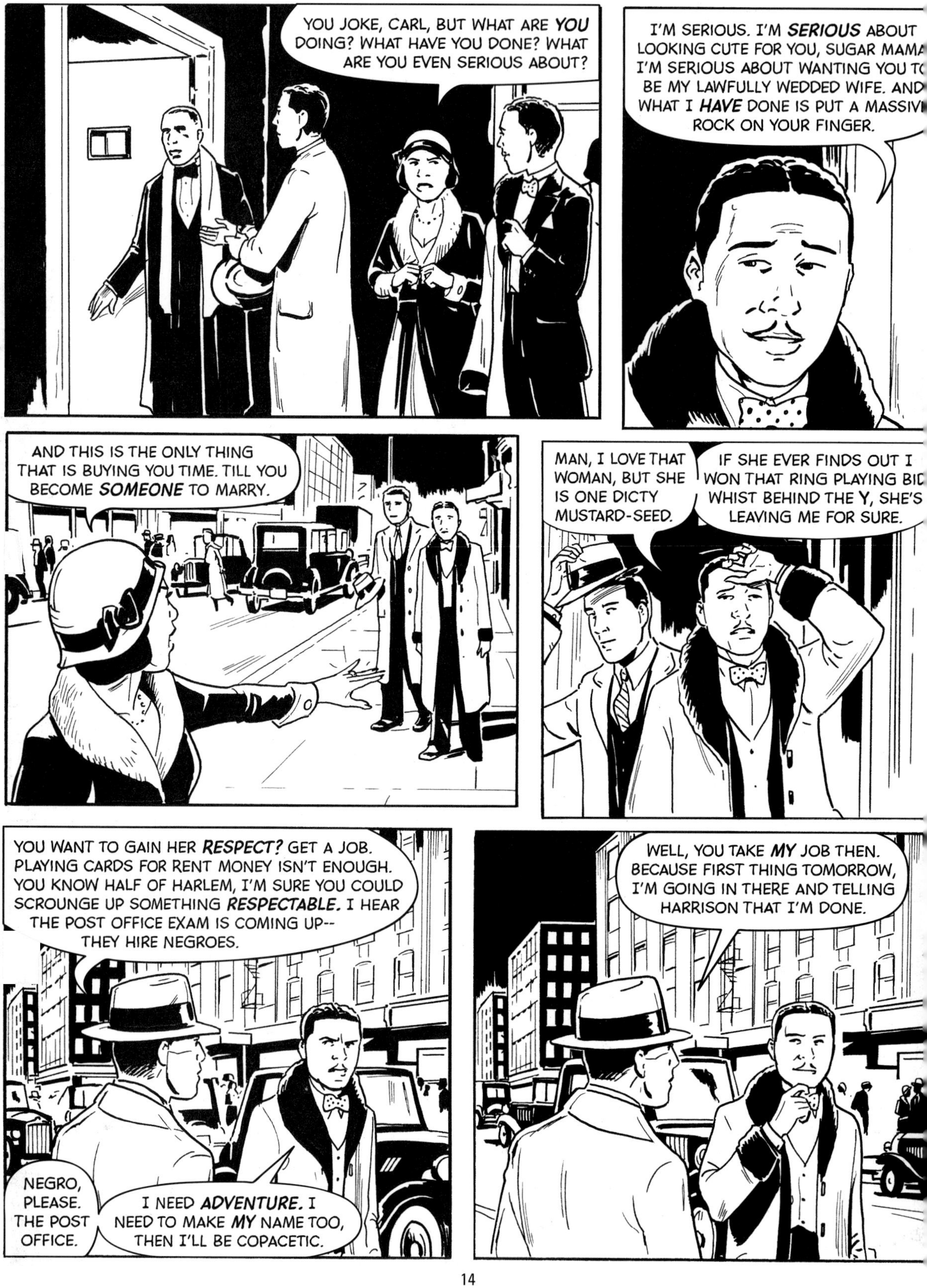
YOU JOKE, CARL, BUT WHAT ARE *YOU* DOING? WHAT HAVE YOU DONE? WHAT ARE YOU EVEN SERIOUS ABOUT?
I'M SERIOUS. I'M ***SERIOUS*** ABOUT LOOKING CUTE FOR YOU, SUGAR MAMA I'M SERIOUS ABOUT WANTING YOU T BE MY LAWFULLY WEDDED WIFE. AND WHAT I ***HAVE*** DONE IS PUT A MASSIV ROCK ON YOUR FINGER.
AND THIS IS THE ONLY THING THAT IS BUYING YOU TIME. TILL YOU BECOME ***SOMEONE*** TO MARRY.
MAN, I LOVE THAT WOMAN, BUT SHE IS ONE DICTY MUSTARD-SEED.
IF SHE EVER FINDS OUT I WON THAT RING PLAYING BI WHIST BEHIND THE **Y**, SHE'S LEAVING ME FOR SURE.
YOU WANT TO GAIN HER ***RESPECT?*** GET A JOB. PLAYING CARDS FOR RENT MONEY ISN'T ENOUGH. YOU KNOW HALF OF HARLEM, I'M SURE YOU COULD SCROUNGE UP SOMETHING ***RESPECTABLE.*** I HEAR THE POST OFFICE EXAM IS COMING UP-- THEY HIRE NEGROES.
NEGRO, PLEASE. THE POST OFFICE.
I NEED ***ADVENTURE.*** I NEED TO MAKE ***MY*** NAME TOO, THEN I'LL BE COPACETIC.
WELL, YOU TAKE ***MY*** JOB THEN. BECAUSE FIRST THING TOMORROW, I'M GOING IN THERE AND TELLING HARRISON THAT I'M DONE.

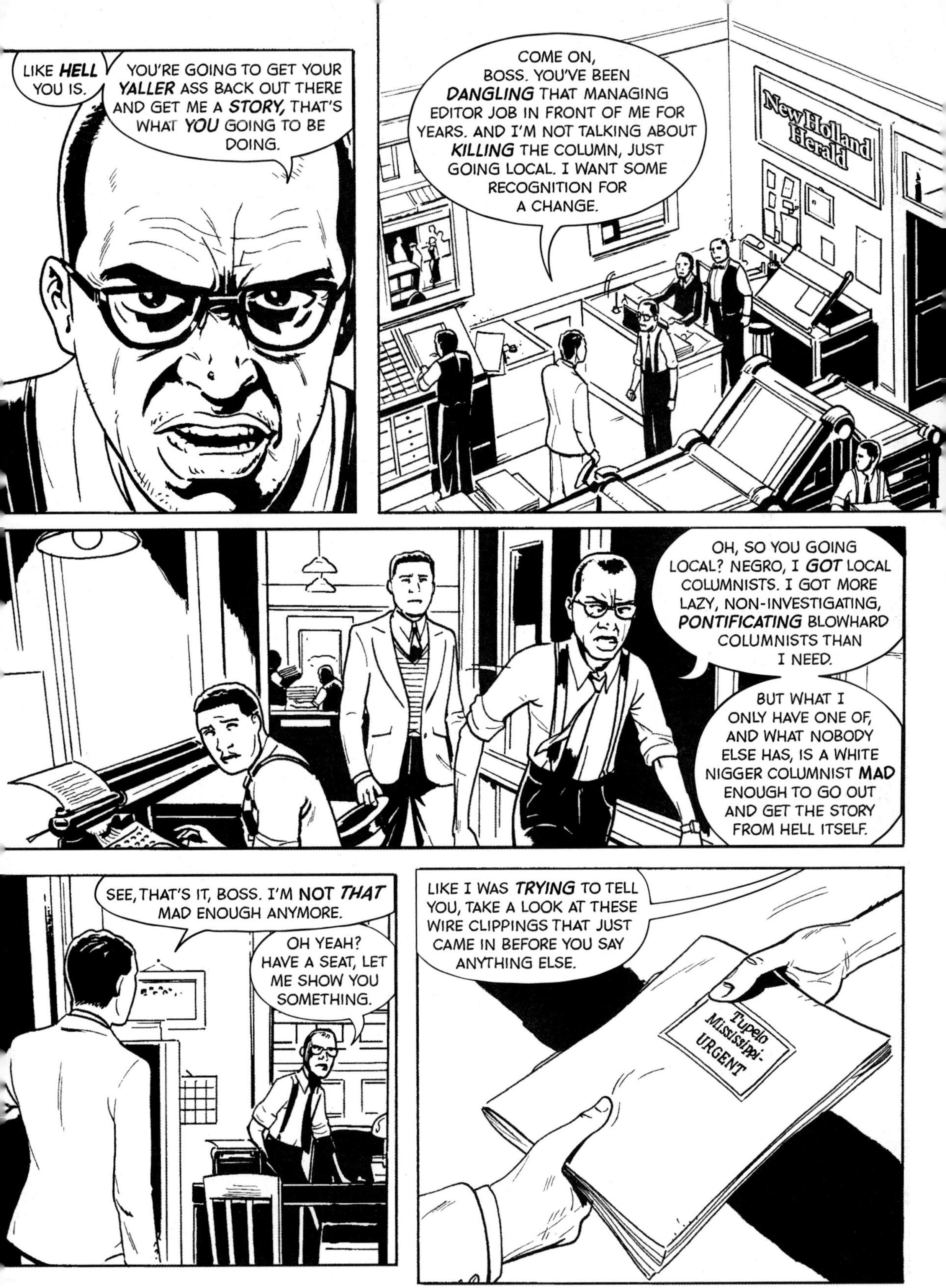
LIKE HELL YOU IS.
YOU'RE GOING TO GET YOUR YALLER ASS BACK OUT THERE AND GET ME A STORY, THAT'S WHAT YOU GOING TO BE DOING.
COME ON, BOSS. YOU'VE BEEN DANGLING THAT MANAGING EDITOR JOB IN FRONT OF ME FOR YEARS. AND I'M NOT TALKING ABOUT KILLING THE COLUMN, JUST GOING LOCAL. I WANT SOME RECOGNITION FOR A CHANGE.
New Holland Herald
OH, SO YOU GOING LOCAL? NEGRO, I GOT LOCAL COLUMNISTS. I GOT MORE LAZY, NON-INVESTIGATING, PONTIFICATING BLOWHARD COLUMNISTS THAN I NEED.
BUT WHAT I ONLY HAVE ONE OF, AND WHAT NOBODY ELSE HAS, IS A WHITE NIGGER COLUMNIST MAD ENOUGH TO GO OUT AND GET THE STORY FROM HELL ITSELF.
SEE, THAT'S IT, BOSS. I'M NOT THAT MAD ENOUGH ANYMORE.
OH YEAH? HAVE A SEAT, LET ME SHOW YOU SOMETHING.
LIKE I WAS TRYING TO TELL YOU, TAKE A LOOK AT THESE WIRE CLIPPINGS THAT JUST CAME IN BEFORE YOU SAY ANYTHING ELSE.
Tupelo Mississippi- URGENT

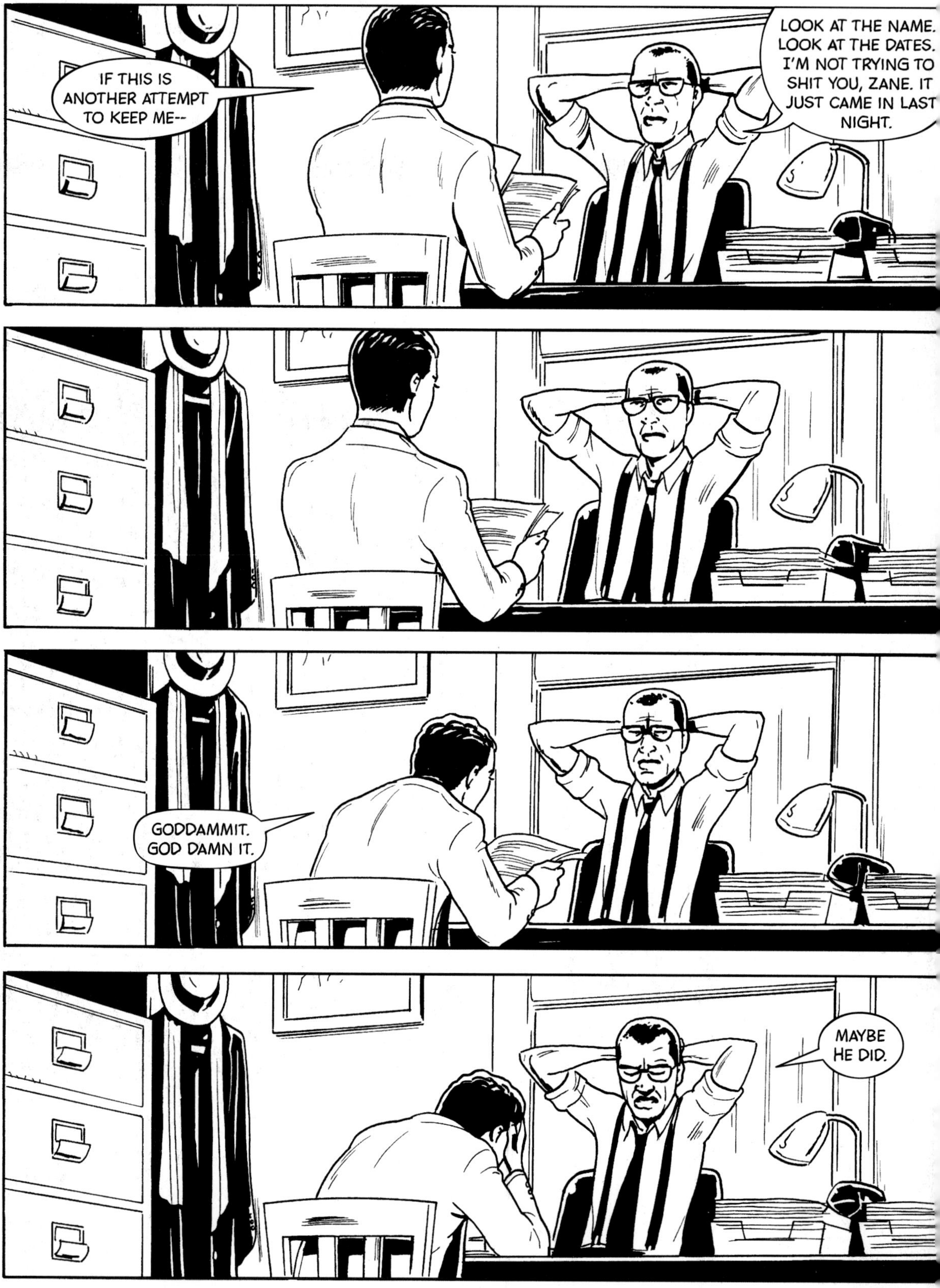
IF THIS IS ANOTHER ATTEMPT TO KEEP ME--
LOOK AT THE NAME. LOOK AT THE DATES. I'M NOT TRYING TO SHIT YOU, ZANE. IT JUST CAME IN LAST NIGHT.
GODDAMMIT. GOD DAMN IT.
MAYBE HE DID.

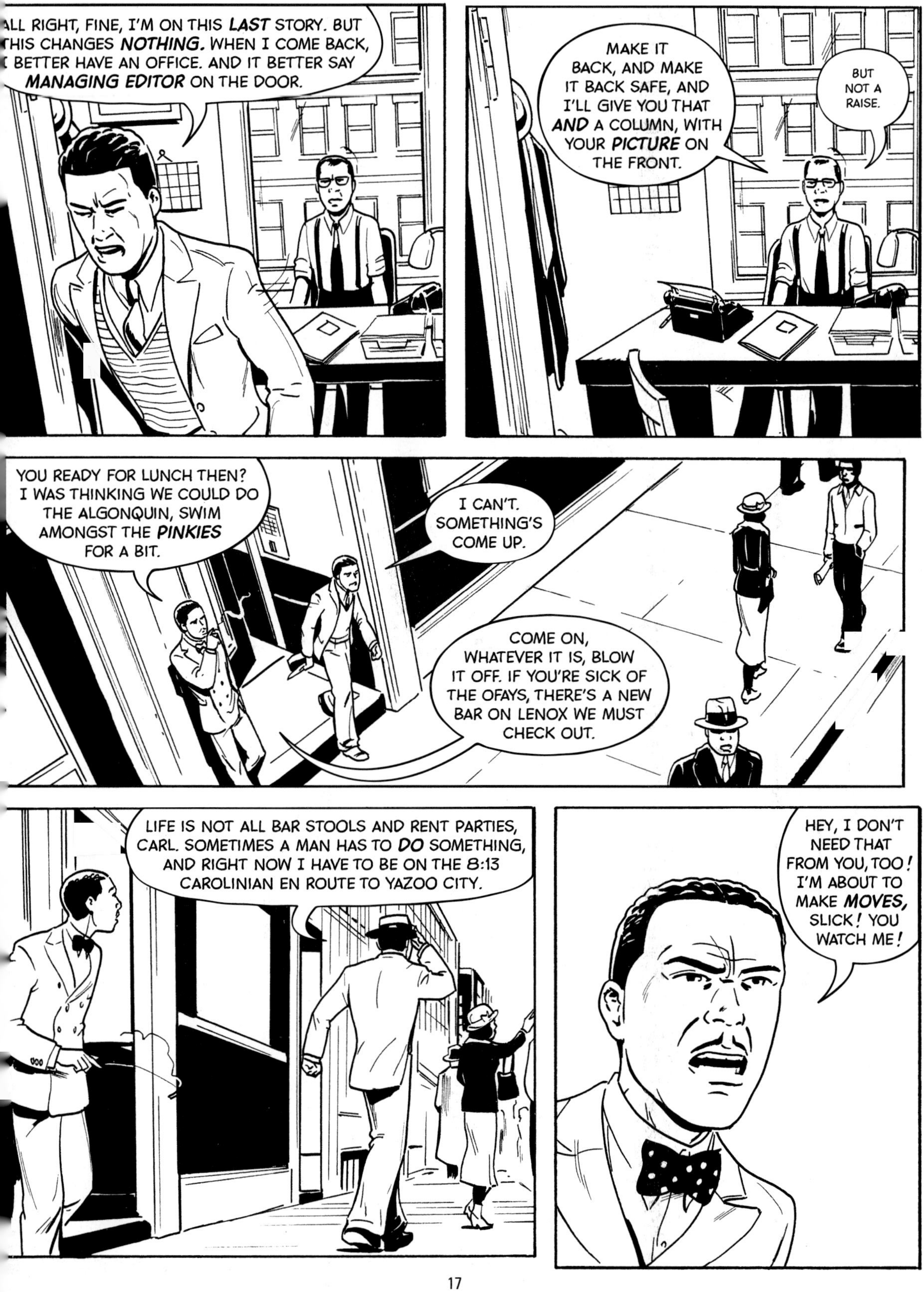
ALL RIGHT, FINE, I'M ON THIS LAST STORY. BUT THIS CHANGES NOTHING. WHEN I COME BACK, I BETTER HAVE AN OFFICE. AND IT BETTER SAY MANAGING EDITOR ON THE DOOR.
MAKE IT BACK, AND MAKE IT BACK SAFE, AND I'LL GIVE YOU THAT AND A COLUMN, WITH YOUR PICTURE ON THE FRONT.
BUT NOT A RAISE.
YOU READY FOR LUNCH THEN? I WAS THINKING WE COULD DO THE ALGONQUIN, SWIM AMONGST THE PINKIES FOR A BIT.
I CAN'T. SOMETHING'S COME UP.
COME ON, WHATEVER IT IS, BLOW IT OFF. IF YOU'RE SICK OF THE OFAYS, THERE'S A NEW BAR ON LENOX WE MUST CHECK OUT.
LIFE IS NOT ALL BAR STOOLS AND RENT PARTIES, CARL. SOMETIMES A MAN HAS TO DO SOMETHING, AND RIGHT NOW I HAVE TO BE ON THE 8:13 CAROLINIAN EN ROUTE TO YAZOO CITY.
HEY, I DON'T NEED THAT FROM YOU, TOO! I'M ABOUT TO MAKE MOVES, SLICK! YOU WATCH ME!

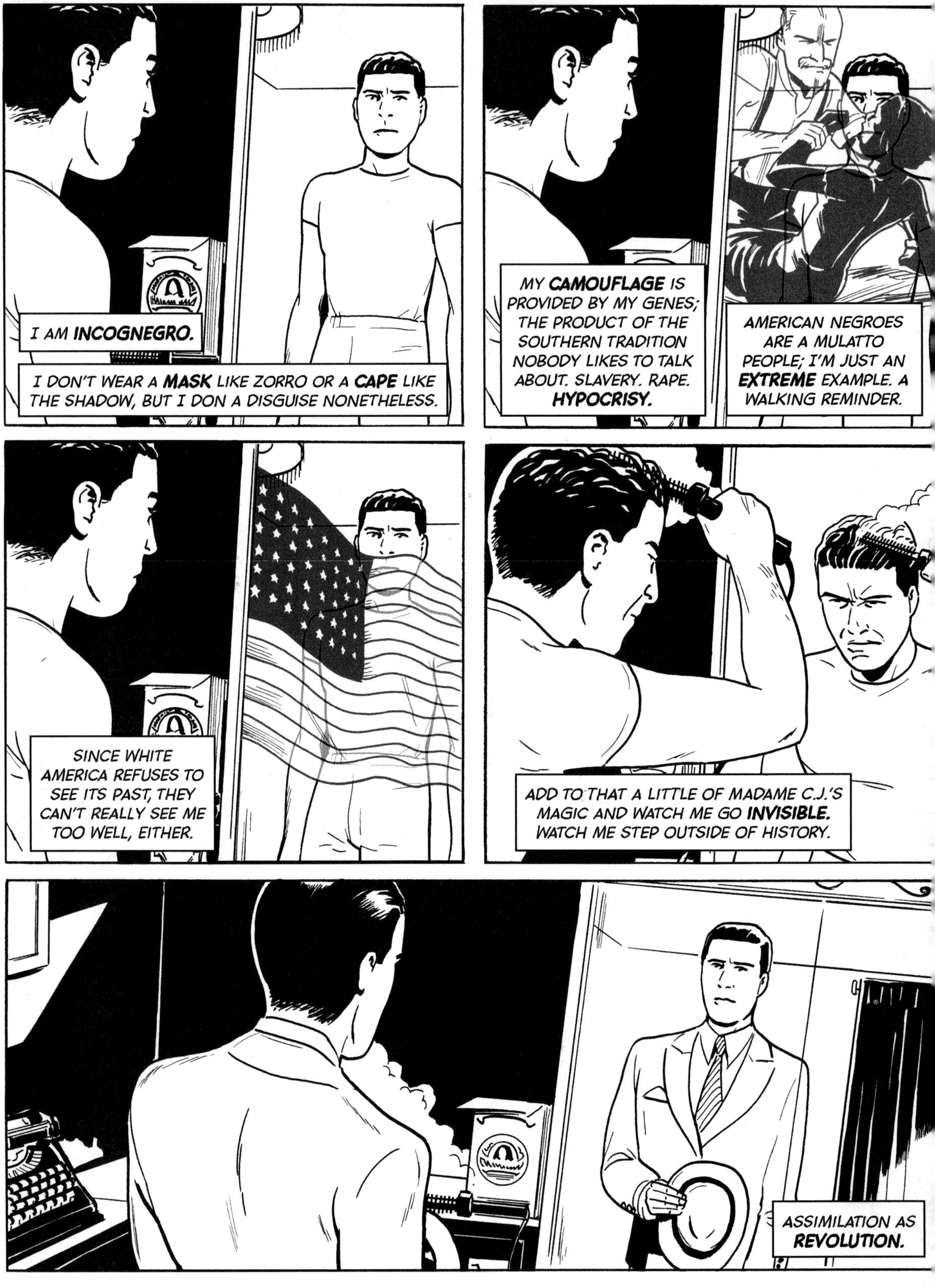
I AM INCOGNEGRO.
I DON'T WEAR A MASK LIKE ZORRO OR A CAPE LIKE THE SHADOW, BUT I DON A DISGUISE NONETHELESS.
MY CAMOUFLAGE IS PROVIDED BY MY GENES; THE PRODUCT OF THE SOUTHERN TRADITION NOBODY LIKES TO TALK ABOUT. SLAVERY. RAPE. HYPOCRISY.
AMERICAN NEGROES ARE A MULATTO PEOPLE; I'M JUST AN EXTREME EXAMPLE. A WALKING REMINDER.
SINCE WHITE AMERICA REFUSES TO SEE ITS PAST, THEY CAN'T REALLY SEE ME TOO WELL, EITHER.
ADD TO THAT A LITTLE OF MADAME C.J.'S MAGIC AND WATCH ME GO INVISIBLE. WATCH ME STEP OUTSIDE OF HISTORY.
ASSIMILATION AS REVOLUTION.

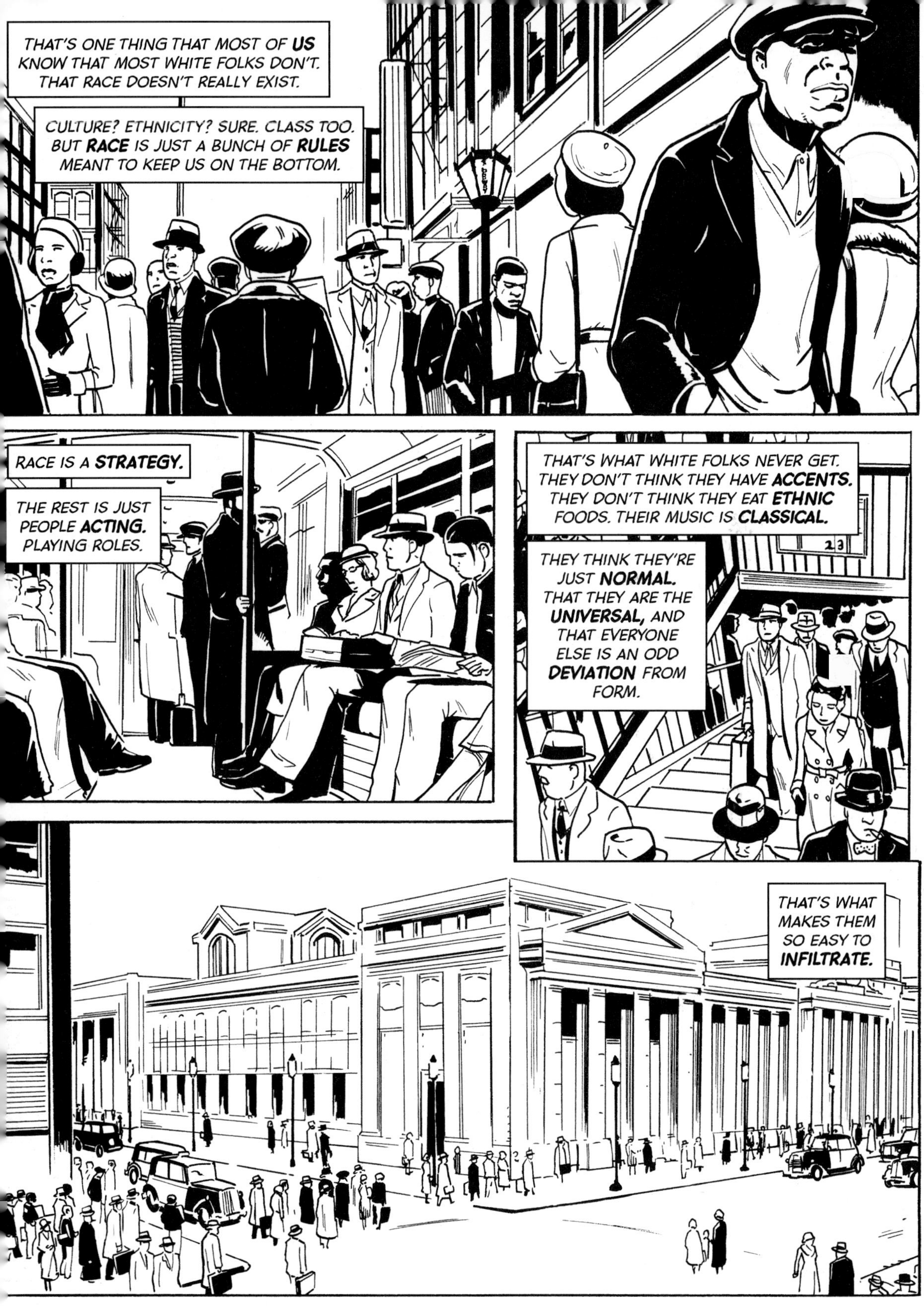
THAT'S ONE THING THAT MOST OF US KNOW THAT MOST WHITE FOLKS DON'T. THAT RACE DOESN'T REALLY EXIST.
CULTURE? ETHNICITY? SURE. CLASS TOO. BUT RACE IS JUST A BUNCH OF RULES MEANT TO KEEP US ON THE BOTTOM.
RACE IS A STRATEGY.
THE REST IS JUST PEOPLE ACTING. PLAYING ROLES.
THAT'S WHAT WHITE FOLKS NEVER GET. THEY DON'T THINK THEY HAVE ACCENTS. THEY DON'T THINK THEY EAT ETHNIC FOODS. THEIR MUSIC IS CLASSICAL.
THEY THINK THEY'RE JUST NORMAL. THAT THEY ARE THE UNIVERSAL, AND THAT EVERYONE ELSE IS AN ODD DEVIATION FROM FORM.
THAT'S WHAT MAKES THEM SO EASY TO INFILTRATE.

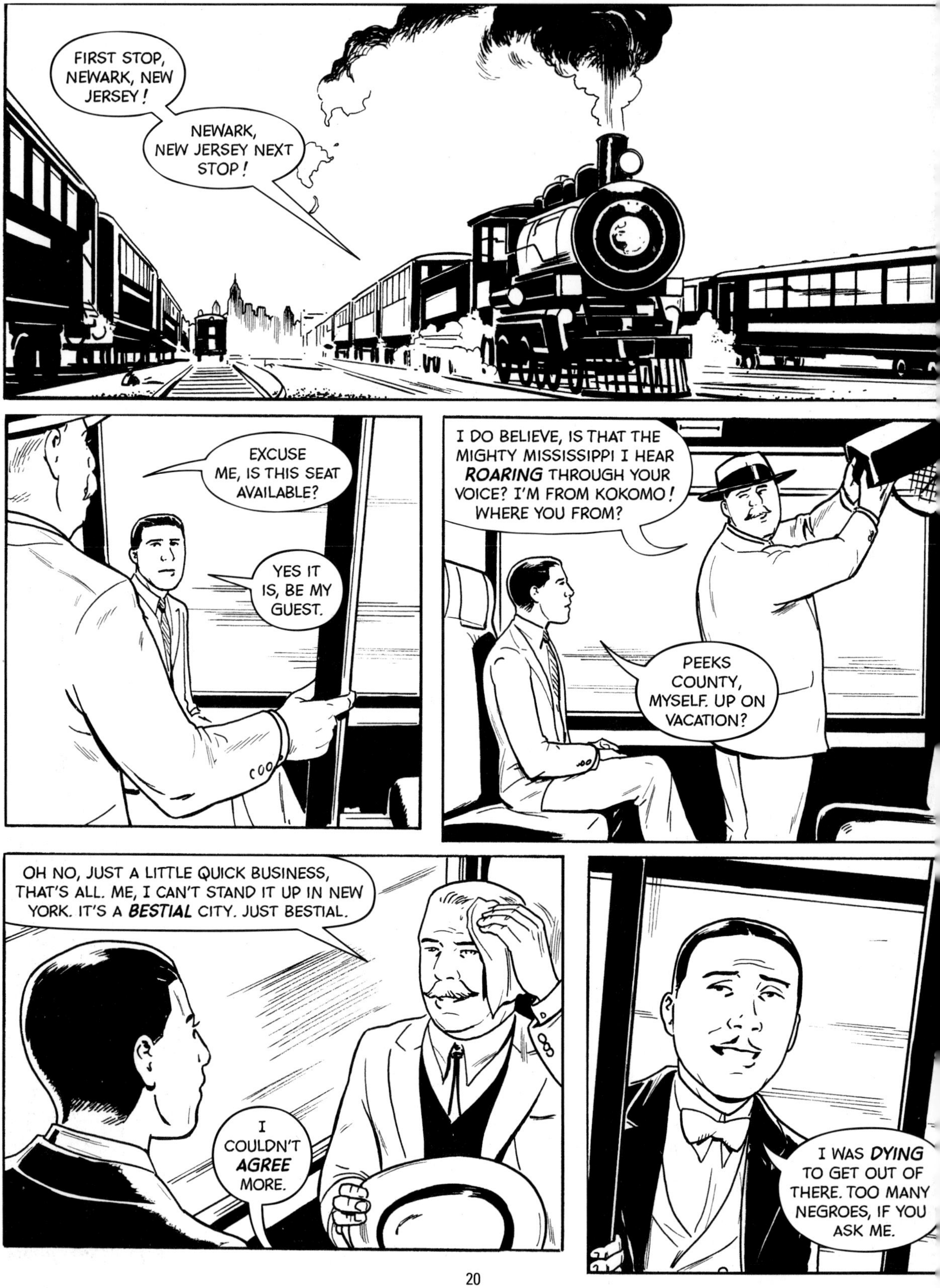
FIRST STOP, NEWARK, NEW JERSEY!
NEWARK, NEW JERSEY NEXT STOP!
EXCUSE ME, IS THIS SEAT AVAILABLE?
YES IT IS, BE MY GUEST.
I DO BELIEVE, IS THAT THE MIGHTY MISSISSIPPI I HEAR ROARING THROUGH YOUR VOICE? I'M FROM KOKOMO! WHERE YOU FROM?
PEEKS COUNTY, MYSELF. UP ON VACATION?
OH NO, JUST A LITTLE QUICK BUSINESS, THAT'S ALL. ME, I CAN'T STAND IT UP IN NEW YORK. IT'S A BESTIAL CITY. JUST BESTIAL.
I COULDN'T AGREE MORE.
I WAS DYING TO GET OUT OF THERE. TOO MANY NEGROES, IF YOU ASK ME.

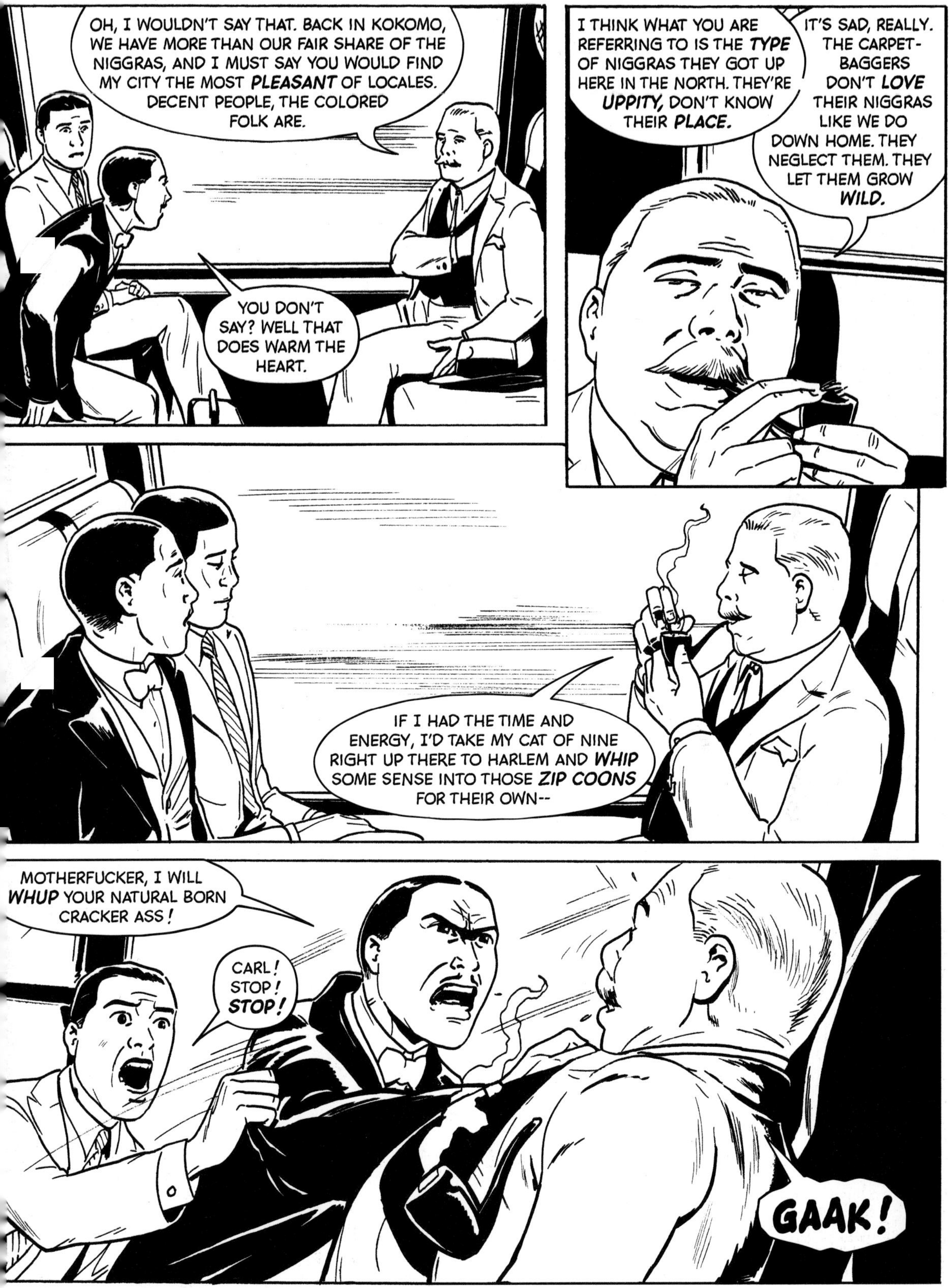

OH, I WOULDN'T SAY THAT. BACK IN KOKOMO, WE HAVE MORE THAN OUR FAIR SHARE OF THE NIGGRAS, AND I MUST SAY YOU WOULD FIND MY CITY THE MOST PLEASANT OF LOCALES. DECENT PEOPLE, THE COLORED FOLK ARE.
YOU DON'T SAY? WELL THAT DOES WARM THE HEART.
I THINK WHAT YOU ARE REFERRING TO IS THE TYPE OF NIGGRAS THEY GOT UP HERE IN THE NORTH. THEY'RE UPPITY, DON'T KNOW THEIR PLACE.
IT'S SAD, REALLY. THE CARPET-BAGGERS DON'T LOVE THEIR NIGGRAS LIKE WE DO DOWN HOME. THEY NEGLECT THEM. THEY LET THEM GROW WILD.
IF I HAD THE TIME AND ENERGY, I'D TAKE MY CAT OF NINE RIGHT UP THERE TO HARLEM AND WHIP SOME SENSE INTO THOSE ZIP COONS FOR THEIR OWN--
MOTHERFUCKER, I WILL WHUP YOUR NATURAL BORN CRACKER ASS!
CARL! STOP! STOP!
GAAK!

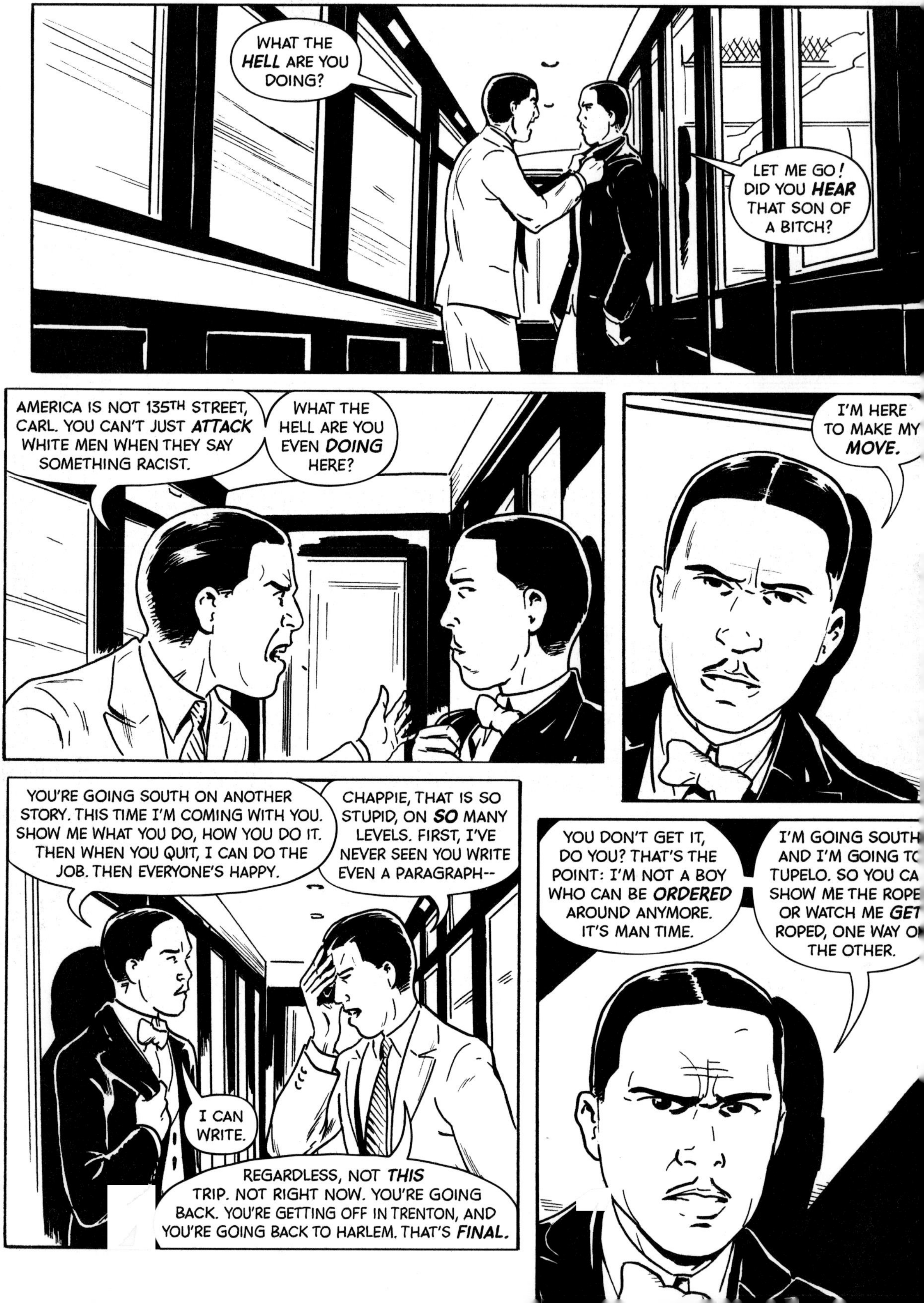
WHAT THE HELL ARE YOU DOING?
LET ME GO! DID YOU HEAR THAT SON OF A BITCH?
AMERICA IS NOT 135TH STREET, CARL. YOU CAN'T JUST ATTACK WHITE MEN WHEN THEY SAY SOMETHING RACIST.
WHAT THE HELL ARE YOU EVEN DOING HERE?
I'M HERE TO MAKE MY MOVE.
YOU'RE GOING SOUTH ON ANOTHER STORY. THIS TIME I'M COMING WITH YOU. SHOW ME WHAT YOU DO, HOW YOU DO IT. THEN WHEN YOU QUIT, I CAN DO THE JOB. THEN EVERYONE'S HAPPY.
CHAPPIE, THAT IS SO STUPID, ON SO MANY LEVELS. FIRST, I'VE NEVER SEEN YOU WRITE EVEN A PARAGRAPH--
I CAN WRITE.
REGARDLESS, NOT THIS TRIP. NOT RIGHT NOW. YOU'RE GOING BACK. YOU'RE GETTING OFF IN TRENTON, AND YOU'RE GOING BACK TO HARLEM. THAT'S FINAL.
YOU DON'T GET IT, DO YOU? THAT'S THE POINT: I'M NOT A BOY WHO CAN BE ORDERED AROUND ANYMORE. IT'S MAN TIME.
I'M GOING SOUTH AND I'M GOING TO TUPELO. SO YOU CA SHOW ME THE ROPE OR WATCH ME GET ROPED, ONE WAY O THE OTHER.

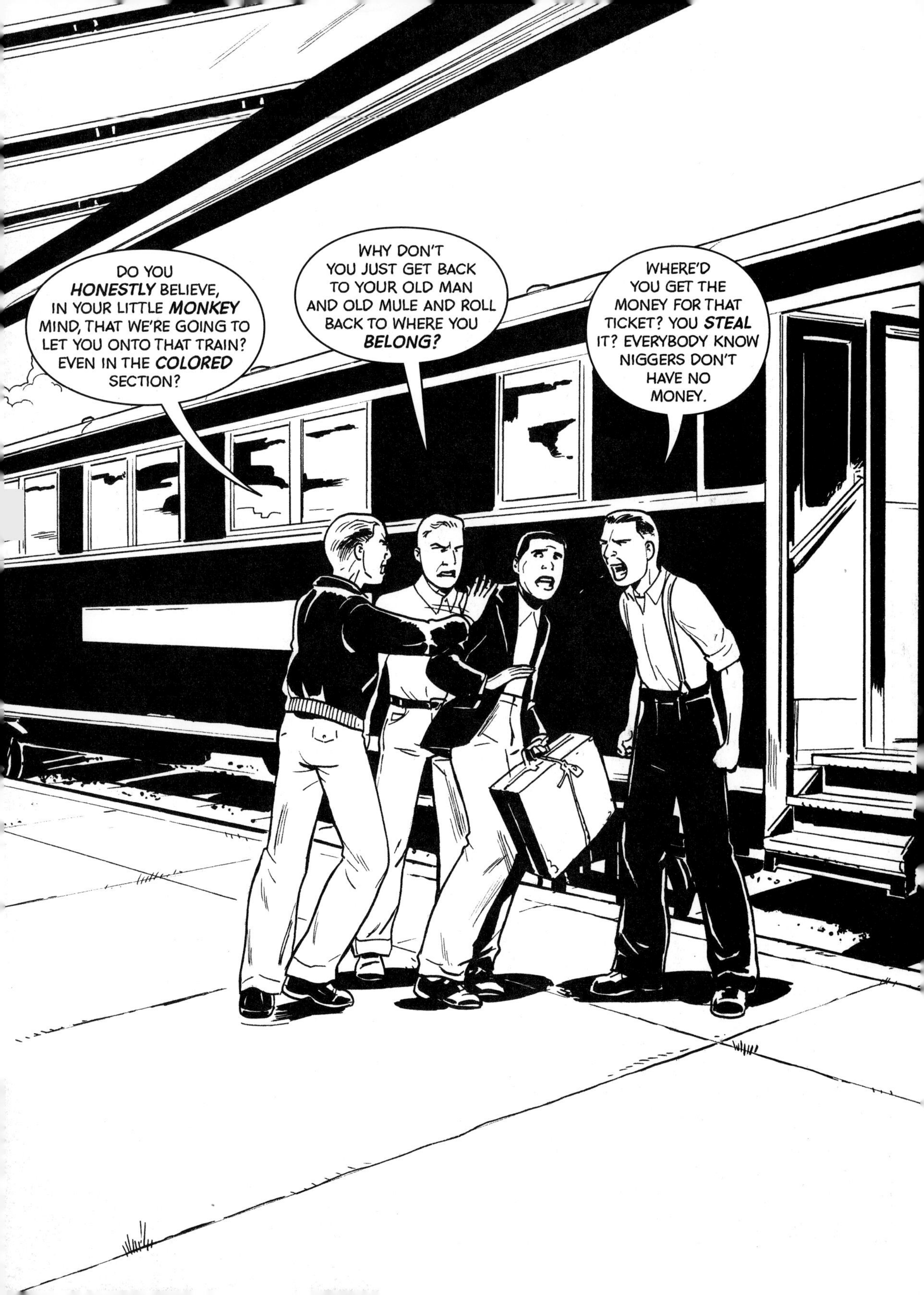
DO YOU HONESTLY BELIEVE, IN YOUR LITTLE MONKEY MIND, THAT WE'RE GOING TO LET YOU ONTO THAT TRAIN? EVEN IN THE COLORED SECTION?
WHY DON'T YOU JUST GET BACK TO YOUR OLD MAN AND OLD MULE AND ROLL BACK TO WHERE YOU BELONG?
WHERE'D YOU GET THE MONEY FOR THAT TICKET? YOU STEAL IT? EVERYBODY KNOW NIGGERS DON'T HAVE NO MONEY.

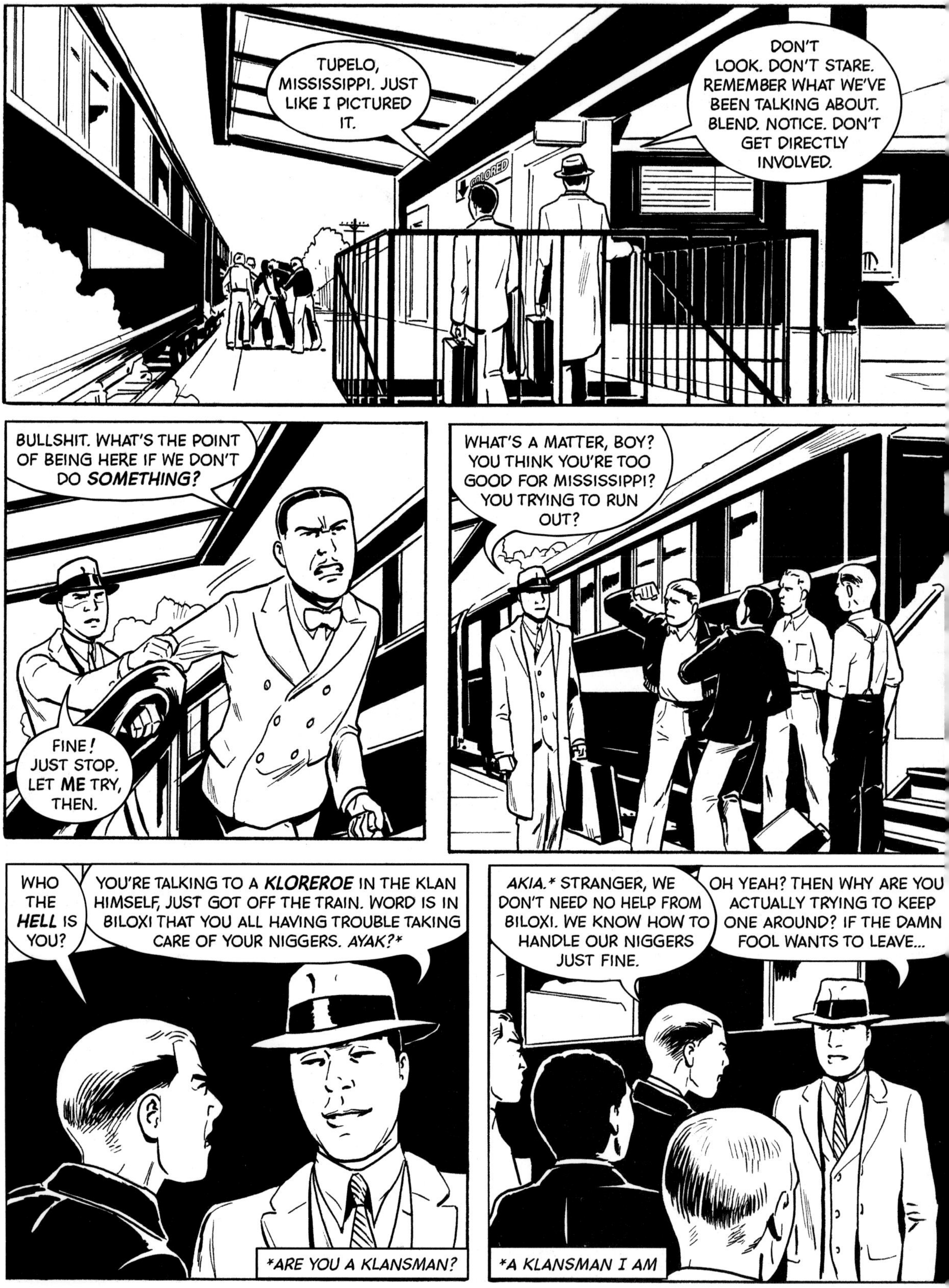

TUPELO, MISSISSIPPI. JUST LIKE I PICTURED IT.
DON'T LOOK. DON'T STARE. REMEMBER WHAT WE'VE BEEN TALKING ABOUT. BLEND. NOTICE. DON'T GET DIRECTLY INVOLVED.
COLORED
BULLSHIT. WHAT'S THE POINT OF BEING HERE IF WE DON'T DO *SOMETHING?*
FINE! JUST STOP. LET **ME** TRY, THEN.
WHAT'S A MATTER, BOY? YOU THINK YOU'RE TOO GOOD FOR MISSISSIPPI? YOU TRYING TO RUN OUT?
WHO THE **HELL** IS YOU?
YOU'RE TALKING TO A **KLOREROE** IN THE KLAN HIMSELF, JUST GOT OFF THE TRAIN. WORD IS IN BILOXI THAT YOU ALL HAVING TROUBLE TAKING CARE OF YOUR NIGGERS. *AYAK?**
*ARE YOU A KLANSMAN?
*AKIA.** STRANGER, WE DON'T NEED NO HELP FROM BILOXI. WE KNOW HOW TO HANDLE OUR NIGGERS JUST FINE.
OH YEAH? THEN WHY ARE YOU ACTUALLY TRYING TO KEEP ONE AROUND? IF THE DAMN FOOL WANTS TO LEAVE...
*A KLANSMAN I AM

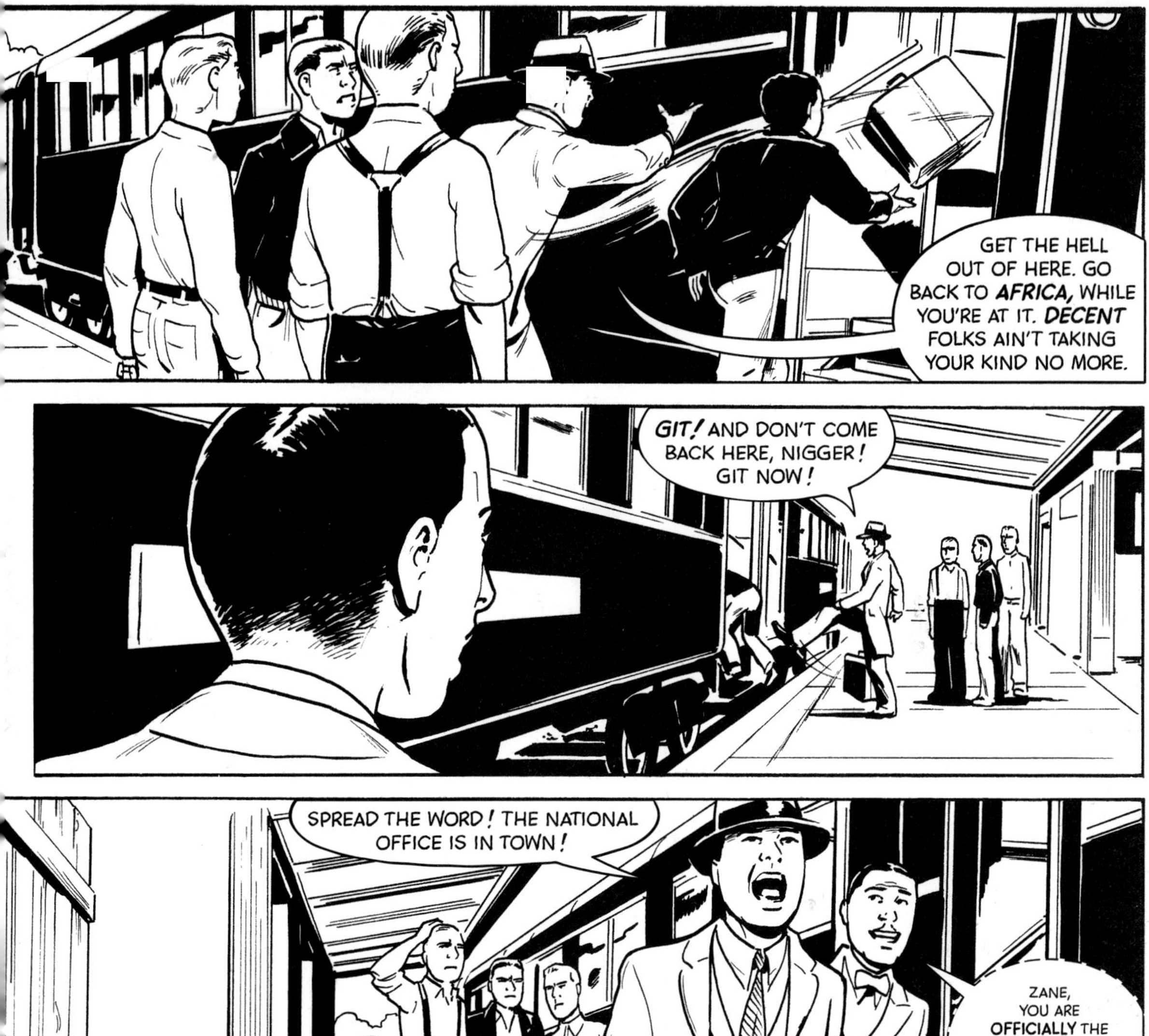
GET THE HELL OUT OF HERE. GO BACK TO AFRICA, WHILE YOU'RE AT IT. DECENT FOLKS AIN'T TAKING YOUR KIND NO MORE.
GIT! AND DON'T COME BACK HERE, NIGGER! GIT NOW!
SPREAD THE WORD! THE NATIONAL OFFICE IS IN TOWN!
ZANE, YOU ARE OFFICIALLY THE CRAZIEST NIGGER SOUTH OF THE MASON-DIXON. MY PAL.
BOSS, YOU NEED A RIDE TO TOWN? I'M GOING.
SEE, THAT'S THE SOUTHERN HOSPITALITY I'D HEARD SO MUCH ABOUT.

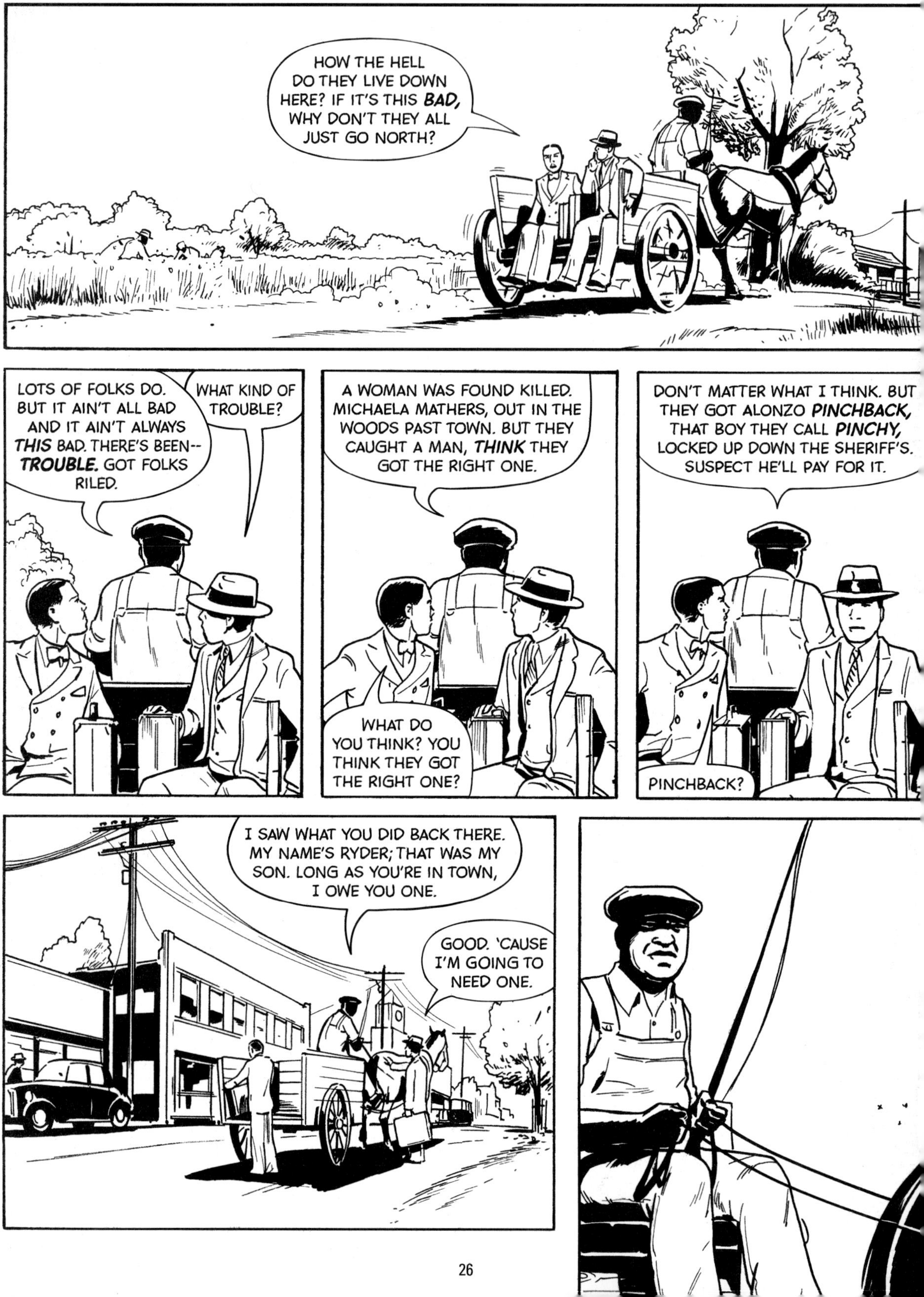
HOW THE HELL DO THEY LIVE DOWN HERE? IF IT'S THIS BAD, WHY DON'T THEY ALL JUST GO NORTH?
LOTS OF FOLKS DO. BUT IT AIN'T ALL BAD AND IT AIN'T ALWAYS THIS BAD. THERE'S BEEN-- TROUBLE. GOT FOLKS RILED.
WHAT KIND OF TROUBLE?
A WOMAN WAS FOUND KILLED. MICHAELA MATHERS, OUT IN THE WOODS PAST TOWN. BUT THEY CAUGHT A MAN, THINK THEY GOT THE RIGHT ONE.
WHAT DO YOU THINK? YOU THINK THEY GOT THE RIGHT ONE?
DON'T MATTER WHAT I THINK. BUT THEY GOT ALONZO PINCHBACK, THAT BOY THEY CALL PINCHY, LOCKED UP DOWN THE SHERIFF'S. SUSPECT HE'LL PAY FOR IT.
PINCHBACK?
I SAW WHAT YOU DID BACK THERE. MY NAME'S RYDER; THAT WAS MY SON. LONG AS YOU'RE IN TOWN, I OWE YOU ONE.
GOOD. 'CAUSE I'M GOING TO NEED ONE.

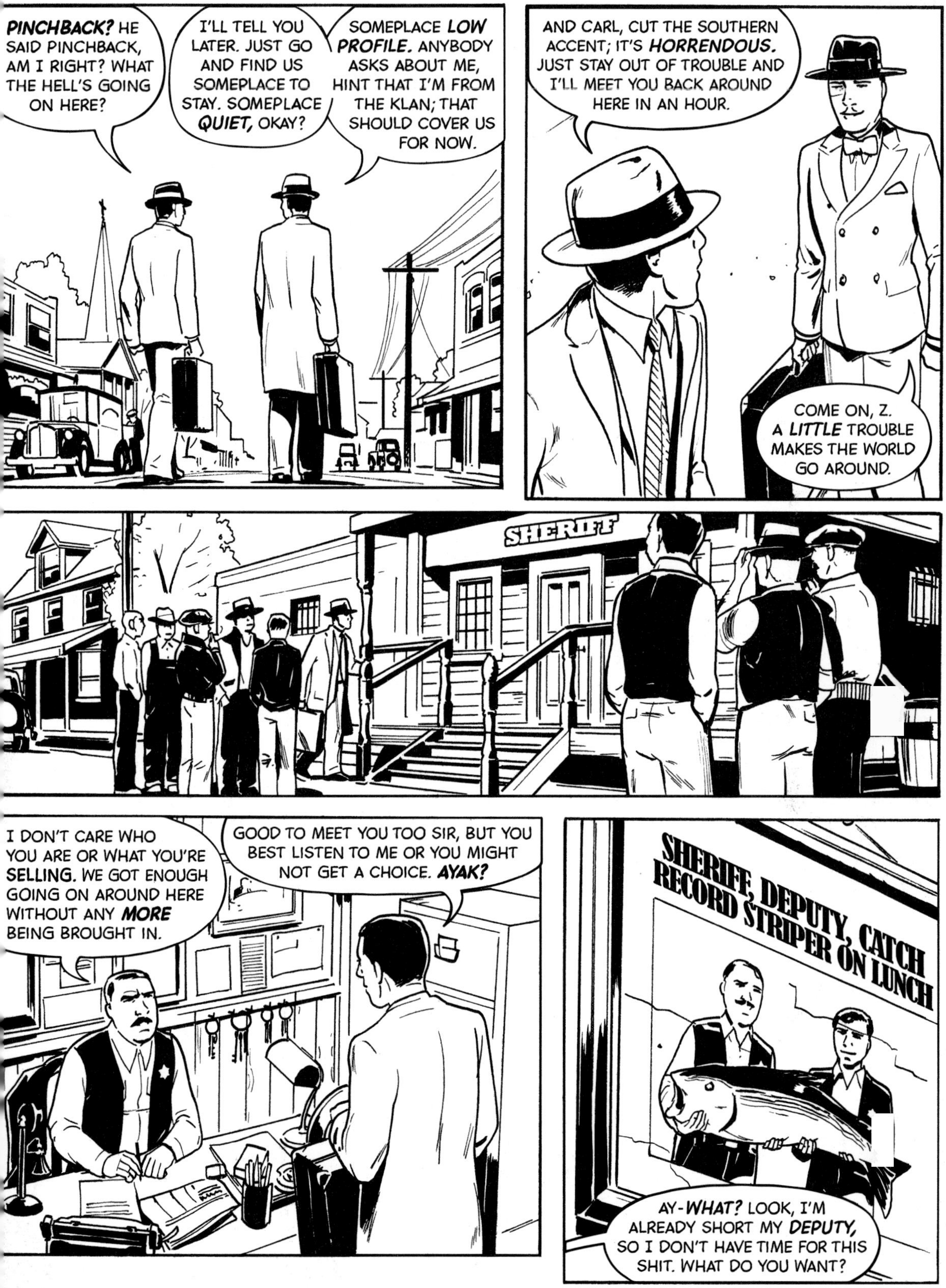
PINCHBACK? HE SAID PINCHBACK, AM I RIGHT? WHAT THE HELL'S GOING ON HERE?
I'LL TELL YOU LATER. JUST GO AND FIND US SOMEPLACE TO STAY. SOMEPLACE QUIET, OKAY?
SOMEPLACE LOW PROFILE. ANYBODY ASKS ABOUT ME, HINT THAT I'M FROM THE KLAN; THAT SHOULD COVER US FOR NOW.
AND CARL, CUT THE SOUTHERN ACCENT; IT'S HORRENDOUS. JUST STAY OUT OF TROUBLE AND I'LL MEET YOU BACK AROUND HERE IN AN HOUR.
COME ON, Z. A LITTLE TROUBLE MAKES THE WORLD GO AROUND.
SHERIFF
I DON'T CARE WHO YOU ARE OR WHAT YOU'RE SELLING. WE GOT ENOUGH GOING ON AROUND HERE WITHOUT ANY MORE BEING BROUGHT IN.
GOOD TO MEET YOU TOO SIR, BUT YOU BEST LISTEN TO ME OR YOU MIGHT NOT GET A CHOICE. AYAK?
SHERIFF, DEPUTY, CATCH RECORD STRIPER ON LUNCH
AY-WHAT? LOOK, I'M ALREADY SHORT MY DEPUTY, SO I DON'T HAVE TIME FOR THIS SHIT. WHAT DO YOU WANT?

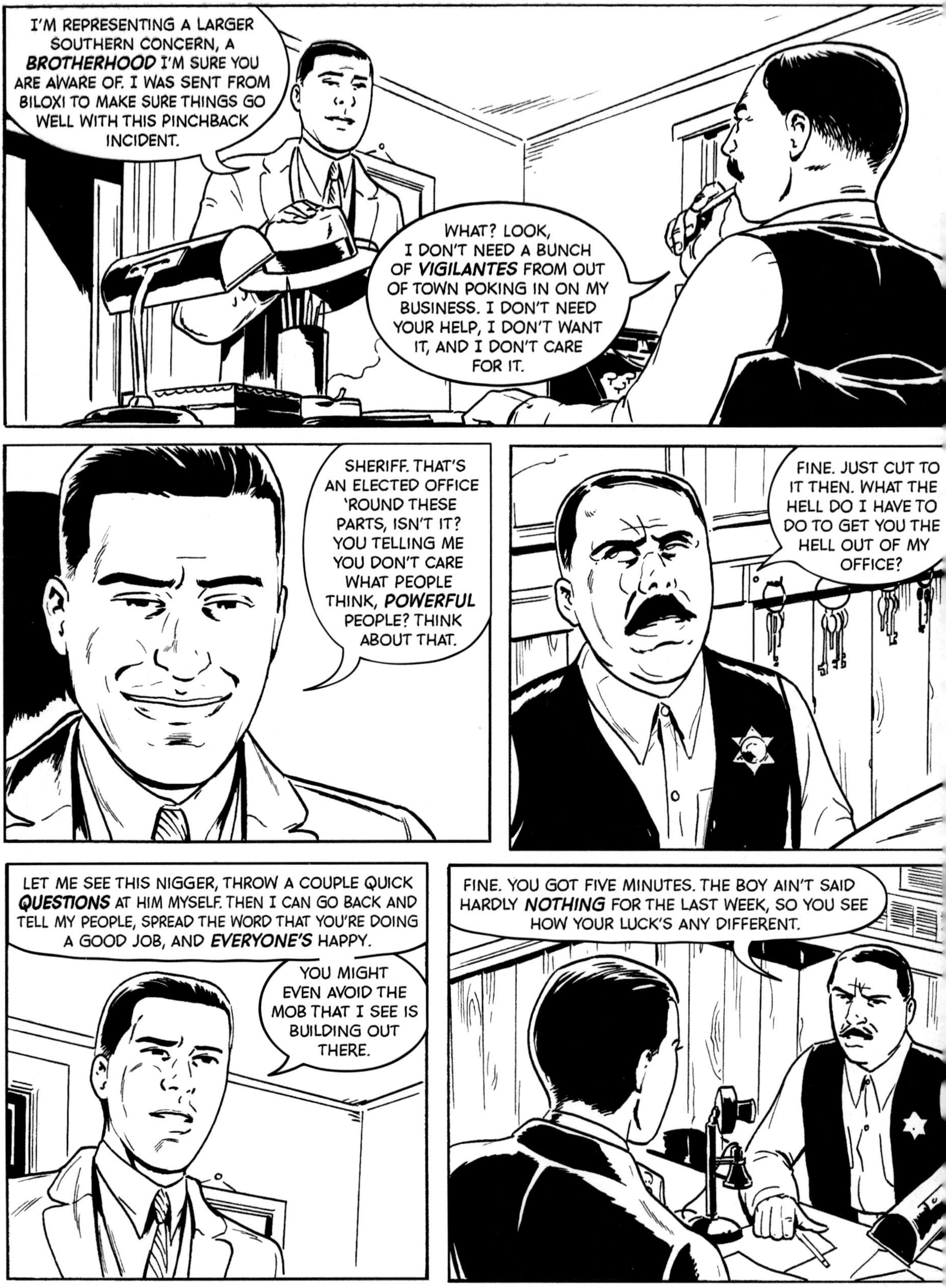
I'M REPRESENTING A LARGER SOUTHERN CONCERN, A BROTHERHOOD I'M SURE YOU ARE AWARE OF. I WAS SENT FROM BILOXI TO MAKE SURE THINGS GO WELL WITH THIS PINCHBACK INCIDENT.
WHAT? LOOK, I DON'T NEED A BUNCH OF VIGILANTES FROM OUT OF TOWN POKING IN ON MY BUSINESS. I DON'T NEED YOUR HELP, I DON'T WANT IT, AND I DON'T CARE FOR IT.
SHERIFF. THAT'S AN ELECTED OFFICE 'ROUND THESE PARTS, ISN'T IT? YOU TELLING ME YOU DON'T CARE WHAT PEOPLE THINK, POWERFUL PEOPLE? THINK ABOUT THAT.
FINE. JUST CUT TO IT THEN. WHAT THE HELL DO I HAVE TO DO TO GET YOU THE HELL OUT OF MY OFFICE?
LET ME SEE THIS NIGGER, THROW A COUPLE QUICK QUESTIONS AT HIM MYSELF. THEN I CAN GO BACK AND TELL MY PEOPLE, SPREAD THE WORD THAT YOU'RE DOING A GOOD JOB, AND EVERYONE'S HAPPY.
YOU MIGHT EVEN AVOID THE MOB THAT I SEE IS BUILDING OUT THERE.
FINE. YOU GOT FIVE MINUTES. THE BOY AIN'T SAID HARDLY NOTHING FOR THE LAST WEEK, SO YOU SEE HOW YOUR LUCK'S ANY DIFFERENT.

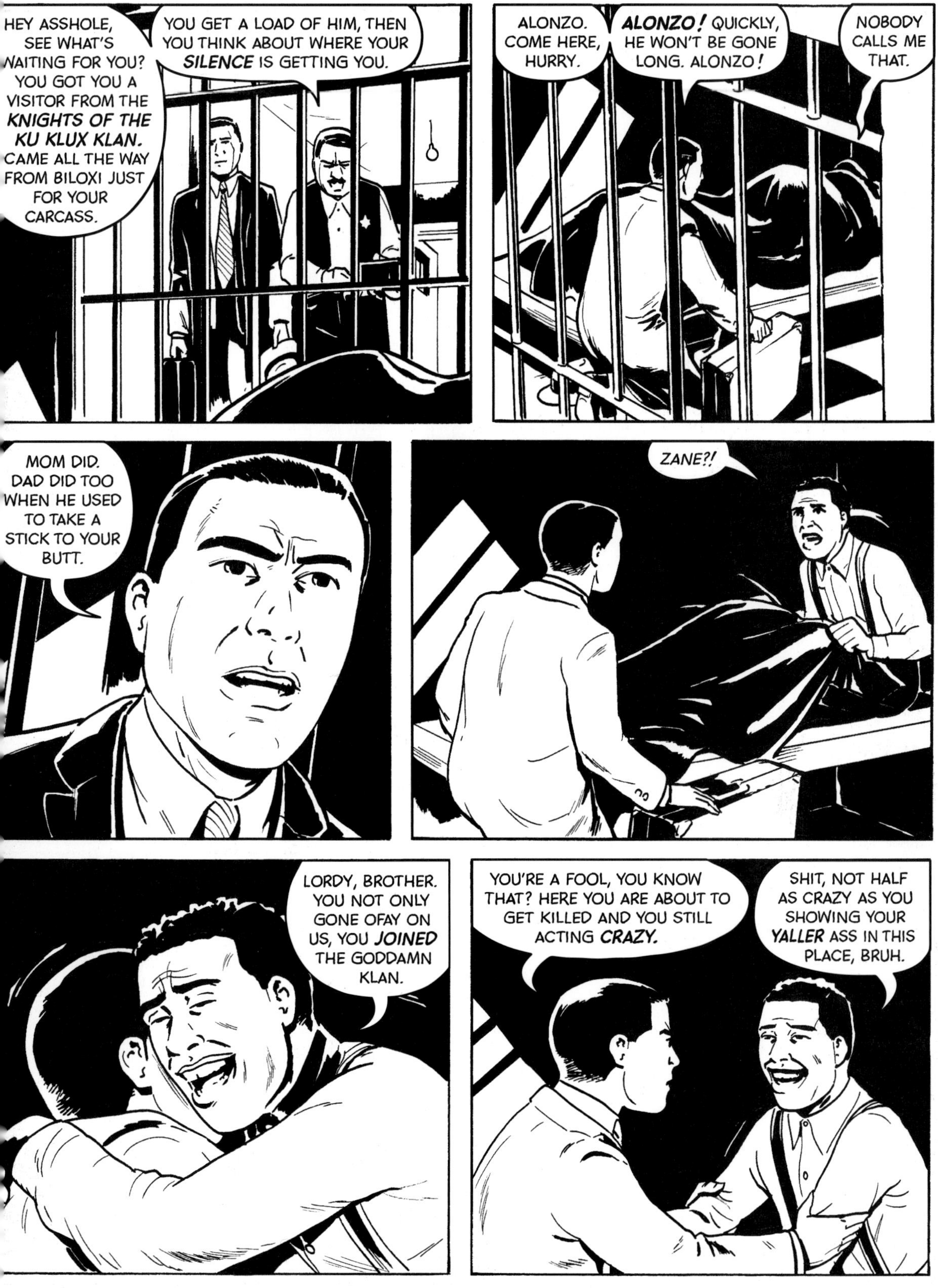
HEY ASSHOLE, SEE WHAT'S WAITING FOR YOU? YOU GOT YOU A VISITOR FROM THE KNIGHTS OF THE KU KLUX KLAN. CAME ALL THE WAY FROM BILOXI JUST FOR YOUR CARCASS.
YOU GET A LOAD OF HIM, THEN YOU THINK ABOUT WHERE YOUR SILENCE IS GETTING YOU.
ALONZO. COME HERE, HURRY.
ALONZO! QUICKLY, HE WON'T BE GONE LONG. ALONZO!
NOBODY CALLS ME THAT.
MOM DID. DAD DID TOO WHEN HE USED TO TAKE A STICK TO YOUR BUTT.
ZANE?!
LORDY, BROTHER. YOU NOT ONLY GONE OFAY ON US, YOU JOINED THE GODDAMN KLAN.
YOU'RE A FOOL, YOU KNOW THAT? HERE YOU ARE ABOUT TO GET KILLED AND YOU STILL ACTING CRAZY.
SHIT, NOT HALF AS CRAZY AS YOU SHOWING YOUR YALLER ASS IN THIS PLACE, BRUH.

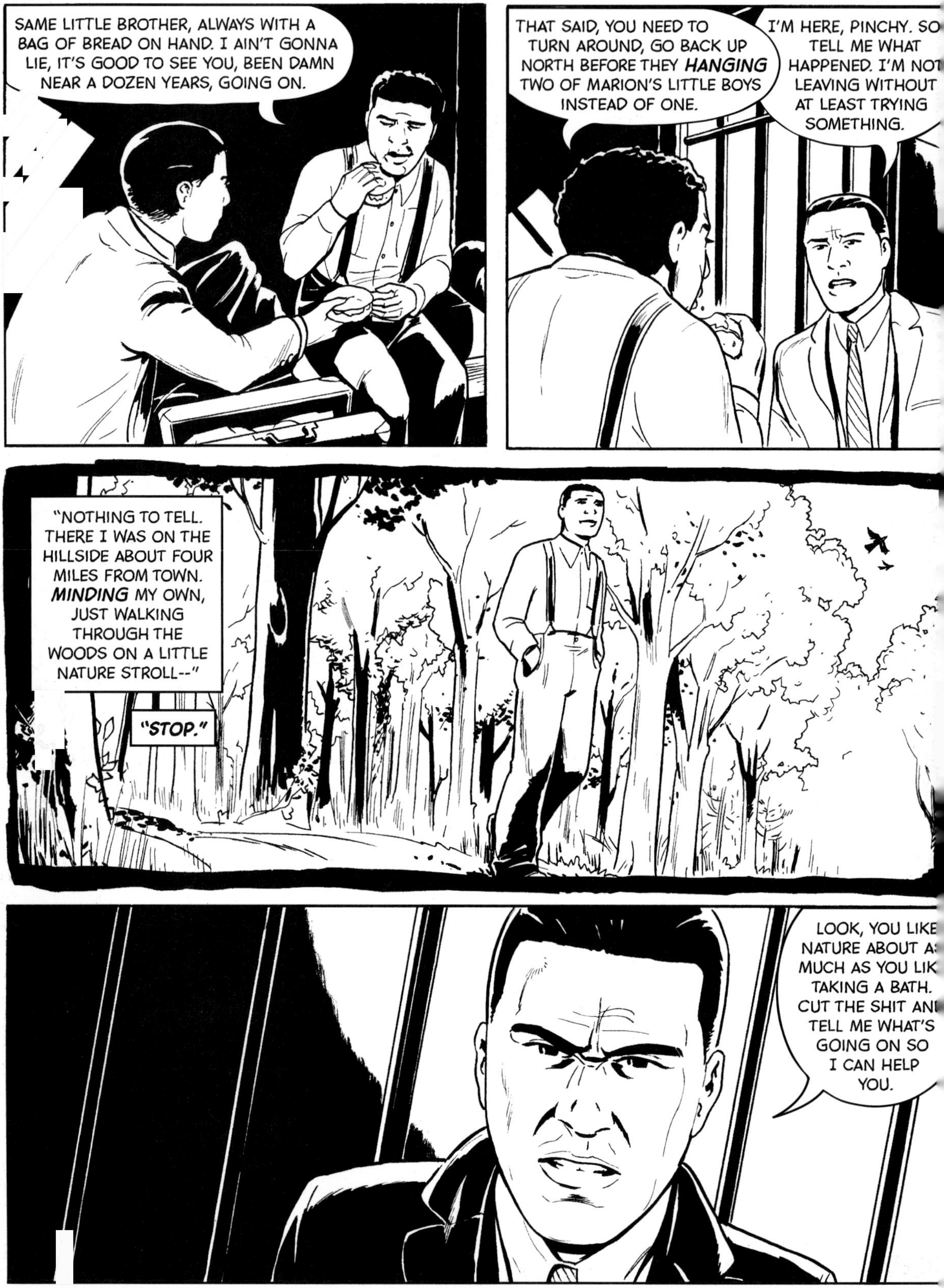
SAME LITTLE BROTHER, ALWAYS WITH A BAG OF BREAD ON HAND. I AIN'T GONNA LIE, IT'S GOOD TO SEE YOU, BEEN DAMN NEAR A DOZEN YEARS, GOING ON.
THAT SAID, YOU NEED TO TURN AROUND, GO BACK UP NORTH BEFORE THEY *HANGING* TWO OF MARION'S LITTLE BOYS INSTEAD OF ONE.
I'M HERE, PINCHY. SO TELL ME WHAT HAPPENED. I'M NOT LEAVING WITHOUT AT LEAST TRYING SOMETHING.
"NOTHING TO TELL. THERE I WAS ON THE HILLSIDE ABOUT FOUR MILES FROM TOWN. *MINDING* MY OWN, JUST WALKING THROUGH THE WOODS ON A LITTLE NATURE STROLL--"
*"STOP."*
LOOK, YOU LIKE NATURE ABOUT AS MUCH AS YOU LIKE TAKING A BATH. CUT THE SHIT AND TELL ME WHAT'S GOING ON SO I CAN HELP YOU.

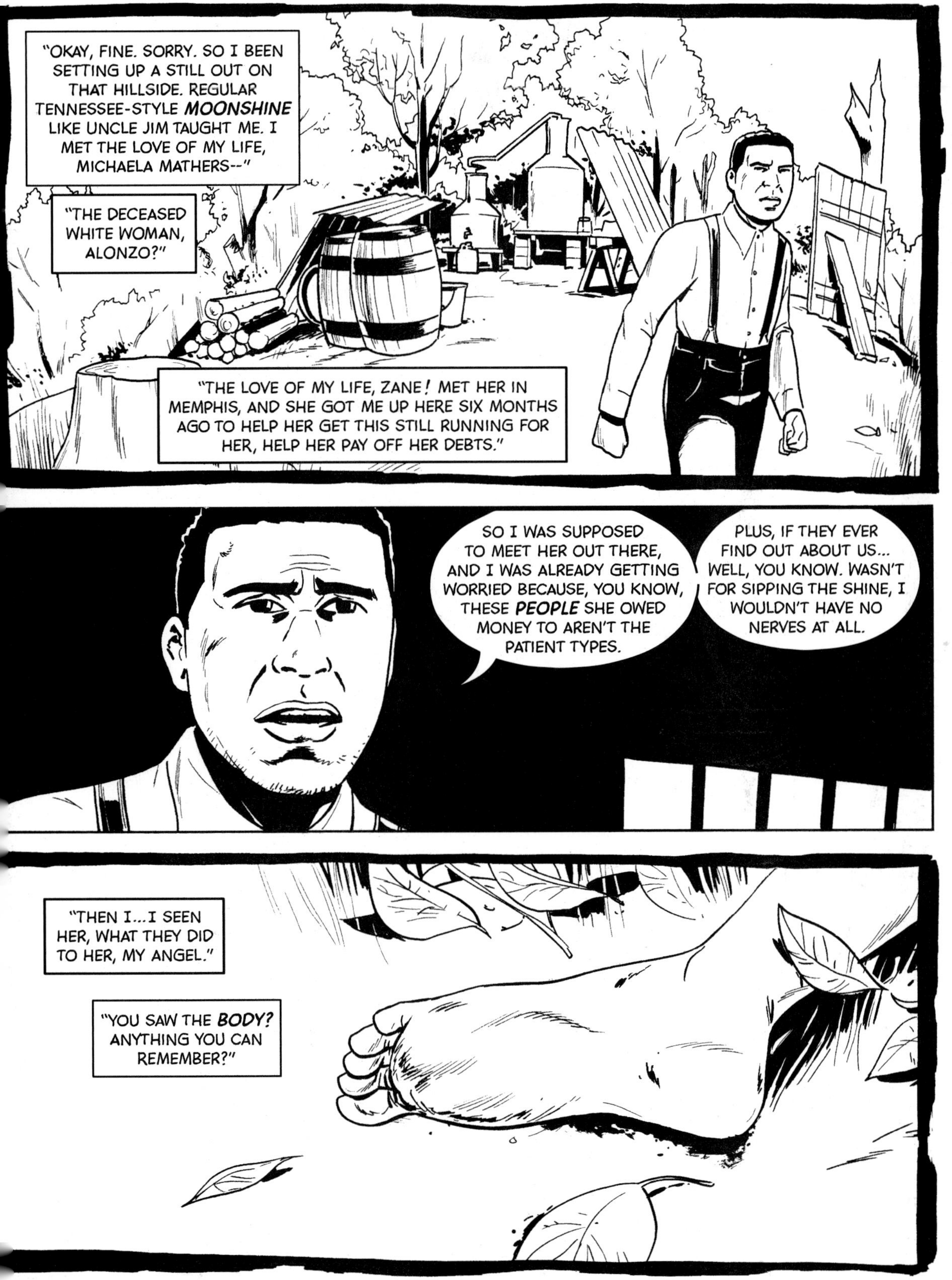
"OKAY, FINE. SORRY. SO I BEEN SETTING UP A STILL OUT ON THAT HILLSIDE. REGULAR TENNESSEE-STYLE MOONSHINE LIKE UNCLE JIM TAUGHT ME. I MET THE LOVE OF MY LIFE, MICHAELA MATHERS--"
"THE DECEASED WHITE WOMAN, ALONZO?"
"THE LOVE OF MY LIFE, ZANE! MET HER IN MEMPHIS, AND SHE GOT ME UP HERE SIX MONTHS AGO TO HELP HER GET THIS STILL RUNNING FOR HER, HELP HER PAY OFF HER DEBTS."
SO I WAS SUPPOSED TO MEET HER OUT THERE, AND I WAS ALREADY GETTING WORRIED BECAUSE, YOU KNOW, THESE PEOPLE SHE OWED MONEY TO AREN'T THE PATIENT TYPES.
PLUS, IF THEY EVER FIND OUT ABOUT US... WELL, YOU KNOW. WASN'T FOR SIPPING THE SHINE, I WOULDN'T HAVE NO NERVES AT ALL.
"THEN I...I SEEN HER, WHAT THEY DID TO HER, MY ANGEL."
"YOU SAW THE BODY? ANYTHING YOU CAN REMEMBER?"

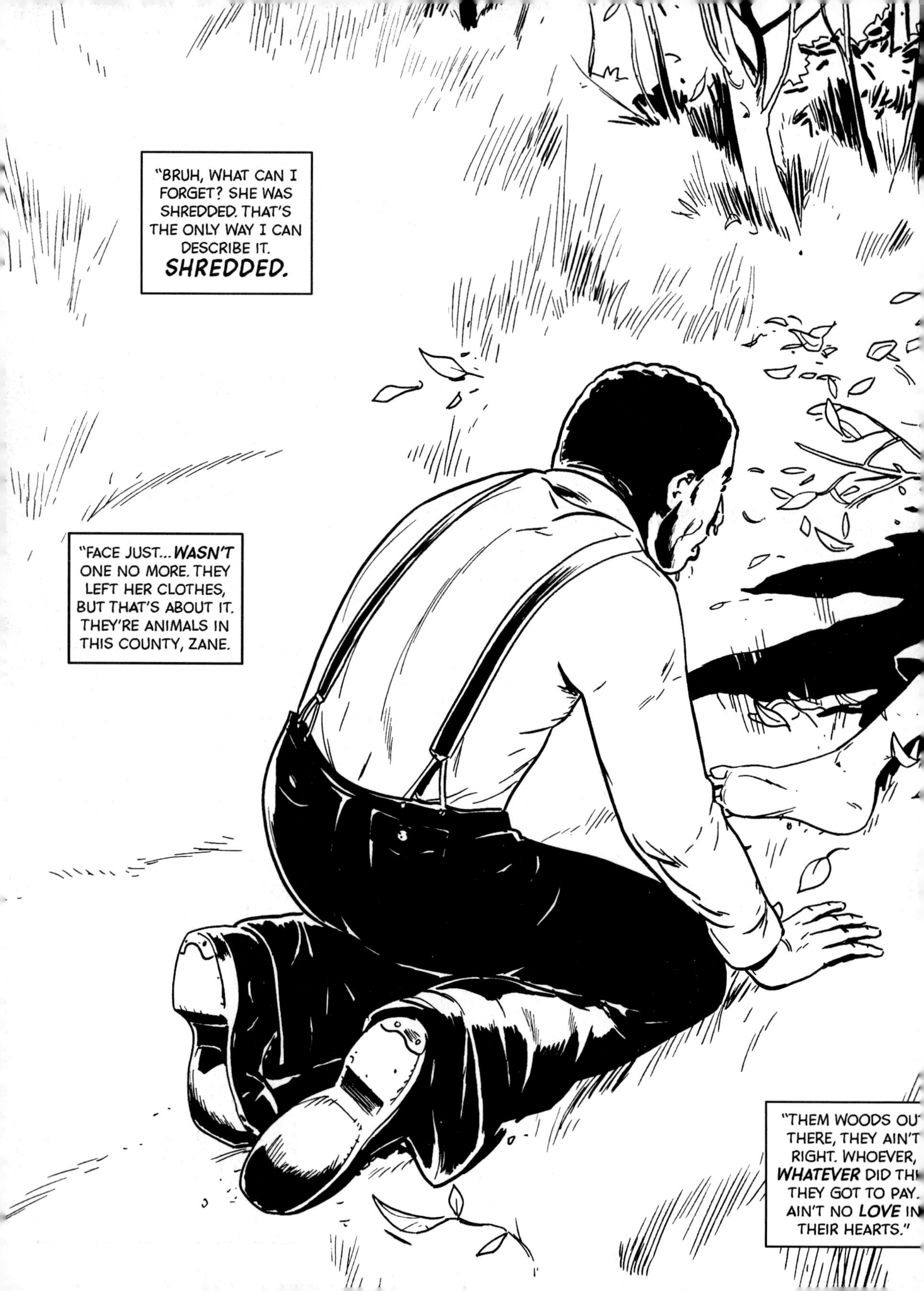
"BRUH, WHAT CAN I FORGET? SHE WAS SHREDDED. THAT'S THE ONLY WAY I CAN DESCRIBE IT. **SHREDDED.**
"FACE JUST... ***WASN'T*** ONE NO MORE. THEY LEFT HER CLOTHES, BUT THAT'S ABOUT IT. THEY'RE ANIMALS IN THIS COUNTY, ZANE.
"THEM WOODS OU THERE, THEY AIN'T RIGHT. WHOEVER, ***WHATEVER*** DID THI THEY GOT TO PAY. AIN'T NO ***LOVE*** IN THEIR HEARTS."

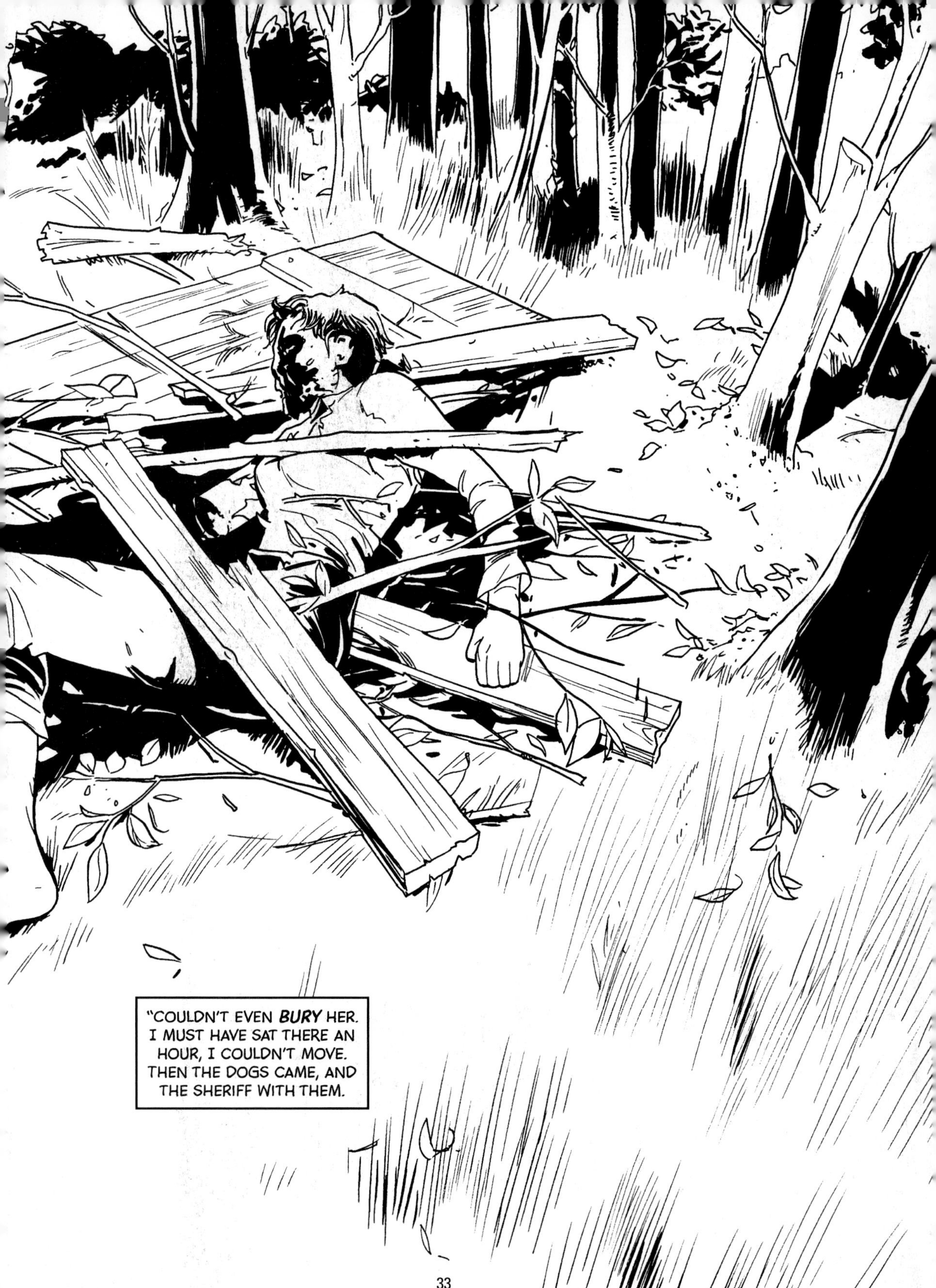
"COULDN'T EVEN *BURY* HER. I MUST HAVE SAT THERE AN HOUR, I COULDN'T MOVE. THEN THE DOGS CAME, AND THE SHERIFF WITH THEM.

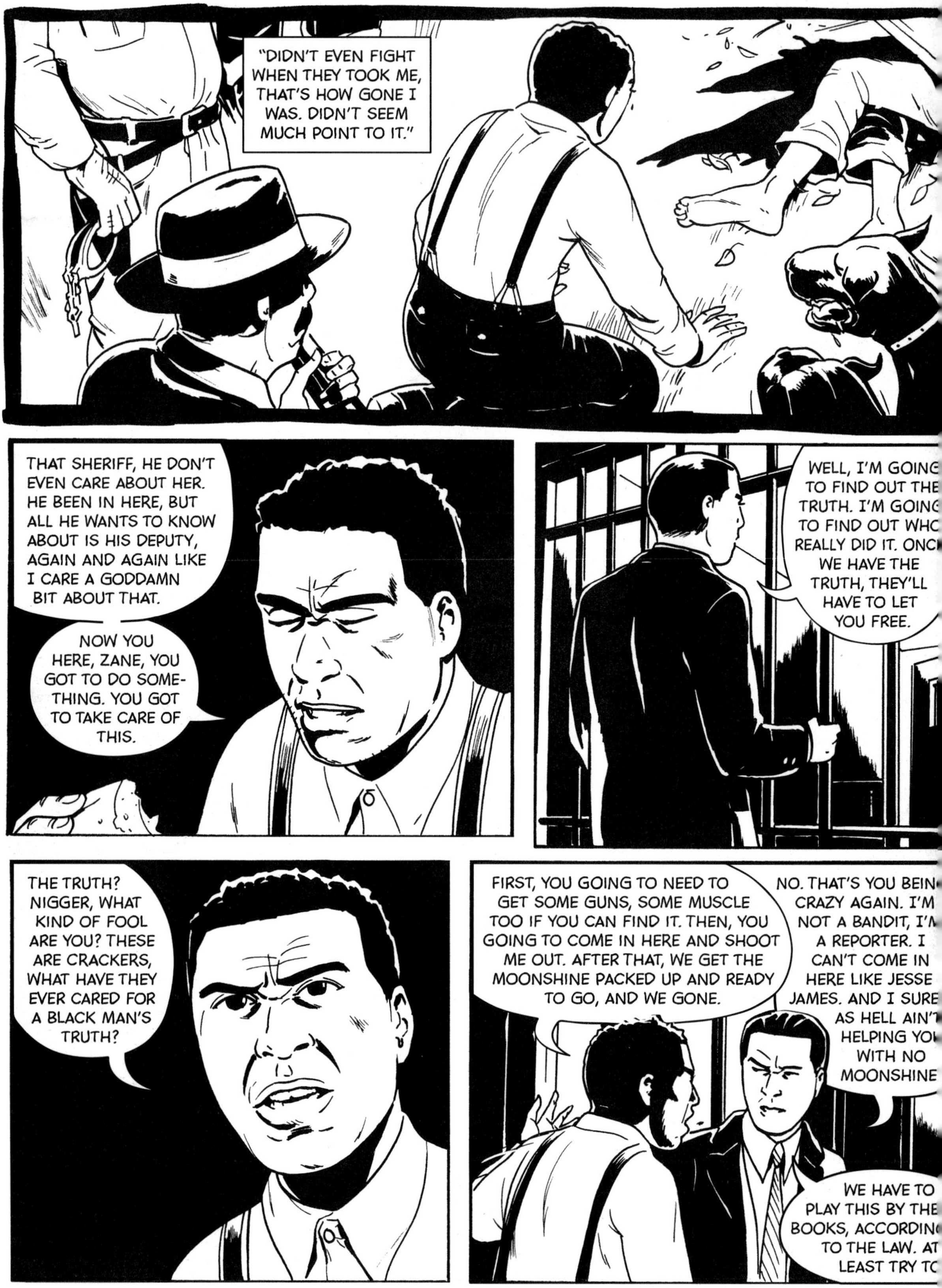
"DIDN'T EVEN FIGHT WHEN THEY TOOK ME, THAT'S HOW GONE I WAS. DIDN'T SEEM MUCH POINT TO IT."
THAT SHERIFF, HE DON'T EVEN CARE ABOUT HER. HE BEEN IN HERE, BUT ALL HE WANTS TO KNOW ABOUT IS HIS DEPUTY, AGAIN AND AGAIN LIKE I CARE A GODDAMN BIT ABOUT THAT.
NOW YOU HERE, ZANE, YOU GOT TO DO SOME-THING. YOU GOT TO TAKE CARE OF THIS.
WELL, I'M GOING TO FIND OUT THE TRUTH. I'M GOING TO FIND OUT WHO REALLY DID IT. ONCE WE HAVE THE TRUTH, THEY'LL HAVE TO LET YOU FREE.
THE TRUTH? NIGGER, WHAT KIND OF FOOL ARE YOU? THESE ARE CRACKERS, WHAT HAVE THEY EVER CARED FOR A BLACK MAN'S TRUTH?
FIRST, YOU GOING TO NEED TO GET SOME GUNS, SOME MUSCLE TOO IF YOU CAN FIND IT. THEN, YOU GOING TO COME IN HERE AND SHOOT ME OUT. AFTER THAT, WE GET THE MOONSHINE PACKED UP AND READY TO GO, AND WE GONE.
NO. THAT'S YOU BEING CRAZY AGAIN. I'M NOT A BANDIT, I'M A REPORTER. I CAN'T COME IN HERE LIKE JESSE JAMES. AND I SURE AS HELL AIN'T HELPING YOU WITH NO MOONSHINE.
WE HAVE TO PLAY THIS BY THE BOOKS, ACCORDING TO THE LAW. AT LEAST TRY TO

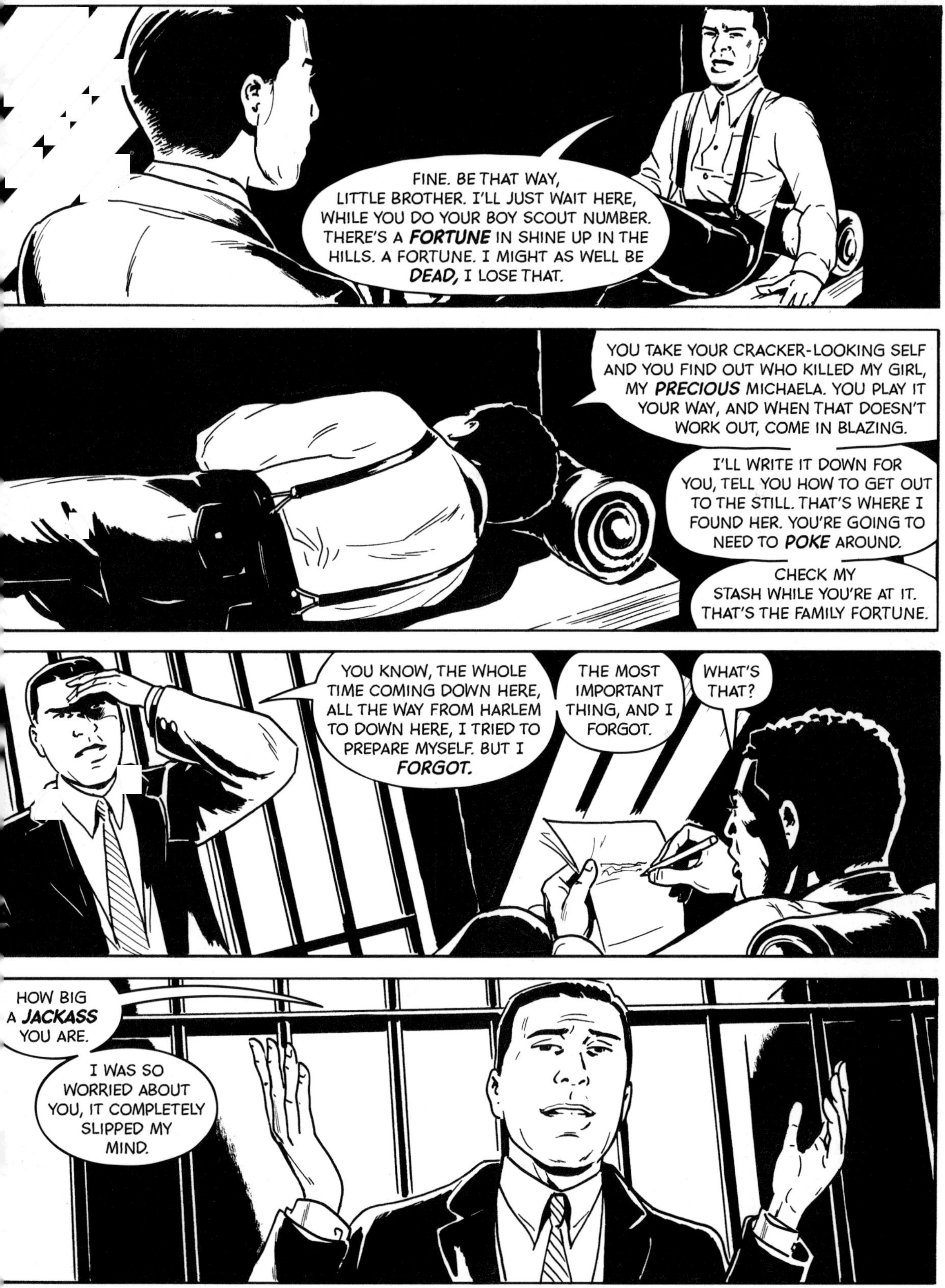
FINE. BE THAT WAY, LITTLE BROTHER. I'LL JUST WAIT HERE, WHILE YOU DO YOUR BOY SCOUT NUMBER. THERE'S A **FORTUNE** IN SHINE UP IN THE HILLS. A FORTUNE. I MIGHT AS WELL BE **DEAD,** I LOSE THAT.
YOU TAKE YOUR CRACKER-LOOKING SELF AND YOU FIND OUT WHO KILLED MY GIRL, MY **PRECIOUS** MICHAELA. YOU PLAY IT YOUR WAY, AND WHEN THAT DOESN'T WORK OUT, COME IN BLAZING.
I'LL WRITE IT DOWN FOR YOU, TELL YOU HOW TO GET OUT TO THE STILL. THAT'S WHERE I FOUND HER. YOU'RE GOING TO NEED TO **POKE** AROUND.
CHECK MY STASH WHILE YOU'RE AT IT. THAT'S THE FAMILY FORTUNE.
YOU KNOW, THE WHOLE TIME COMING DOWN HERE, ALL THE WAY FROM HARLEM TO DOWN HERE, I TRIED TO PREPARE MYSELF. BUT I **FORGOT.**
THE MOST IMPORTANT THING, AND I FORGOT.
WHAT'S THAT?
HOW BIG A **JACKASS** YOU ARE.
I WAS SO WORRIED ABOUT YOU, IT COMPLETELY SLIPPED MY MIND.

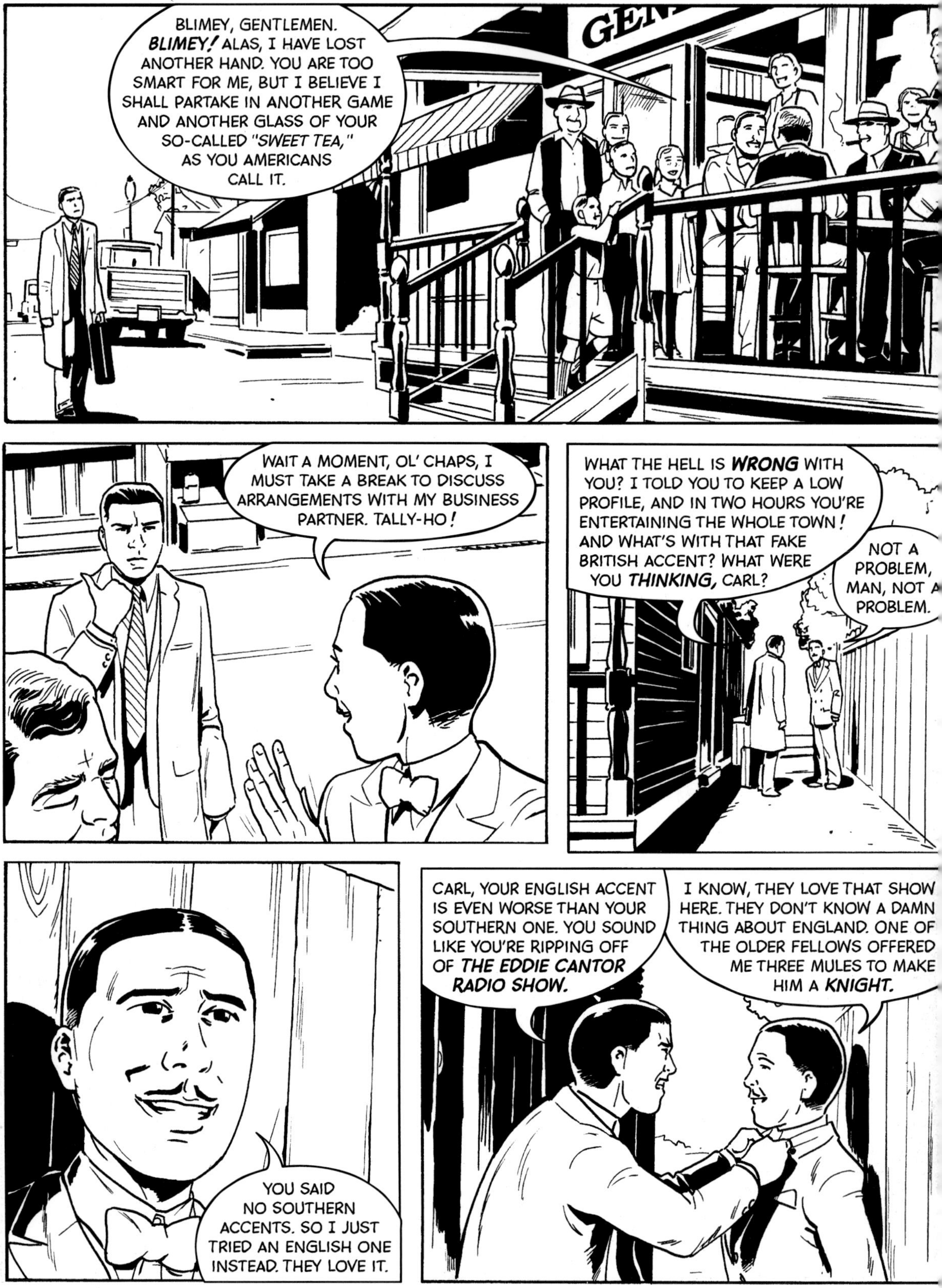

BLIMEY, GENTLEMEN. **BLIMEY!** ALAS, I HAVE LOST ANOTHER HAND. YOU ARE TOO SMART FOR ME, BUT I BELIEVE I SHALL PARTAKE IN ANOTHER GAME AND ANOTHER GLASS OF YOUR SO-CALLED *"SWEET TEA,"* AS YOU AMERICANS CALL IT.
WAIT A MOMENT, OL' CHAPS, I MUST TAKE A BREAK TO DISCUSS ARRANGEMENTS WITH MY BUSINESS PARTNER. TALLY-HO!
WHAT THE HELL IS **WRONG** WITH YOU? I TOLD YOU TO KEEP A LOW PROFILE, AND IN TWO HOURS YOU'RE ENTERTAINING THE WHOLE TOWN! AND WHAT'S WITH THAT FAKE BRITISH ACCENT? WHAT WERE YOU **THINKING,** CARL?
NOT A PROBLEM, MAN, NOT A PROBLEM.
YOU SAID NO SOUTHERN ACCENTS. SO I JUST TRIED AN ENGLISH ONE INSTEAD. THEY LOVE IT.
CARL, YOUR ENGLISH ACCENT IS EVEN WORSE THAN YOUR SOUTHERN ONE. YOU SOUND LIKE YOU'RE RIPPING OFF OF **THE EDDIE CANTOR RADIO SHOW.**
I KNOW, THEY LOVE THAT SHOW HERE. THEY DON'T KNOW A DAMN THING ABOUT ENGLAND. ONE OF THE OLDER FELLOWS OFFERED ME THREE MULES TO MAKE HIM A **KNIGHT.**

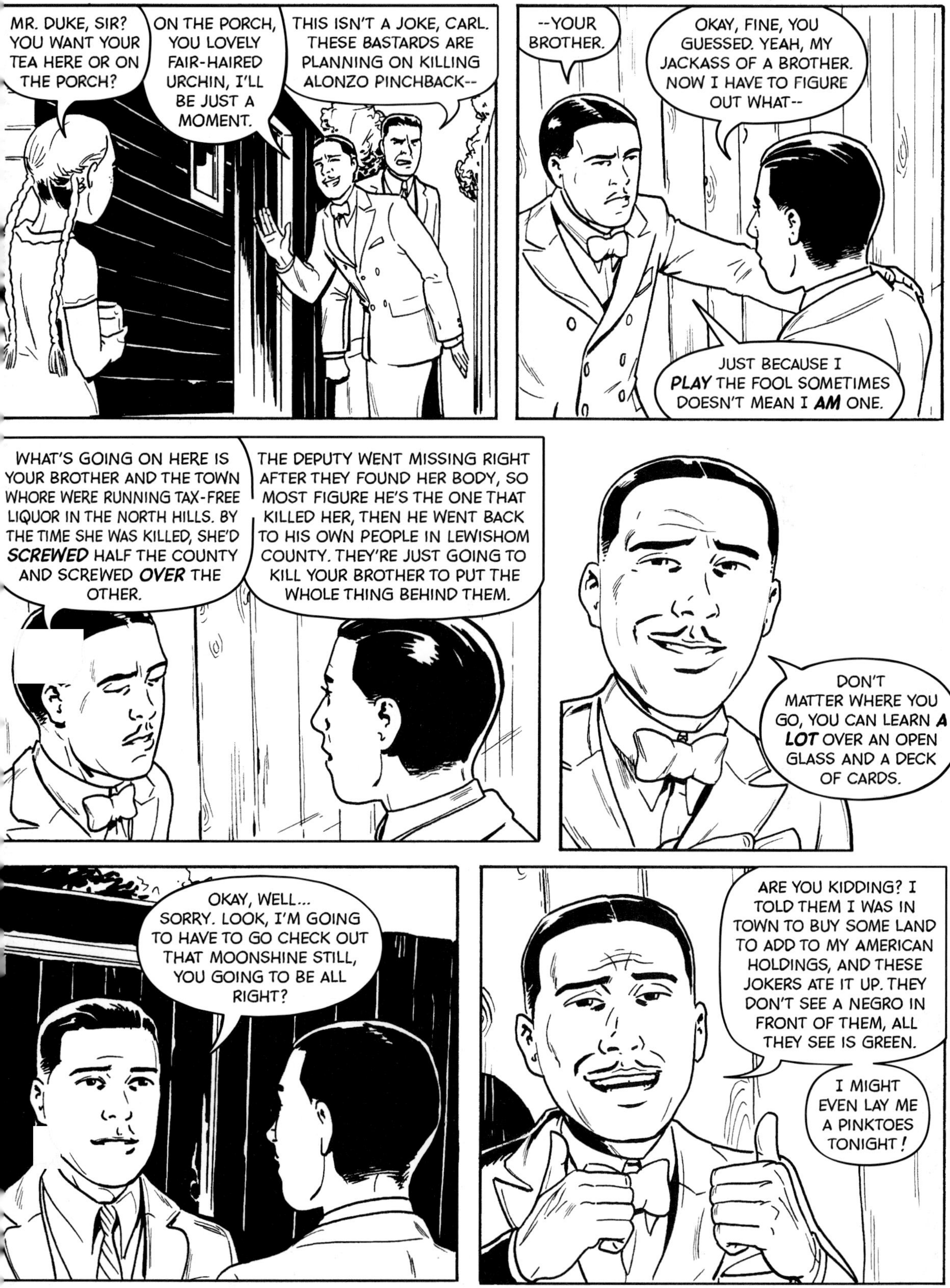
MR. DUKE, SIR? YOU WANT YOUR TEA HERE OR ON THE PORCH?
ON THE PORCH, YOU LOVELY FAIR-HAIRED URCHIN, I'LL BE JUST A MOMENT.
THIS ISN'T A JOKE, CARL. THESE BASTARDS ARE PLANNING ON KILLING ALONZO PINCHBACK--
--YOUR BROTHER.
OKAY, FINE, YOU GUESSED. YEAH, MY JACKASS OF A BROTHER. NOW I HAVE TO FIGURE OUT WHAT--
JUST BECAUSE I PLAY THE FOOL SOMETIMES DOESN'T MEAN I AM ONE.
WHAT'S GOING ON HERE IS YOUR BROTHER AND THE TOWN WHORE WERE RUNNING TAX-FREE LIQUOR IN THE NORTH HILLS. BY THE TIME SHE WAS KILLED, SHE'D SCREWED HALF THE COUNTY AND SCREWED OVER THE OTHER.
THE DEPUTY WENT MISSING RIGHT AFTER THEY FOUND HER BODY, SO MOST FIGURE HE'S THE ONE THAT KILLED HER, THEN HE WENT BACK TO HIS OWN PEOPLE IN LEWISHOM COUNTY. THEY'RE JUST GOING TO KILL YOUR BROTHER TO PUT THE WHOLE THING BEHIND THEM.
DON'T MATTER WHERE YOU GO, YOU CAN LEARN A LOT OVER AN OPEN GLASS AND A DECK OF CARDS.
OKAY, WELL... SORRY. LOOK, I'M GOING TO HAVE TO GO CHECK OUT THAT MOONSHINE STILL, YOU GOING TO BE ALL RIGHT?
ARE YOU KIDDING? I TOLD THEM I WAS IN TOWN TO BUY SOME LAND TO ADD TO MY AMERICAN HOLDINGS, AND THESE JOKERS ATE IT UP. THEY DON'T SEE A NEGRO IN FRONT OF THEM, ALL THEY SEE IS GREEN.
I MIGHT EVEN LAY ME A PINKTOES TONIGHT!

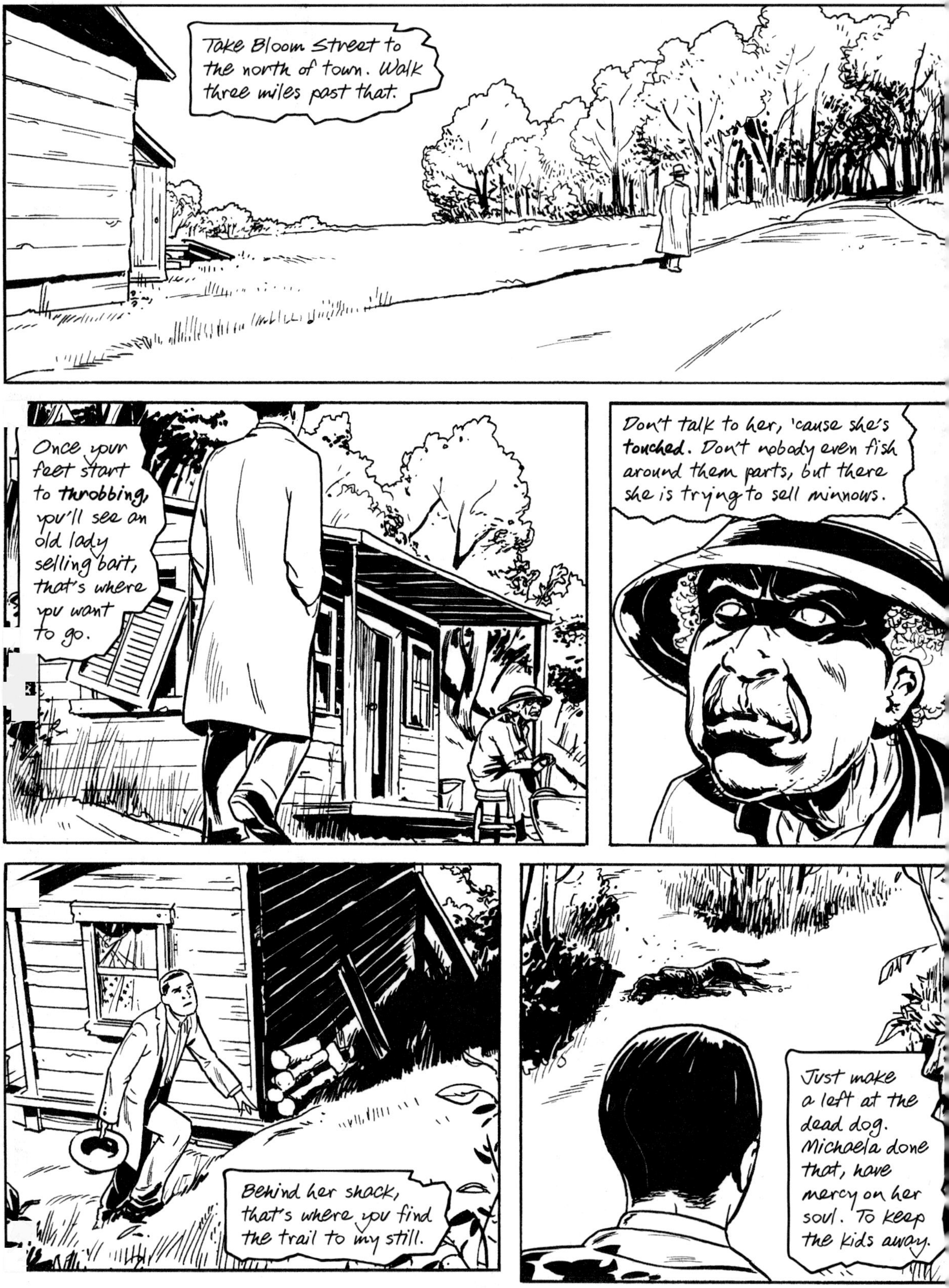
Take Bloom Street to the north of town. Walk three miles past that.
Once your feet start to throbbing, you'll see an old lady selling bait, that's where you want to go.
Don't talk to her, 'cause she's touched. Don't nobody even fish around them parts, but there she is trying to sell minnows.
Behind her shack, that's where you find the trail to my still.
Just make a left at the dead dog. Michaela done that, have mercy on her soul. To keep the kids away.

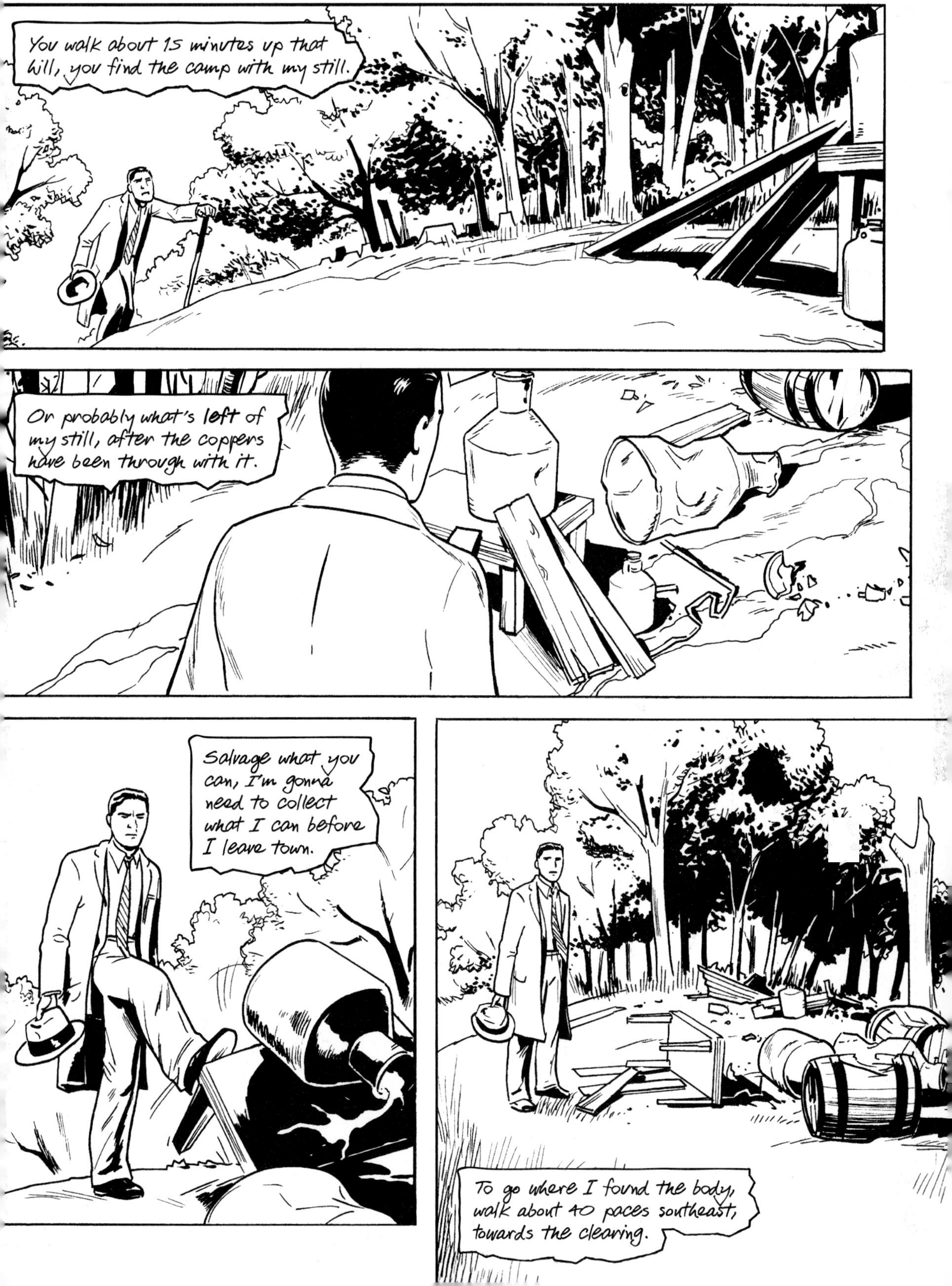
You walk about 15 minutes up that hill, you find the camp with my still.
Or probably what's **left** of my still, after the coppers have been through with it.
Salvage what you can, I'm gonna need to collect what I can before I leave town.
To go where I found the body, walk about 40 paces southeast, towards the clearing.

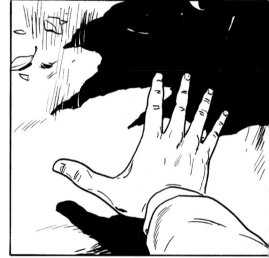

POWWW

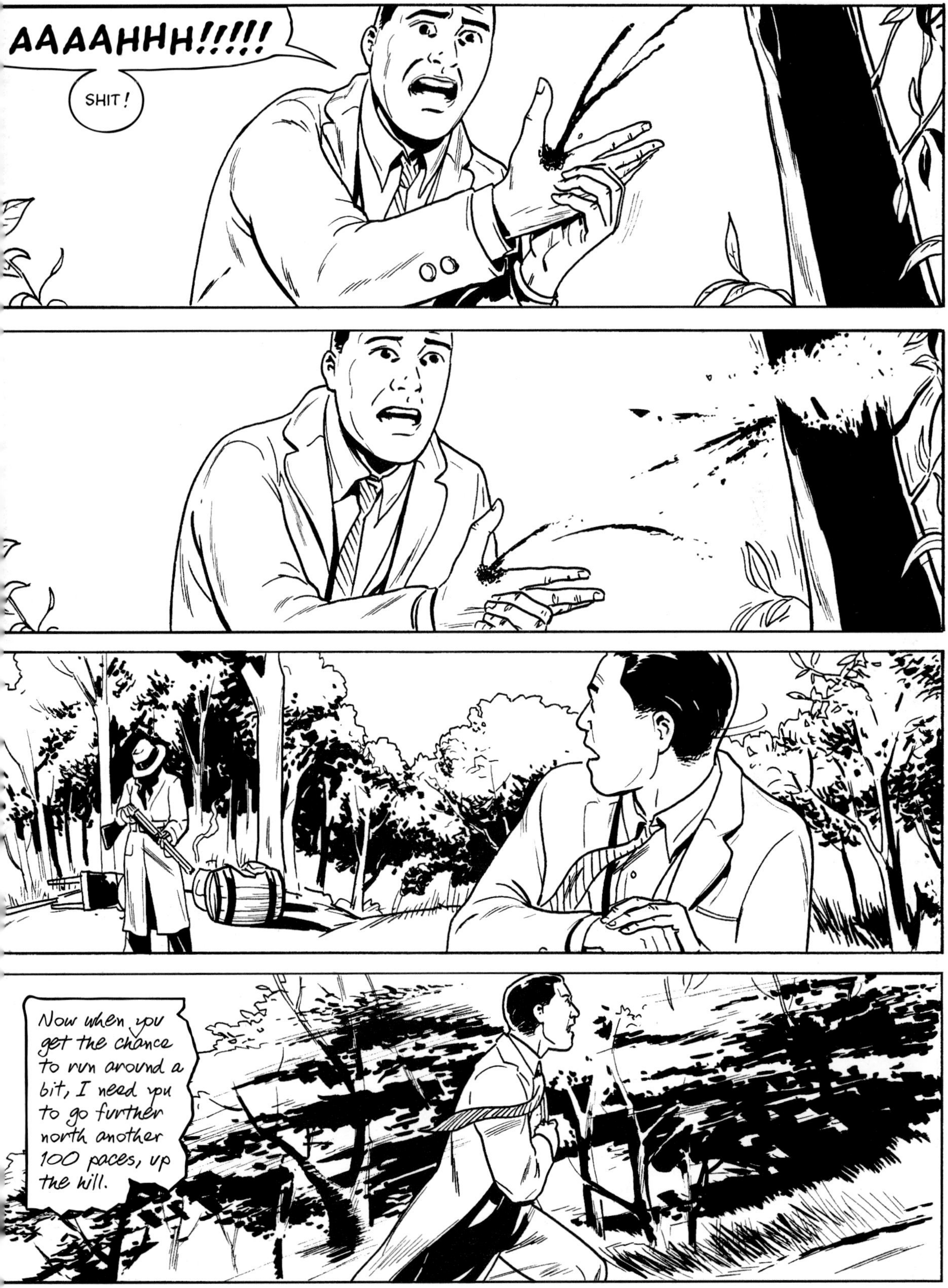
AAAAHHH!!!!!
SHIT!
Now when you get the chance to run around a bit, I need you to go further north another 100 paces, up the hill.

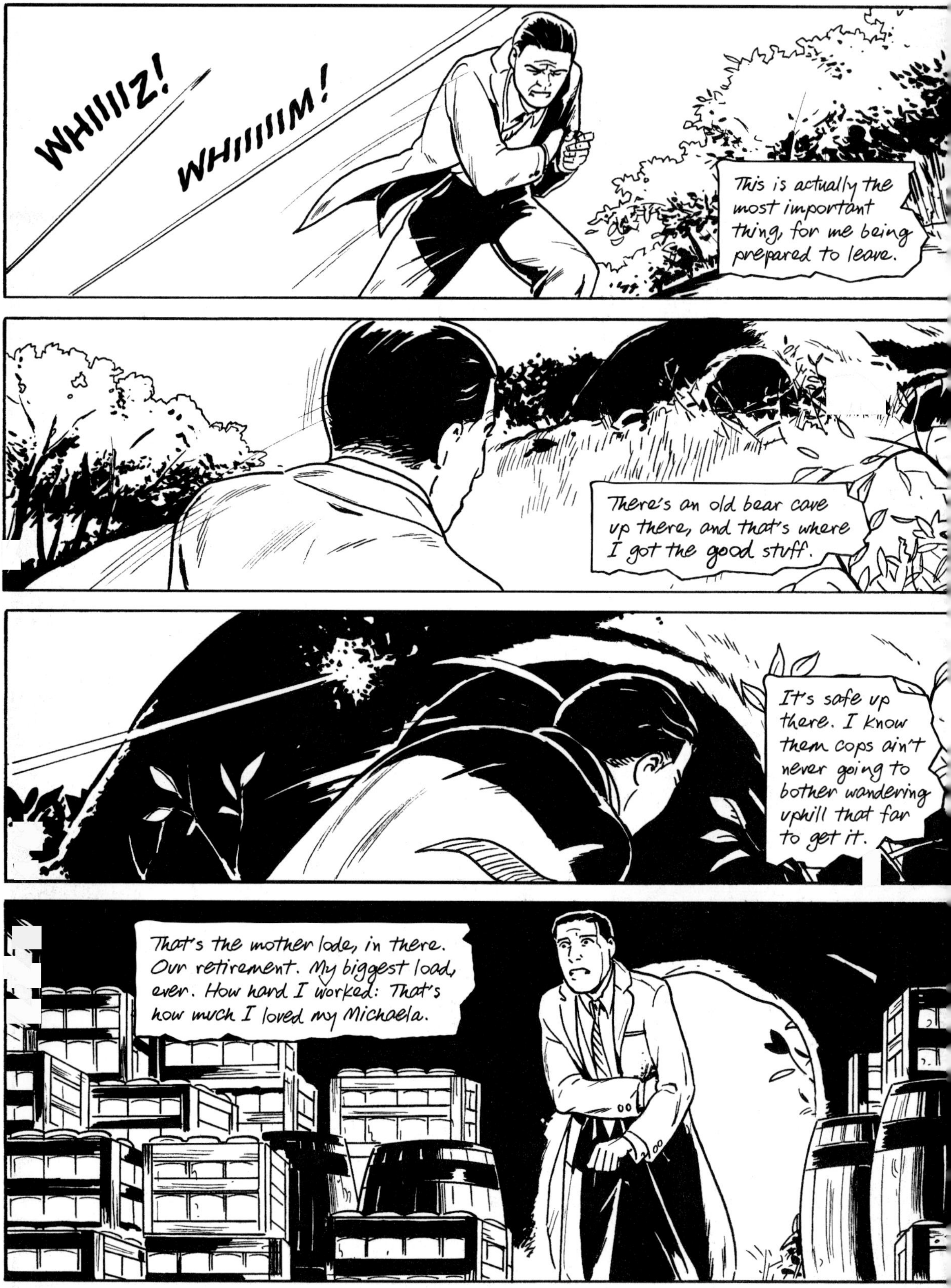
WHIIIIZ!
WHIIIIIM!
This is actually the most important thing, for me being prepared to leave.
There's an old bear cave up there, and that's where I got the good stuff.
It's safe up there. I know them cops ain't never going to bother wandering uphill that far to get it.
That's the mother lode, in there. Our retirement. My biggest load, ever. How hard I worked: That's how much I loved my Michaela.

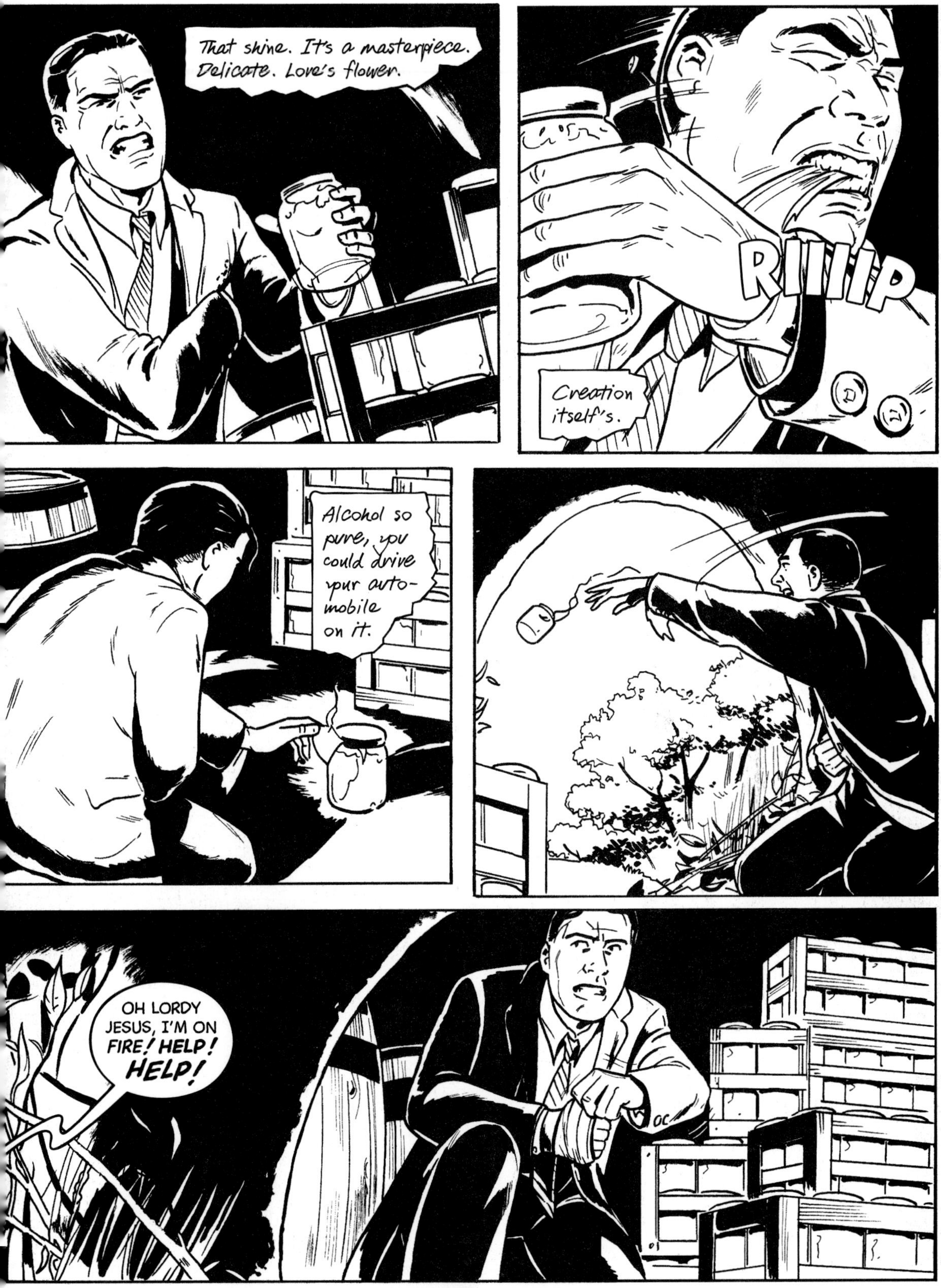
That shine. It's a masterpiece. Delicate. Love's flower.
RIIIIP
Creation itself's.
Alcohol so pure, you could drive your auto-mobile on it.
OH LORDY JESUS, I'M ON FIRE! HELP! HELP!

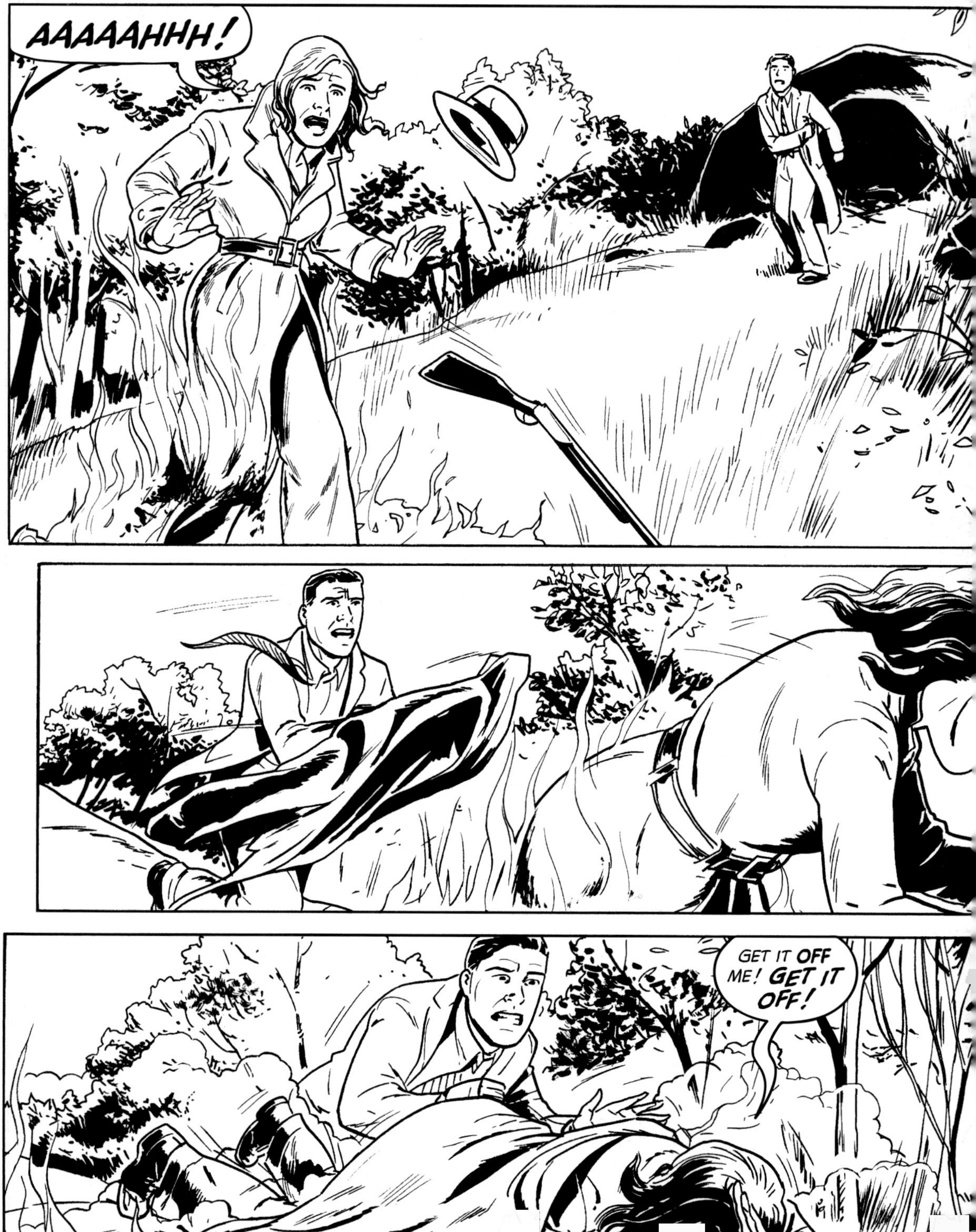
AAAAAHHH!
GET IT OFF ME! GET IT OFF!

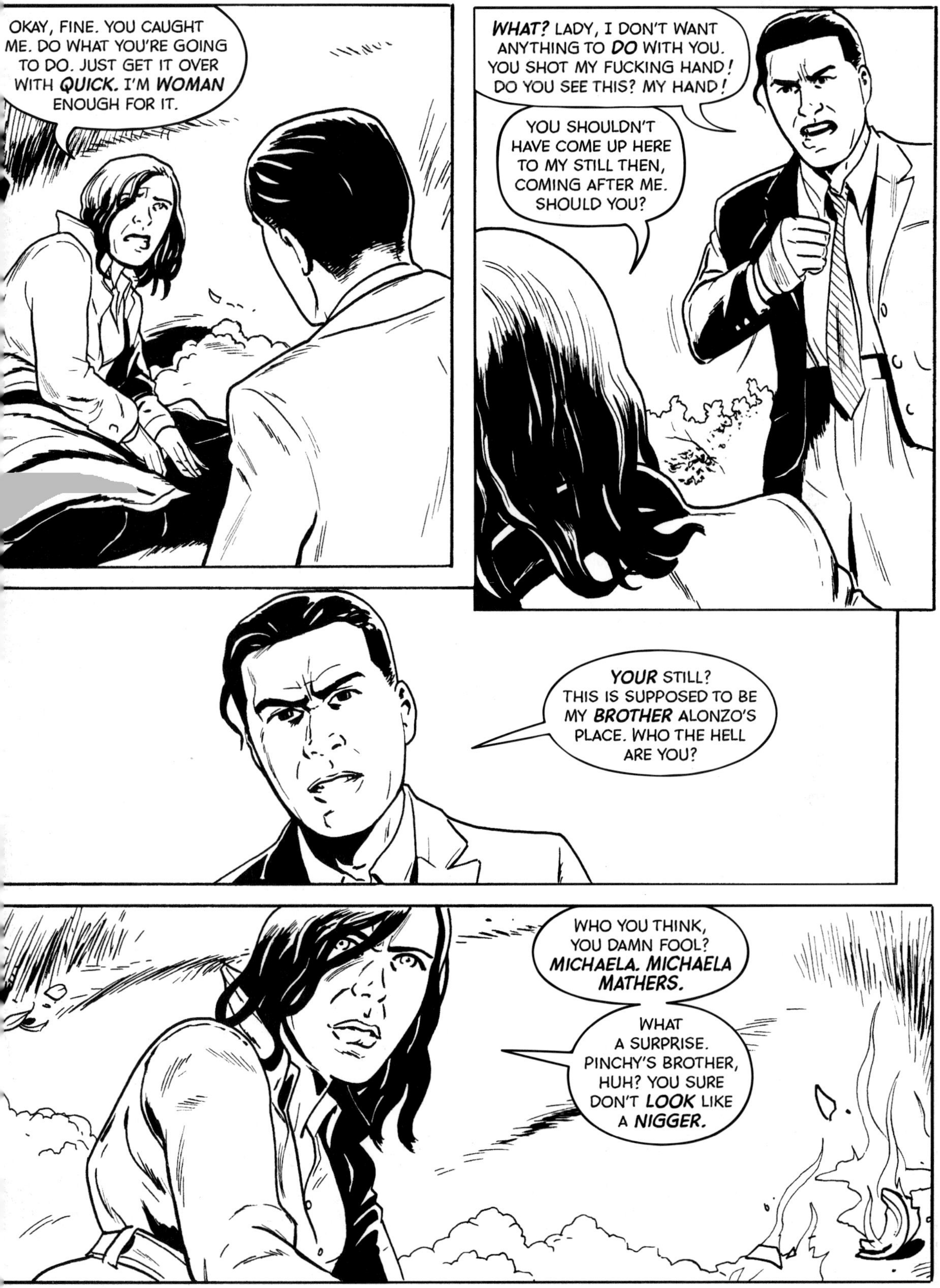

OKAY, FINE. YOU CAUGHT ME. DO WHAT YOU'RE GOING TO DO. JUST GET IT OVER WITH QUICK. I'M WOMAN ENOUGH FOR IT.
WHAT? LADY, I DON'T WANT ANYTHING TO DO WITH YOU. YOU SHOT MY FUCKING HAND! DO YOU SEE THIS? MY HAND!
YOU SHOULDN'T HAVE COME UP HERE TO MY STILL THEN, COMING AFTER ME. SHOULD YOU?
YOUR STILL? THIS IS SUPPOSED TO BE MY BROTHER ALONZO'S PLACE. WHO THE HELL ARE YOU?
WHO YOU THINK, YOU DAMN FOOL? MICHAELA. MICHAELA MATHERS.
WHAT A SURPRISE. PINCHY'S BROTHER, HUH? YOU SURE DON'T LOOK LIKE A NIGGER.

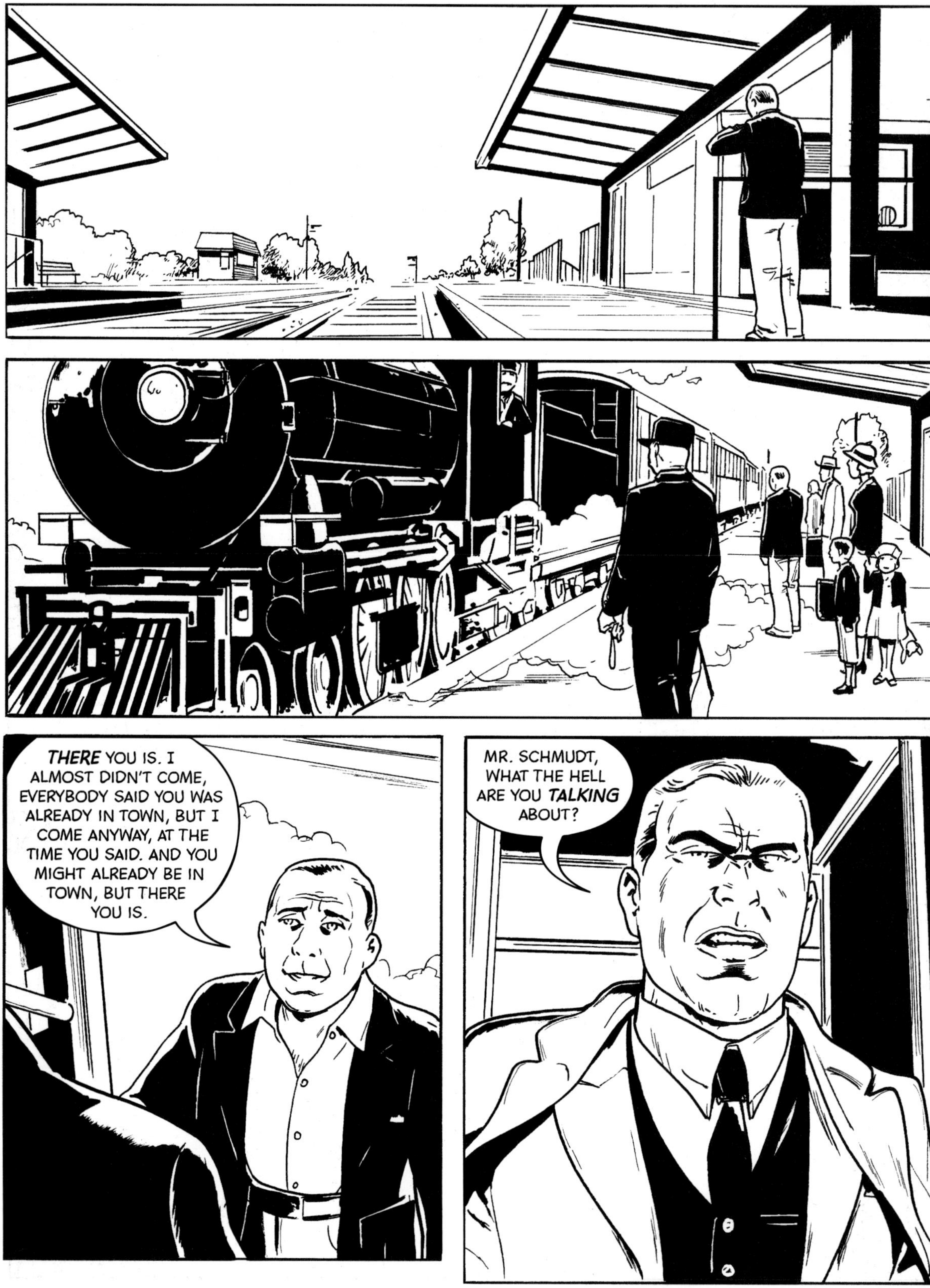
THERE YOU IS. I ALMOST DIDN'T COME, EVERYBODY SAID YOU WAS ALREADY IN TOWN, BUT I COME ANYWAY, AT THE TIME YOU SAID. AND YOU MIGHT ALREADY BE IN TOWN, BUT THERE YOU IS.
MR. SCHMUDT, WHAT THE HELL ARE YOU TALKING ABOUT?

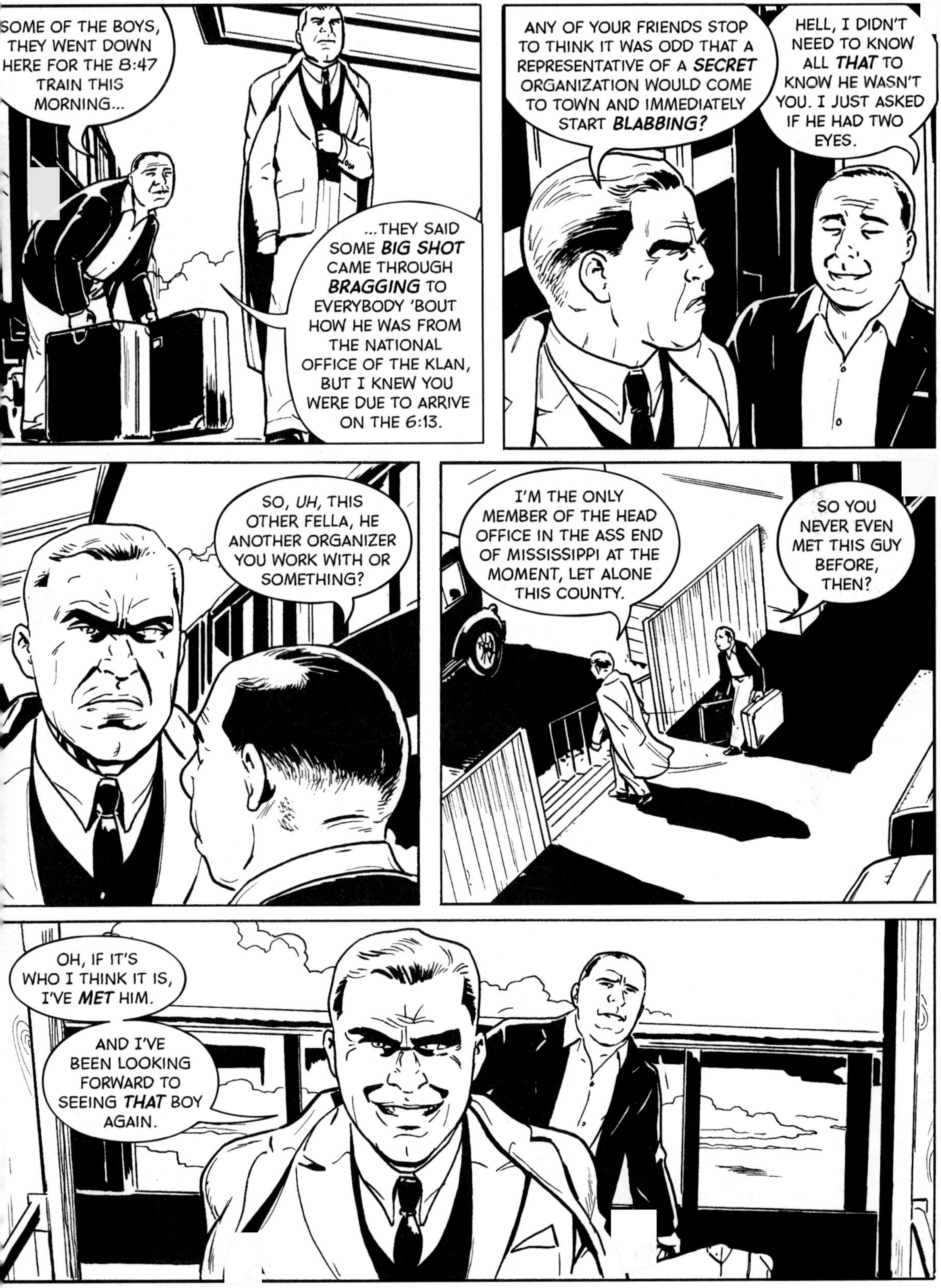
SOME OF THE BOYS, THEY WENT DOWN HERE FOR THE 8:47 TRAIN THIS MORNING...
...THEY SAID SOME BIG SHOT CAME THROUGH BRAGGING TO EVERYBODY 'BOUT HOW HE WAS FROM THE NATIONAL OFFICE OF THE KLAN, BUT I KNEW YOU WERE DUE TO ARRIVE ON THE 6:13.
ANY OF YOUR FRIENDS STOP TO THINK IT WAS ODD THAT A REPRESENTATIVE OF A SECRET ORGANIZATION WOULD COME TO TOWN AND IMMEDIATELY START BLABBING?
HELL, I DIDN'T NEED TO KNOW ALL THAT TO KNOW HE WASN'T YOU. I JUST ASKED IF HE HAD TWO EYES.
SO, UH, THIS OTHER FELLA, HE ANOTHER ORGANIZER YOU WORK WITH OR SOMETHING?
I'M THE ONLY MEMBER OF THE HEAD OFFICE IN THE ASS END OF MISSISSIPPI AT THE MOMENT, LET ALONE THIS COUNTY.
SO YOU NEVER EVEN MET THIS GUY BEFORE, THEN?
OH, IF IT'S WHO I THINK IT IS, I'VE MET HIM.
AND I'VE BEEN LOOKING FORWARD TO SEEING THAT BOY AGAIN.

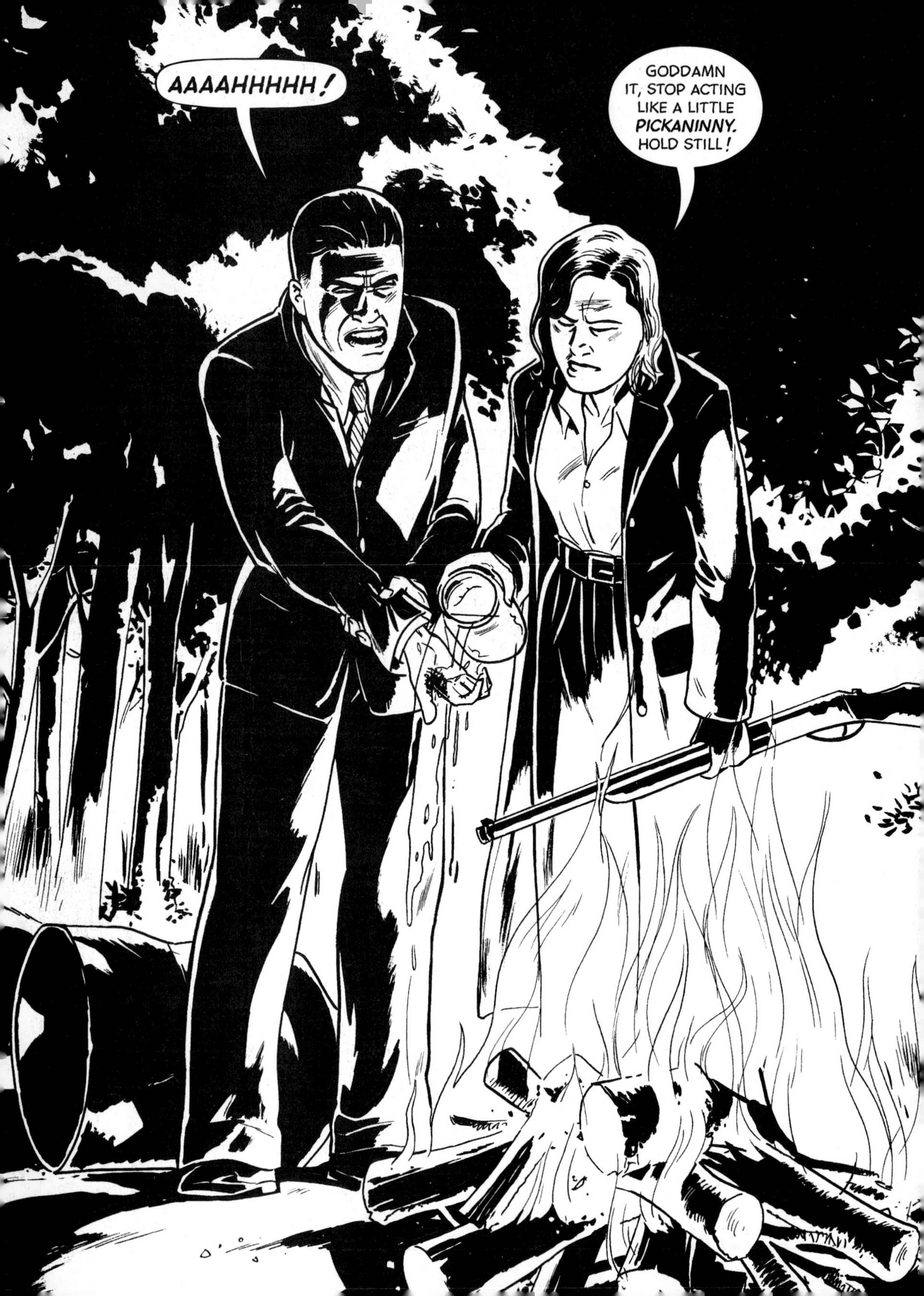
AAAAHHHHH!
GODDAMN IT, STOP ACTING LIKE A LITTLE PICKANINNY. HOLD STILL!

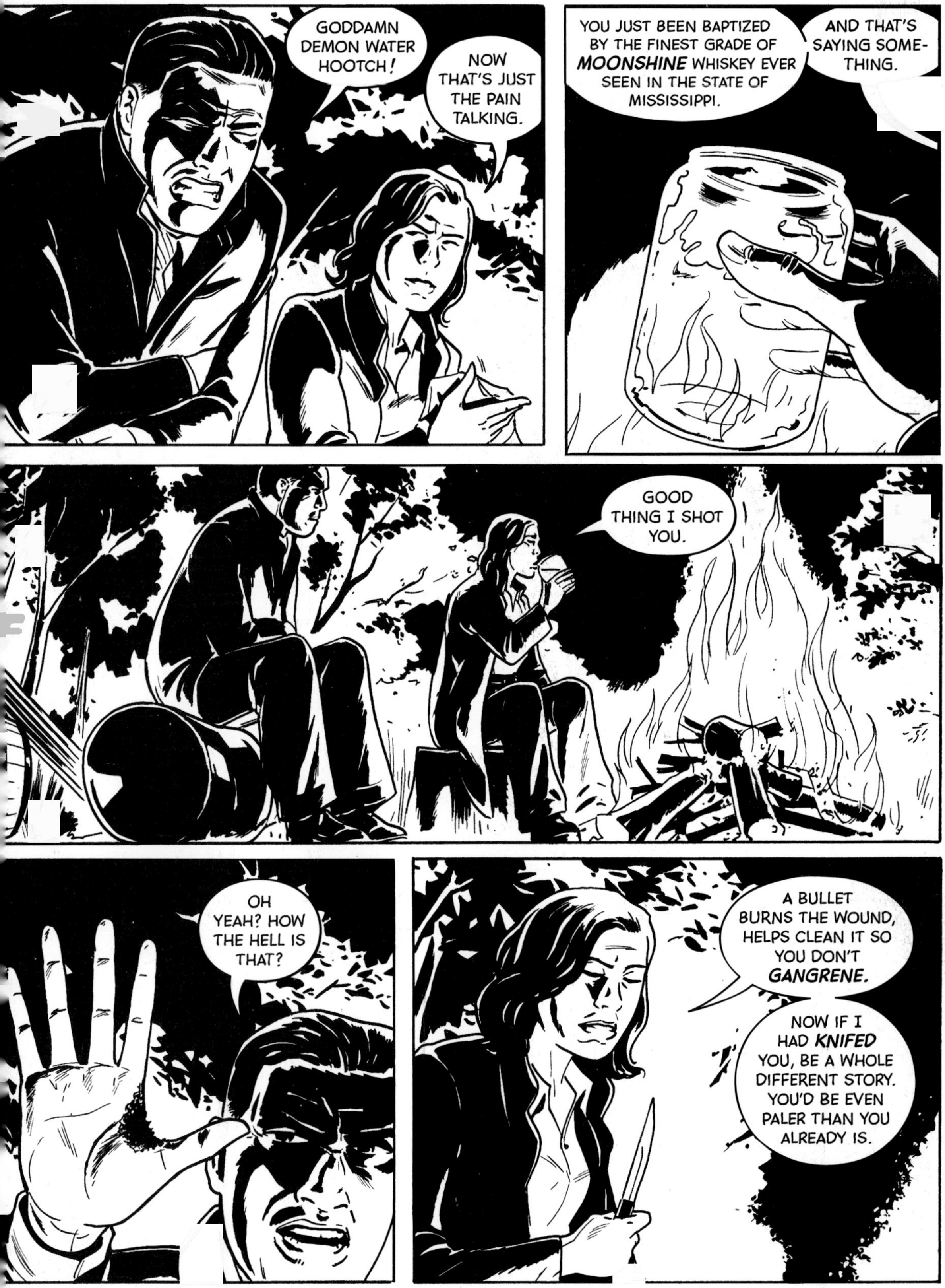
GODDAMN DEMON WATER HOOTCH!
NOW THAT'S JUST THE PAIN TALKING.
YOU JUST BEEN BAPTIZED BY THE FINEST GRADE OF MOONSHINE WHISKEY EVER SEEN IN THE STATE OF MISSISSIPPI.
AND THAT'S SAYING SOME-THING.
GOOD THING I SHOT YOU.
OH YEAH? HOW THE HELL IS THAT?
A BULLET BURNS THE WOUND, HELPS CLEAN IT SO YOU DON'T GANGRENE.
NOW IF I HAD KNIFED YOU, BE A WHOLE DIFFERENT STORY. YOU'D BE EVEN PALER THAN YOU ALREADY IS.

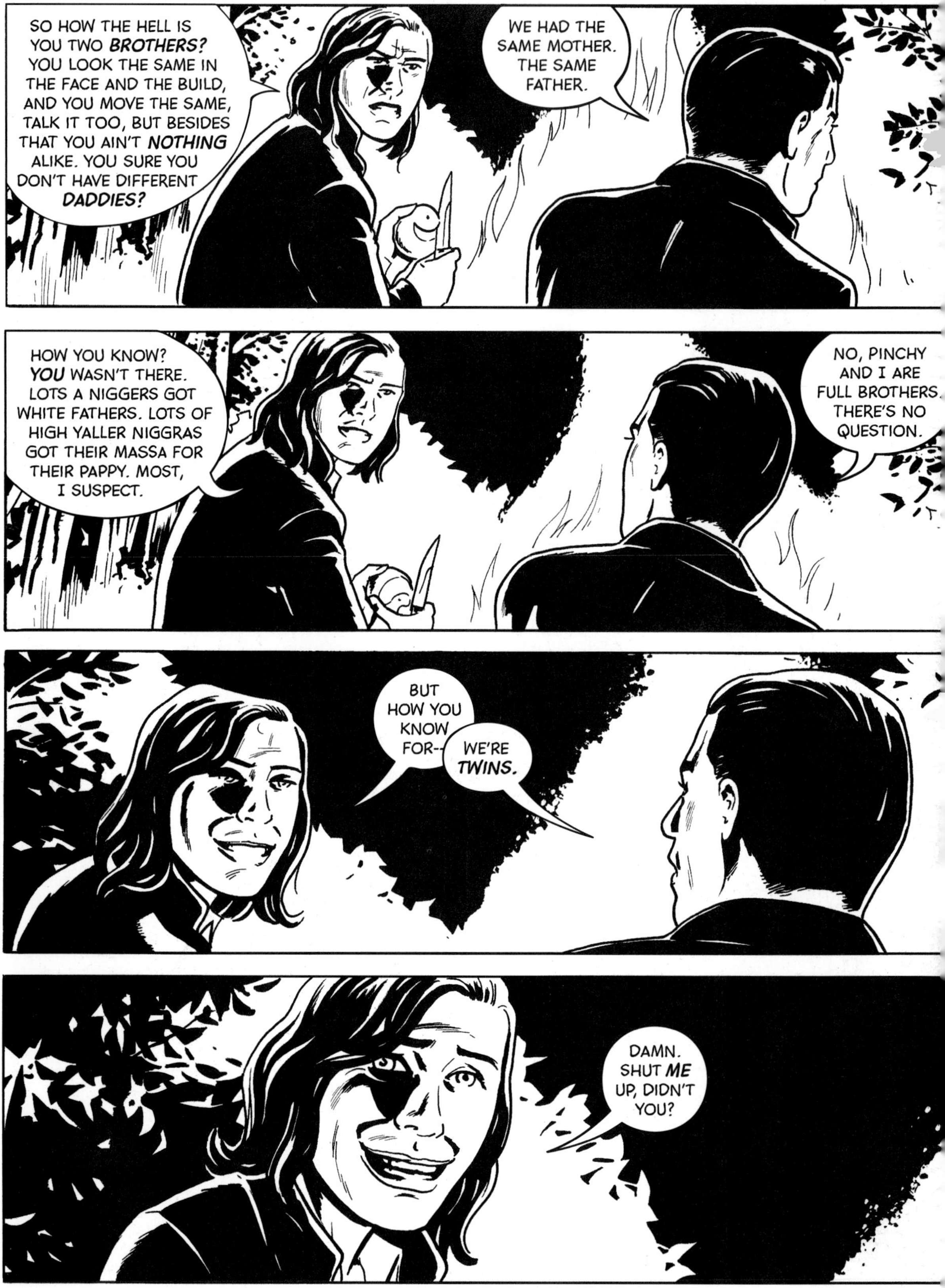
SO HOW THE HELL IS YOU TWO BROTHERS? YOU LOOK THE SAME IN THE FACE AND THE BUILD, AND YOU MOVE THE SAME, TALK IT TOO, BUT BESIDES THAT YOU AIN'T NOTHING ALIKE. YOU SURE YOU DON'T HAVE DIFFERENT DADDIES?
WE HAD THE SAME MOTHER. THE SAME FATHER.
HOW YOU KNOW? YOU WASN'T THERE. LOTS A NIGGERS GOT WHITE FATHERS. LOTS OF HIGH YALLER NIGGRAS GOT THEIR MASSA FOR THEIR PAPPY. MOST, I SUSPECT.
NO, PINCHY AND I ARE FULL BROTHERS. THERE'S NO QUESTION.
BUT HOW YOU KNOW FOR--
WE'RE TWINS.
DAMN. SHUT ME UP, DIDN'T YOU?

51

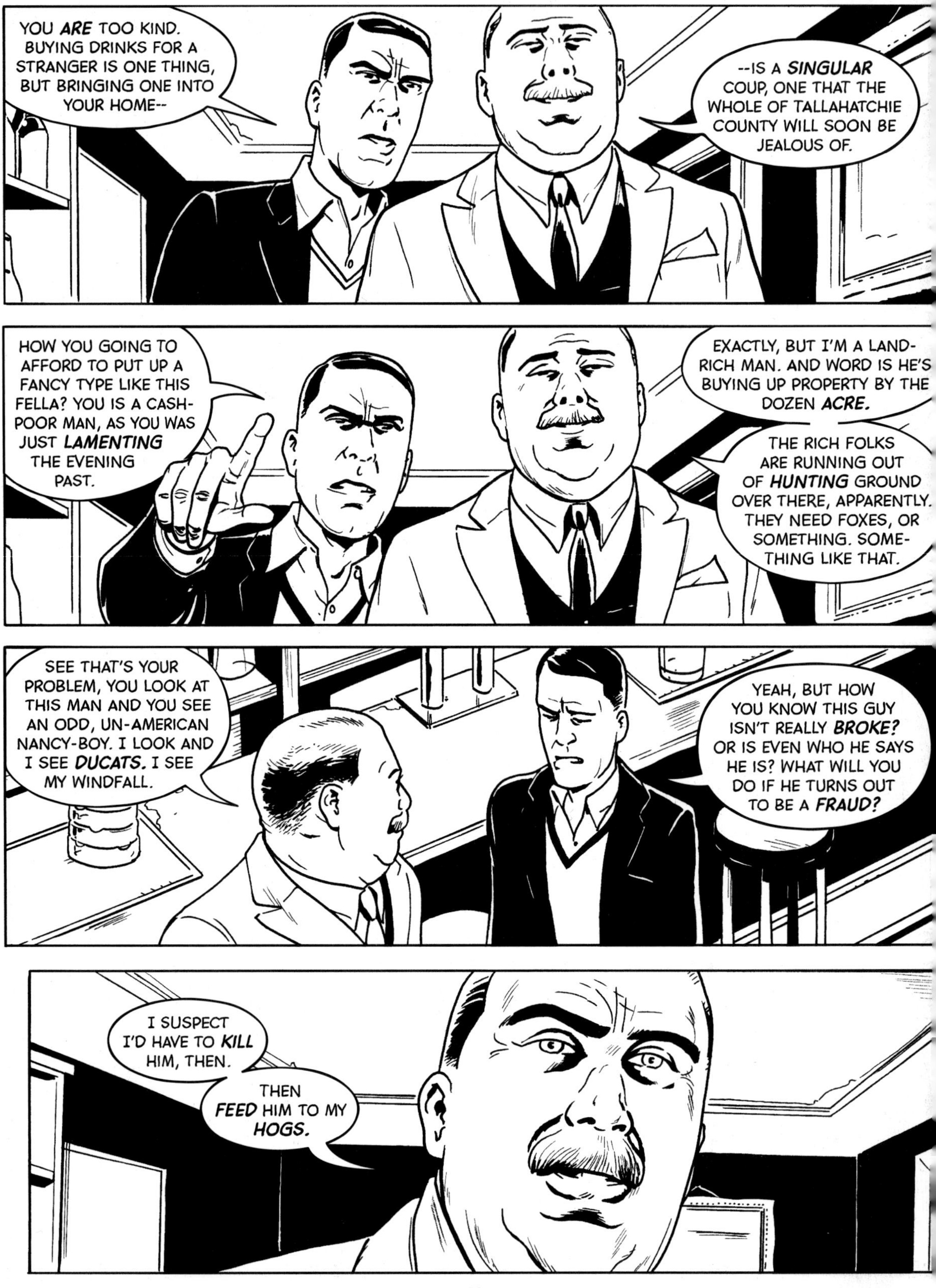
YOU ARE TOO KIND. BUYING DRINKS FOR A STRANGER IS ONE THING, BUT BRINGING ONE INTO YOUR HOME--
--IS A SINGULAR COUP, ONE THAT THE WHOLE OF TALLAHATCHIE COUNTY WILL SOON BE JEALOUS OF.
HOW YOU GOING TO AFFORD TO PUT UP A FANCY TYPE LIKE THIS FELLA? YOU IS A CASH-POOR MAN, AS YOU WAS JUST LAMENTING THE EVENING PAST.
EXACTLY, BUT I'M A LAND-RICH MAN. AND WORD IS HE'S BUYING UP PROPERTY BY THE DOZEN ACRE.
THE RICH FOLKS ARE RUNNING OUT OF HUNTING GROUND OVER THERE, APPARENTLY. THEY NEED FOXES, OR SOMETHING. SOMETHING LIKE THAT.
SEE THAT'S YOUR PROBLEM, YOU LOOK AT THIS MAN AND YOU SEE AN ODD, UN-AMERICAN NANCY-BOY. I LOOK AND I SEE DUCATS. I SEE MY WINDFALL.
YEAH, BUT HOW YOU KNOW THIS GUY ISN'T REALLY BROKE? OR IS EVEN WHO HE SAYS HE IS? WHAT WILL YOU DO IF HE TURNS OUT TO BE A FRAUD?
I SUSPECT I'D HAVE TO KILL HIM, THEN.
THEN FEED HIM TO MY HOGS.

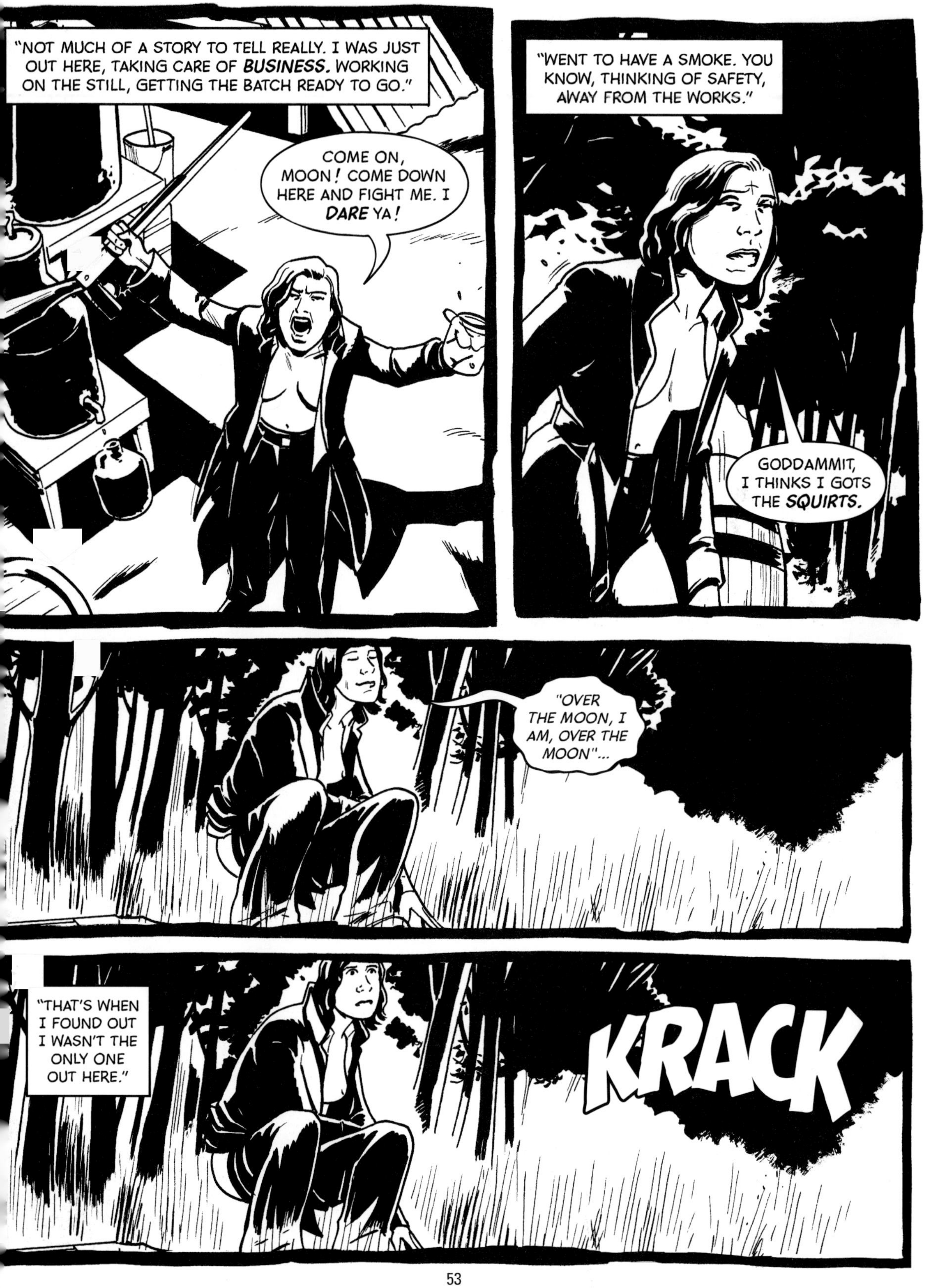
"NOT MUCH OF A STORY TO TELL REALLY. I WAS JUST OUT HERE, TAKING CARE OF BUSINESS. WORKING ON THE STILL, GETTING THE BATCH READY TO GO."
COME ON, MOON! COME DOWN HERE AND FIGHT ME. I DARE YA!
"WENT TO HAVE A SMOKE. YOU KNOW, THINKING OF SAFETY, AWAY FROM THE WORKS."
GODDAMMIT, I THINKS I GOTS THE SQUIRTS.
"OVER THE MOON, I AM, OVER THE MOON"...
"THAT'S WHEN I FOUND OUT I WASN'T THE ONLY ONE OUT HERE."
KRACK

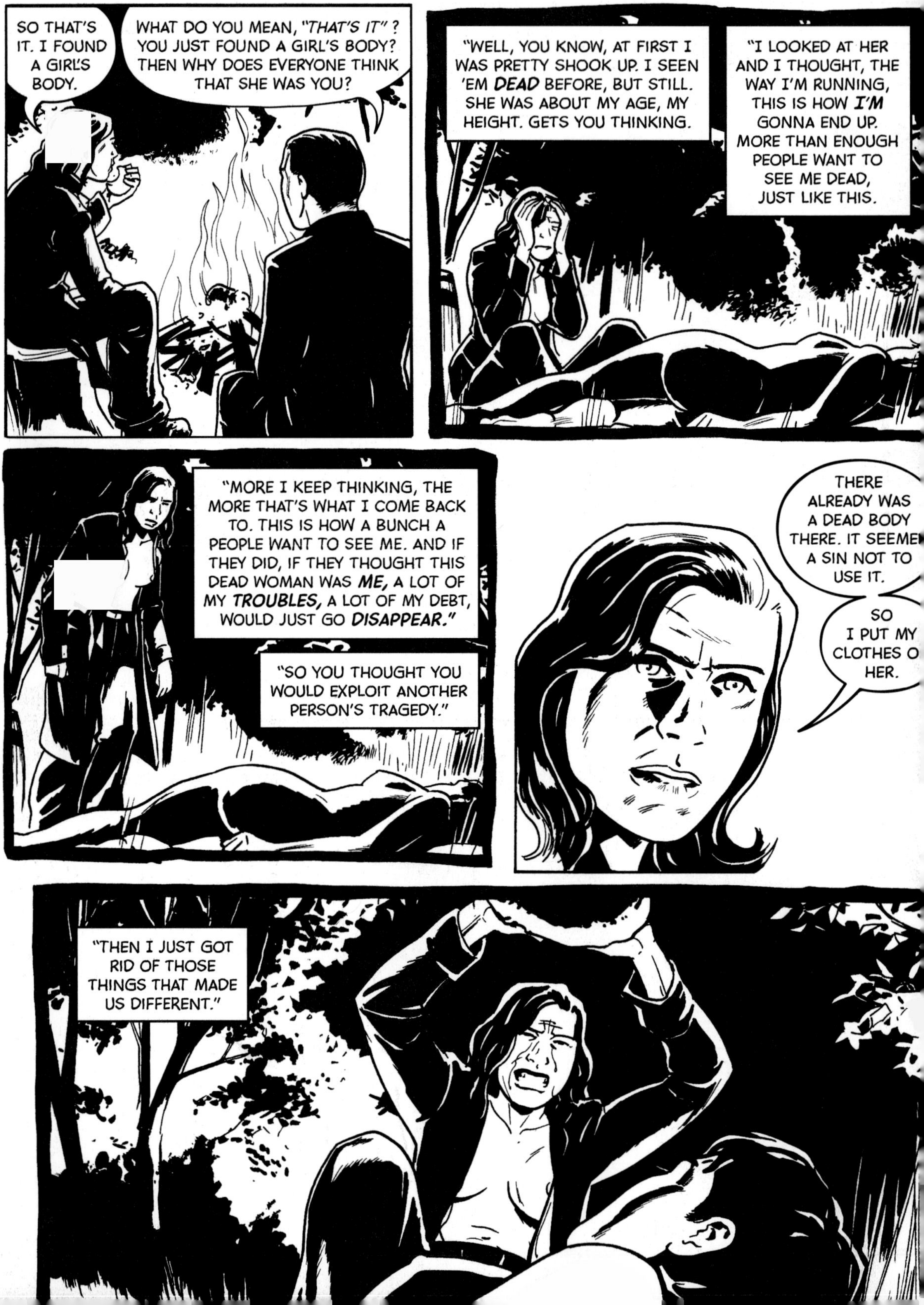
SO THAT'S IT. I FOUND A GIRL'S BODY.
WHAT DO YOU MEAN, "THAT'S IT"? YOU JUST FOUND A GIRL'S BODY? THEN WHY DOES EVERYONE THINK THAT SHE WAS YOU?
"WELL, YOU KNOW, AT FIRST I WAS PRETTY SHOOK UP. I SEEN 'EM DEAD BEFORE, BUT STILL. SHE WAS ABOUT MY AGE, MY HEIGHT. GETS YOU THINKING.
"I LOOKED AT HER AND I THOUGHT, THE WAY I'M RUNNING, THIS IS HOW I'M GONNA END UP. MORE THAN ENOUGH PEOPLE WANT TO SEE ME DEAD, JUST LIKE THIS.
"MORE I KEEP THINKING, THE MORE THAT'S WHAT I COME BACK TO. THIS IS HOW A BUNCH A PEOPLE WANT TO SEE ME. AND IF THEY DID, IF THEY THOUGHT THIS DEAD WOMAN WAS ME, A LOT OF MY TROUBLES, A LOT OF MY DEBT, WOULD JUST GO DISAPPEAR."
"SO YOU THOUGHT YOU WOULD EXPLOIT ANOTHER PERSON'S TRAGEDY."
THERE ALREADY WAS A DEAD BODY THERE. IT SEEME A SIN NOT TO USE IT.
SO I PUT MY CLOTHES O HER.
"THEN I JUST GOT RID OF THOSE THINGS THAT MADE US DIFFERENT."

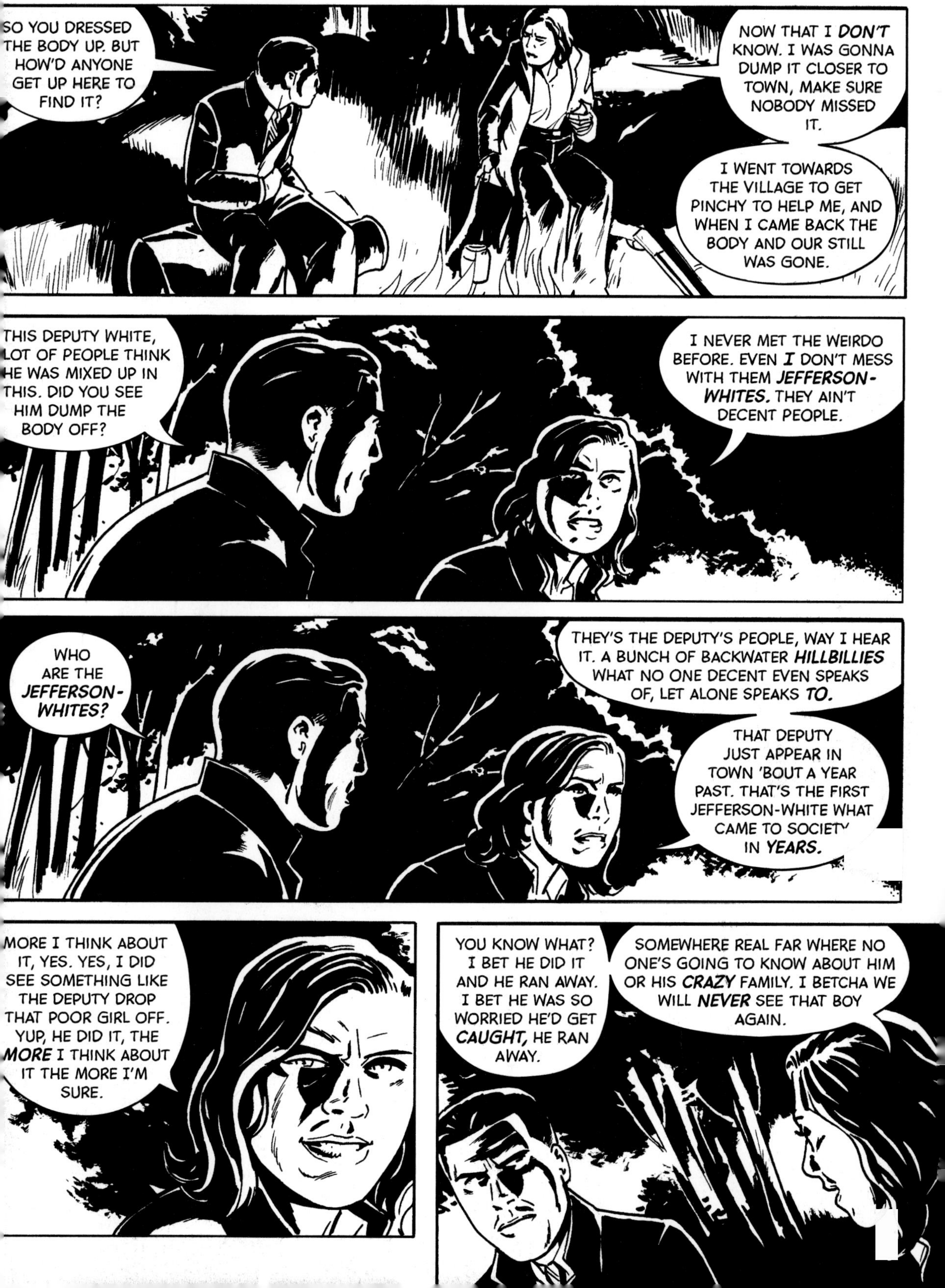
SO YOU DRESSED THE BODY UP. BUT HOW'D ANYONE GET UP HERE TO FIND IT?
NOW THAT I DON'T KNOW. I WAS GONNA DUMP IT CLOSER TO TOWN, MAKE SURE NOBODY MISSED IT.
I WENT TOWARDS THE VILLAGE TO GET PINCHY TO HELP ME, AND WHEN I CAME BACK THE BODY AND OUR STILL WAS GONE.
THIS DEPUTY WHITE, LOT OF PEOPLE THINK HE WAS MIXED UP IN THIS. DID YOU SEE HIM DUMP THE BODY OFF?
I NEVER MET THE WEIRDO BEFORE. EVEN I DON'T MESS WITH THEM JEFFERSON-WHITES. THEY AIN'T DECENT PEOPLE.
WHO ARE THE JEFFERSON-WHITES?
THEY'S THE DEPUTY'S PEOPLE, WAY I HEAR IT. A BUNCH OF BACKWATER HILLBILLIES WHAT NO ONE DECENT EVEN SPEAKS OF, LET ALONE SPEAKS TO.
THAT DEPUTY JUST APPEAR IN TOWN 'BOUT A YEAR PAST. THAT'S THE FIRST JEFFERSON-WHITE WHAT CAME TO SOCIETY IN YEARS.
MORE I THINK ABOUT IT, YES. YES, I DID SEE SOMETHING LIKE THE DEPUTY DROP THAT POOR GIRL OFF. YUP, HE DID IT, THE MORE I THINK ABOUT IT THE MORE I'M SURE.
YOU KNOW WHAT? I BET HE DID IT AND HE RAN AWAY. I BET HE WAS SO WORRIED HE'D GET CAUGHT, HE RAN AWAY.
SOMEWHERE REAL FAR WHERE NO ONE'S GOING TO KNOW ABOUT HIM OR HIS CRAZY FAMILY. I BETCHA WE WILL NEVER SEE THAT BOY AGAIN.

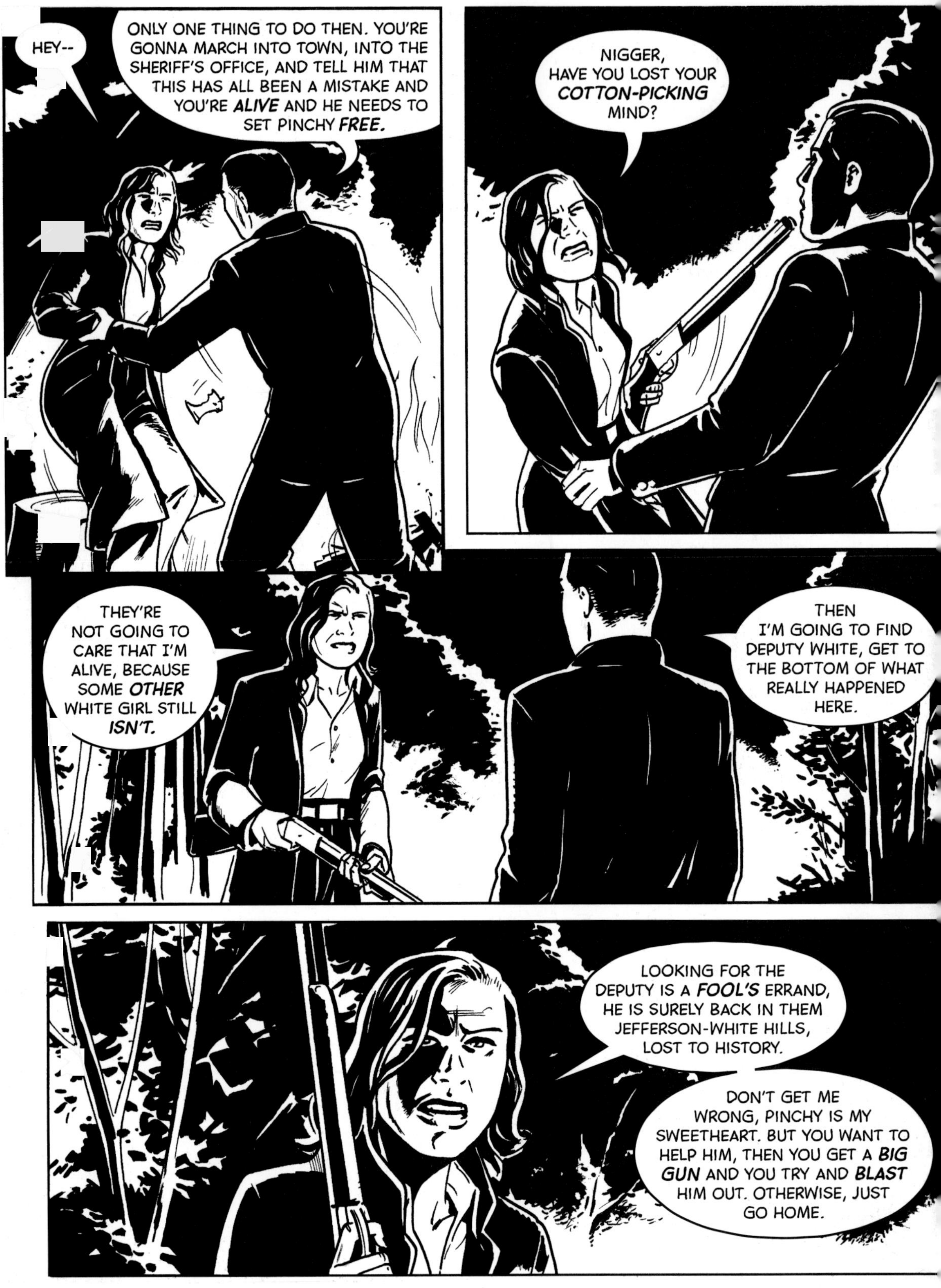
HEY--
ONLY ONE THING TO DO THEN. YOU'RE GONNA MARCH INTO TOWN, INTO THE SHERIFF'S OFFICE, AND TELL HIM THAT THIS HAS ALL BEEN A MISTAKE AND YOU'RE ***ALIVE*** AND HE NEEDS TO SET PINCHY ***FREE.***
NIGGER, HAVE YOU LOST YOUR ***COTTON-PICKING*** MIND?
THEY'RE NOT GOING TO CARE THAT I'M ALIVE, BECAUSE SOME ***OTHER*** WHITE GIRL STILL ***ISN'T.***
THEN I'M GOING TO FIND DEPUTY WHITE, GET TO THE BOTTOM OF WHAT REALLY HAPPENED HERE.
LOOKING FOR THE DEPUTY IS A ***FOOL'S*** ERRAND, HE IS SURELY BACK IN THEM JEFFERSON-WHITE HILLS, LOST TO HISTORY.
DON'T GET ME WRONG, PINCHY IS MY SWEETHEART. BUT YOU WANT TO HELP HIM, THEN YOU GET A ***BIG GUN*** AND YOU TRY AND ***BLAST*** HIM OUT. OTHERWISE, JUST GO HOME.

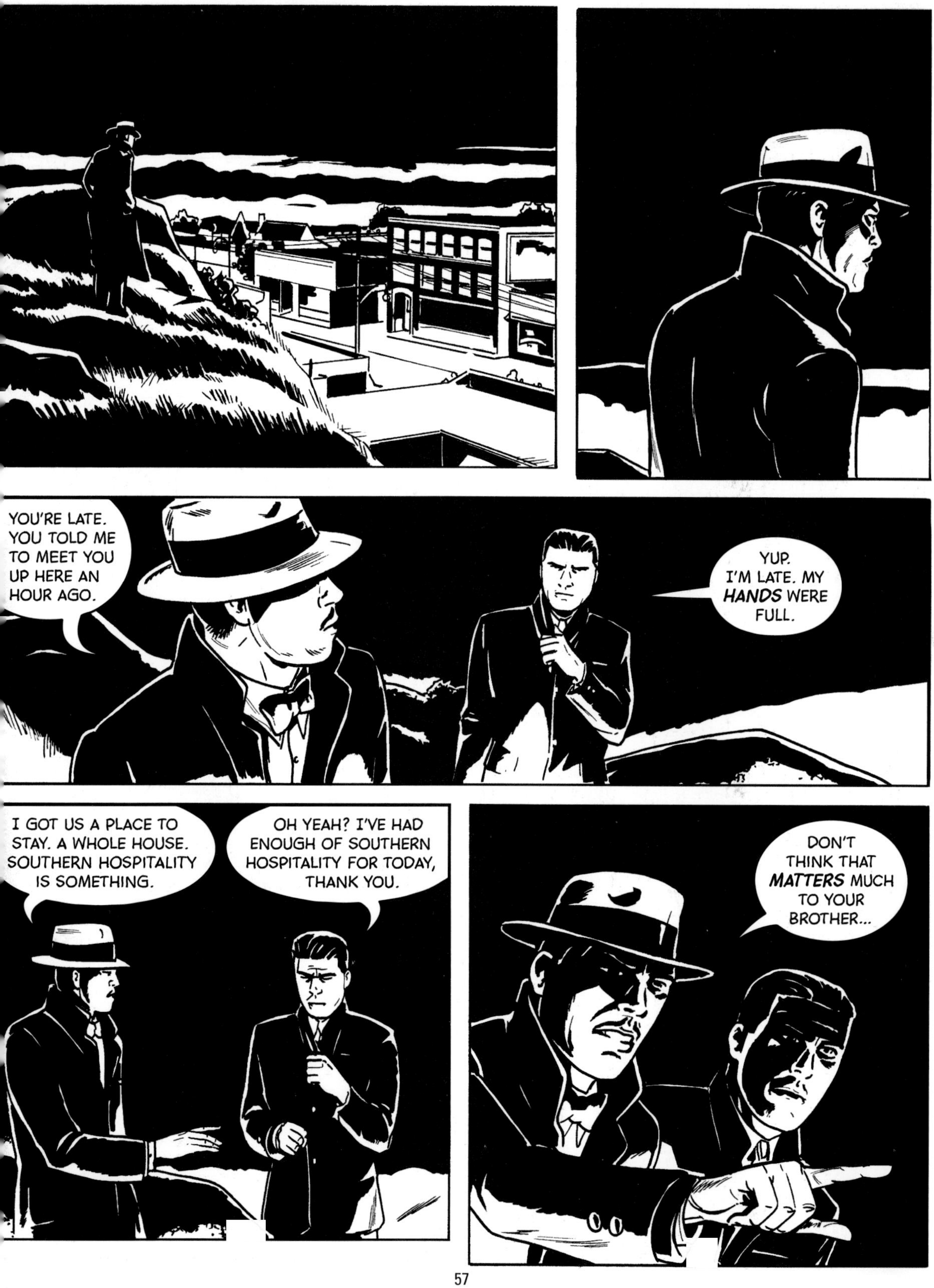
YOU'RE LATE. YOU TOLD ME TO MEET YOU UP HERE AN HOUR AGO.
YUP. I'M LATE. MY *HANDS* WERE FULL.
I GOT US A PLACE TO STAY. A WHOLE HOUSE. SOUTHERN HOSPITALITY IS SOMETHING.
OH YEAH? I'VE HAD ENOUGH OF SOUTHERN HOSPITALITY FOR TODAY, THANK YOU.
DON'T THINK THAT *MATTERS* MUCH TO YOUR BROTHER...

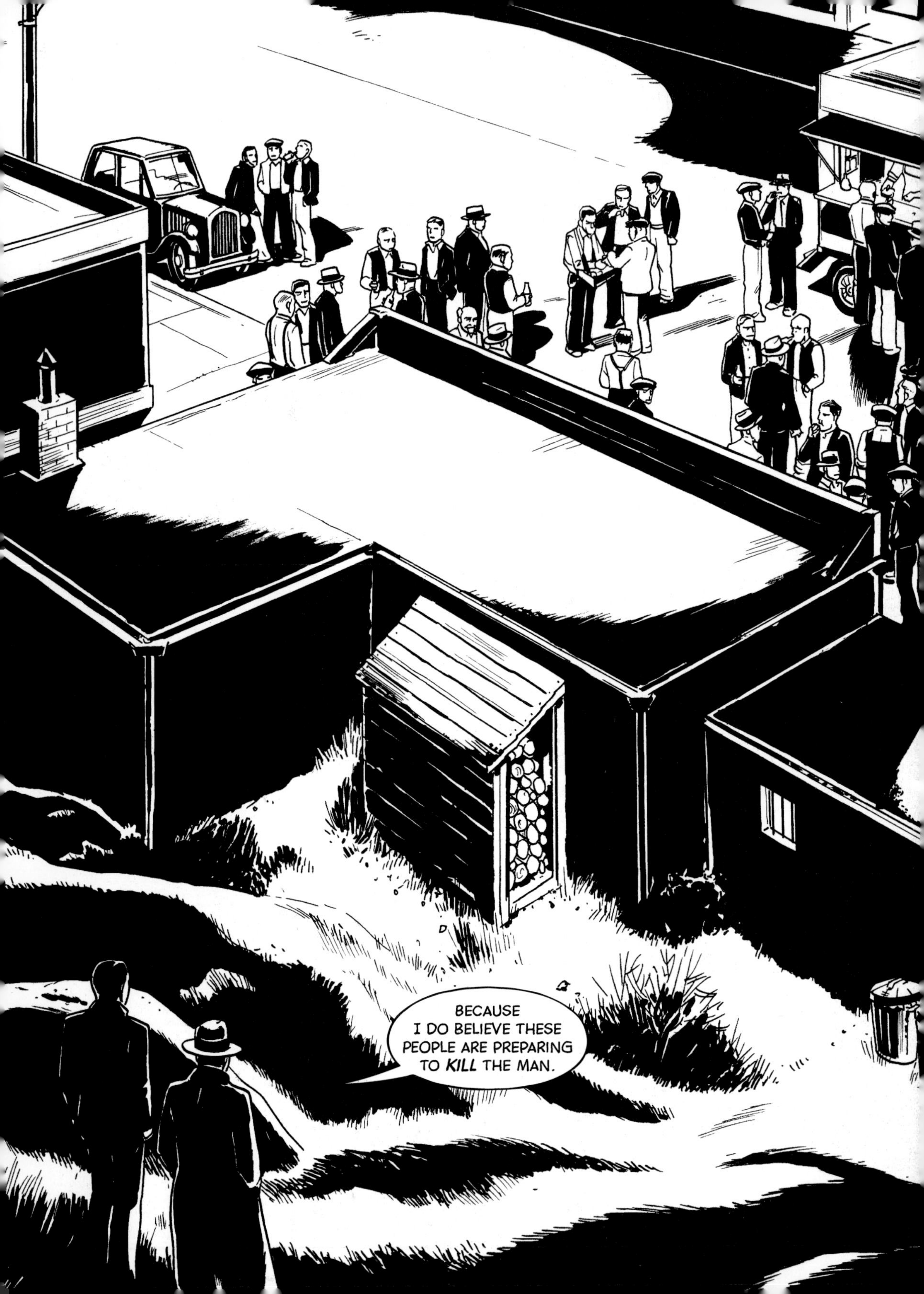
BECAUSE I DO BELIEVE THESE PEOPLE ARE PREPARING TO *KILL* THE MAN.

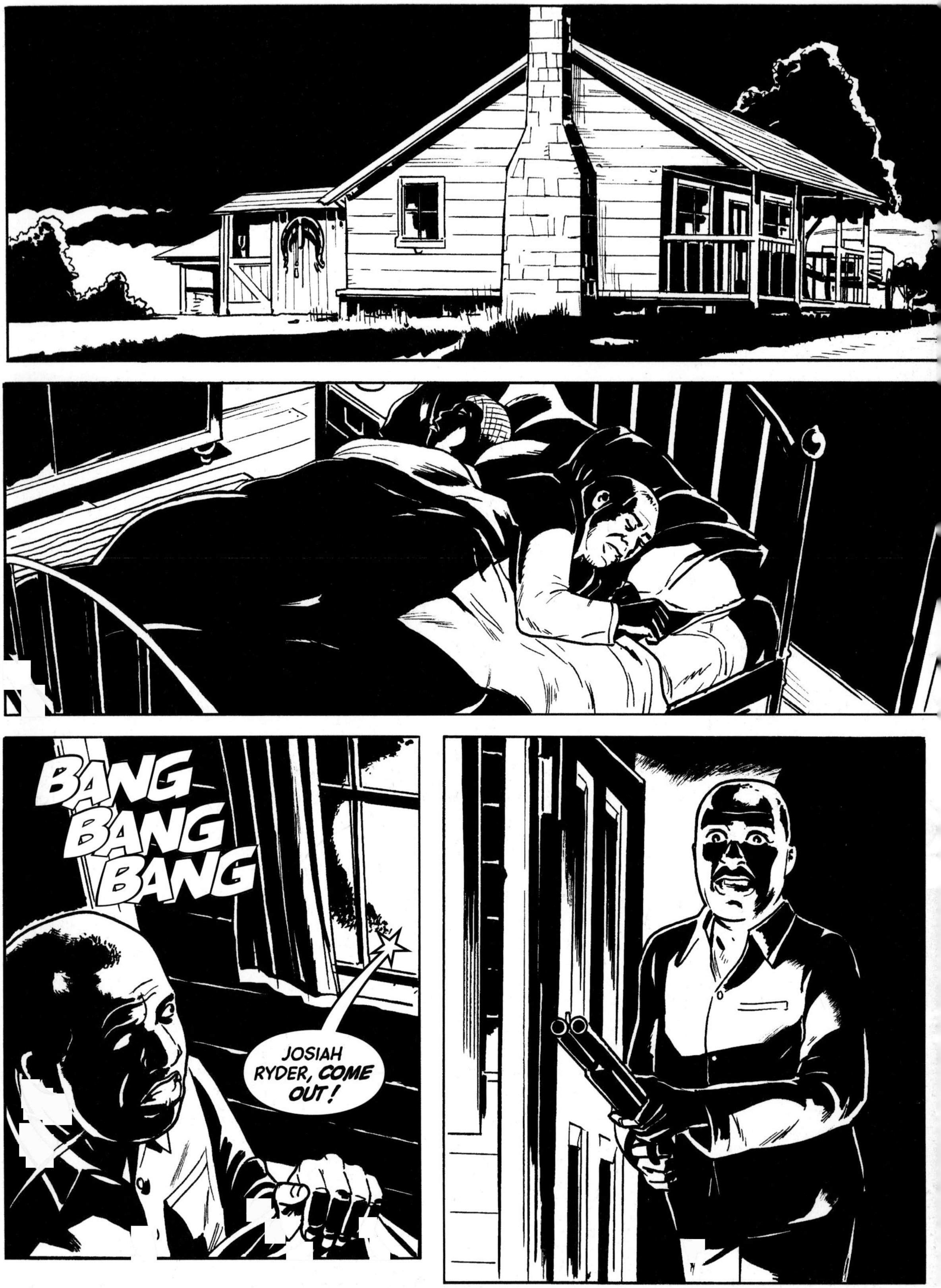
BANG
BANG
BANG
JOSIAH RYDER, COME OUT!

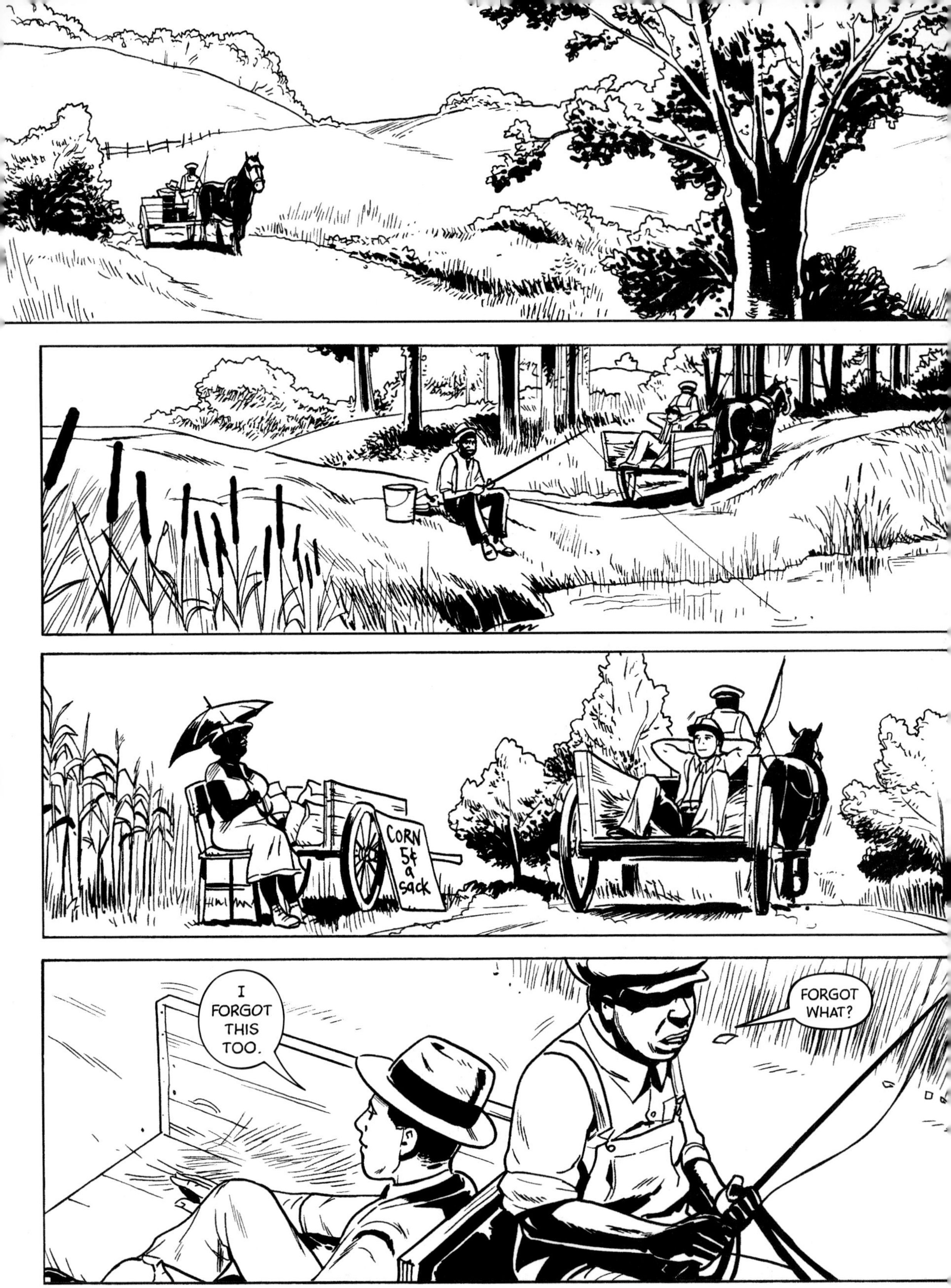
CORN 5¢ a sack
I FORGOT THIS TOO.
FORGOT WHAT?

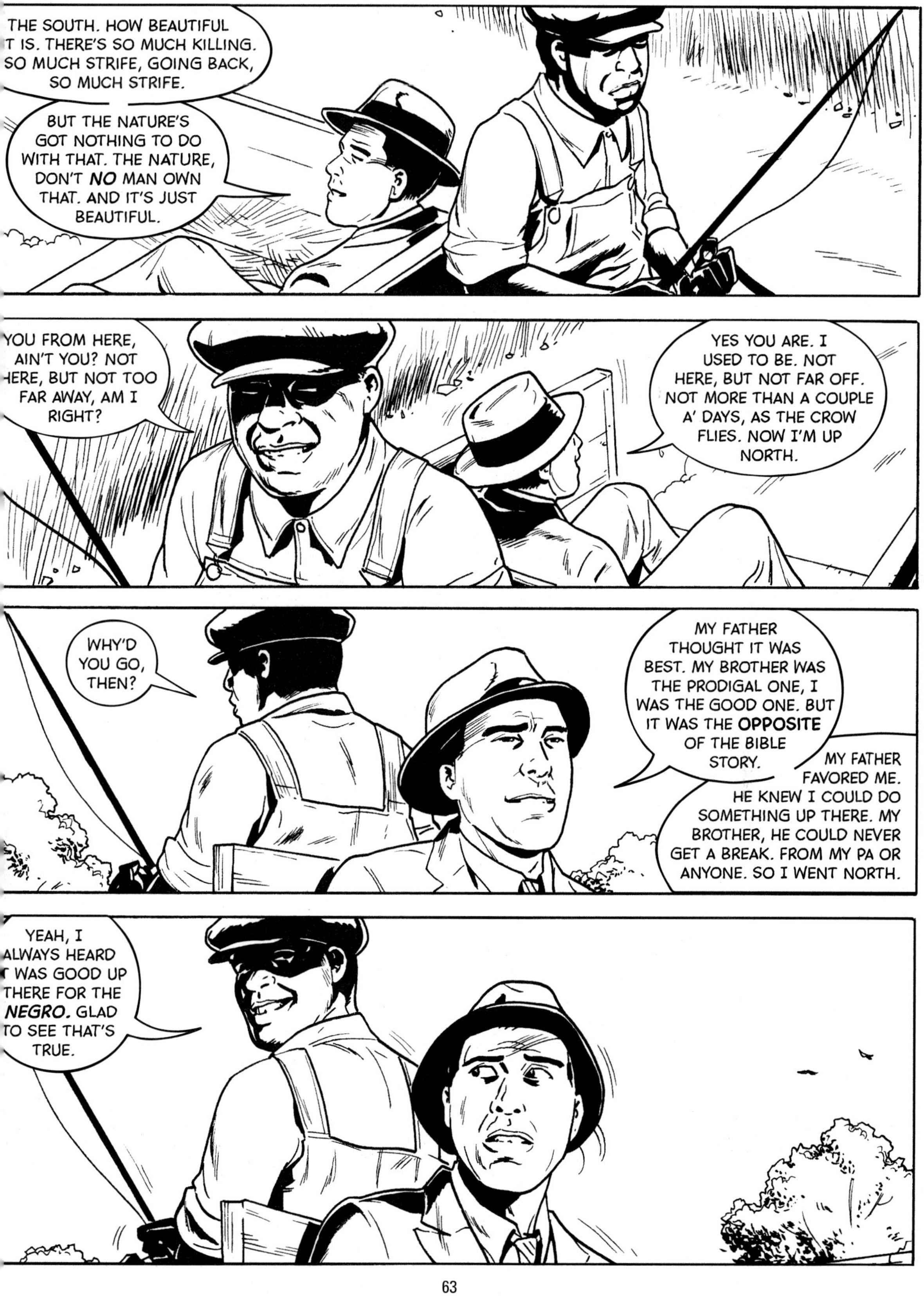
THE SOUTH. HOW BEAUTIFUL T IS. THERE'S SO MUCH KILLING. SO MUCH STRIFE, GOING BACK, SO MUCH STRIFE.
BUT THE NATURE'S GOT NOTHING TO DO WITH THAT. THE NATURE, DON'T ***NO*** MAN OWN THAT. AND IT'S JUST BEAUTIFUL.
YOU FROM HERE, AIN'T YOU? NOT HERE, BUT NOT TOO FAR AWAY, AM I RIGHT?
YES YOU ARE. I USED TO BE. NOT HERE, BUT NOT FAR OFF. NOT MORE THAN A COUPLE A' DAYS, AS THE CROW FLIES. NOW I'M UP NORTH.
WHY'D YOU GO, THEN?
MY FATHER THOUGHT IT WAS BEST. MY BROTHER WAS THE PRODIGAL ONE, I WAS THE GOOD ONE. BUT IT WAS THE **OPPOSITE** OF THE BIBLE STORY.
MY FATHER FAVORED ME. HE KNEW I COULD DO SOMETHING UP THERE. MY BROTHER, HE COULD NEVER GET A BREAK. FROM MY PA OR ANYONE. SO I WENT NORTH.
YEAH, I ALWAYS HEARD T WAS GOOD UP THERE FOR THE ***NEGRO.*** GLAD TO SEE THAT'S TRUE.

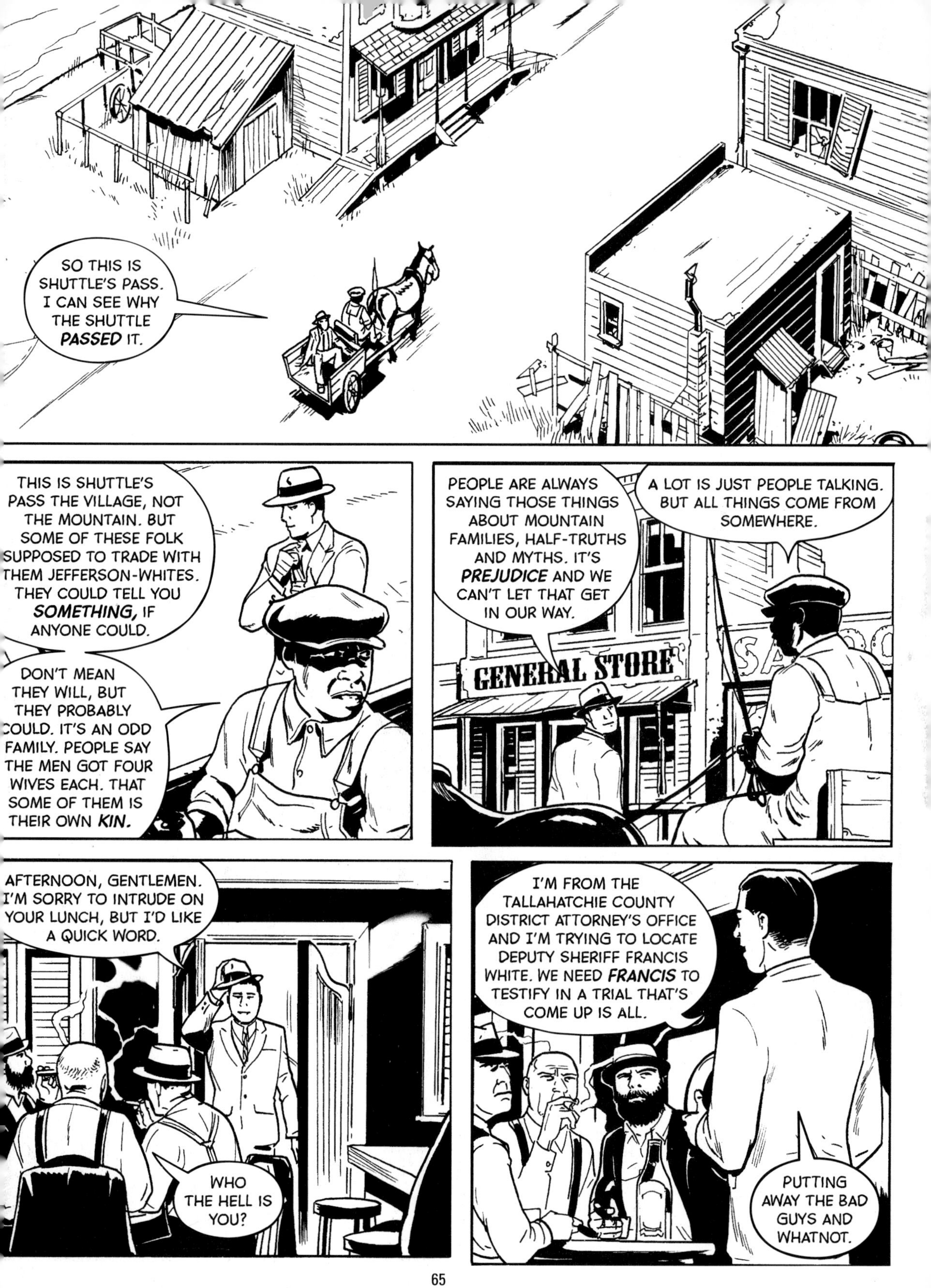
SO THIS IS SHUTTLE'S PASS. I CAN SEE WHY THE SHUTTLE *PASSED* IT.
THIS IS SHUTTLE'S PASS THE VILLAGE, NOT THE MOUNTAIN. BUT SOME OF THESE FOLK SUPPOSED TO TRADE WITH THEM JEFFERSON-WHITES. THEY COULD TELL YOU *SOMETHING,* IF ANYONE COULD.
DON'T MEAN THEY WILL, BUT THEY PROBABLY COULD. IT'S AN ODD FAMILY. PEOPLE SAY THE MEN GOT FOUR WIVES EACH. THAT SOME OF THEM IS THEIR OWN *KIN.*
PEOPLE ARE ALWAYS SAYING THOSE THINGS ABOUT MOUNTAIN FAMILIES, HALF-TRUTHS AND MYTHS. IT'S *PREJUDICE* AND WE CAN'T LET THAT GET IN OUR WAY.
A LOT IS JUST PEOPLE TALKING. BUT ALL THINGS COME FROM SOMEWHERE.
GENERAL STORE
AFTERNOON, GENTLEMEN. I'M SORRY TO INTRUDE ON YOUR LUNCH, BUT I'D LIKE A QUICK WORD.
WHO THE HELL IS YOU?
I'M FROM THE TALLAHATCHIE COUNTY DISTRICT ATTORNEY'S OFFICE AND I'M TRYING TO LOCATE DEPUTY SHERIFF FRANCIS WHITE. WE NEED *FRANCIS* TO TESTIFY IN A TRIAL THAT'S COME UP IS ALL.
PUTTING AWAY THE BAD GUYS AND WHATNOT.

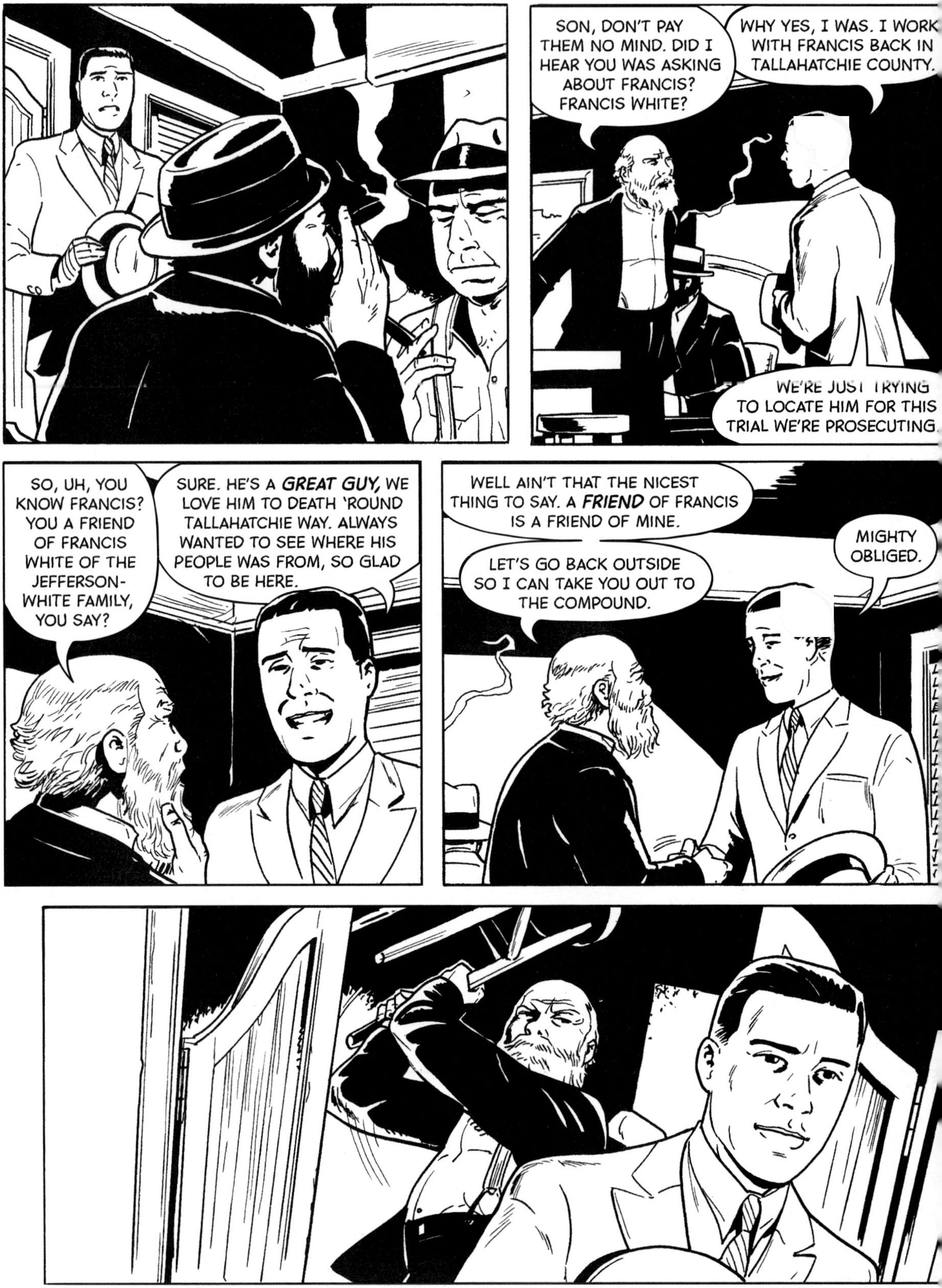
SON, DON'T PAY THEM NO MIND. DID I HEAR YOU WAS ASKING ABOUT FRANCIS? FRANCIS WHITE?
WHY YES, I WAS. I WORK WITH FRANCIS BACK IN TALLAHATCHIE COUNTY.
WE'RE JUST TRYING TO LOCATE HIM FOR THIS TRIAL WE'RE PROSECUTING.
SO, UH, YOU KNOW FRANCIS? YOU A FRIEND OF FRANCIS WHITE OF THE JEFFERSON-WHITE FAMILY, YOU SAY?
SURE. HE'S A ***GREAT GUY,*** WE LOVE HIM TO DEATH 'ROUND TALLAHATCHIE WAY. ALWAYS WANTED TO SEE WHERE HIS PEOPLE WAS FROM, SO GLAD TO BE HERE.
WELL AIN'T THAT THE NICEST THING TO SAY. A ***FRIEND*** OF FRANCIS IS A FRIEND OF MINE.
LET'S GO BACK OUTSIDE SO I CAN TAKE YOU OUT TO THE COMPOUND.
MIGHTY OBLIGED.

# PART II

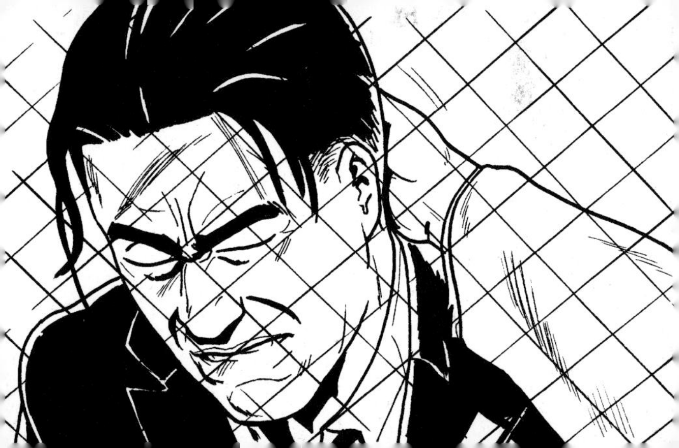

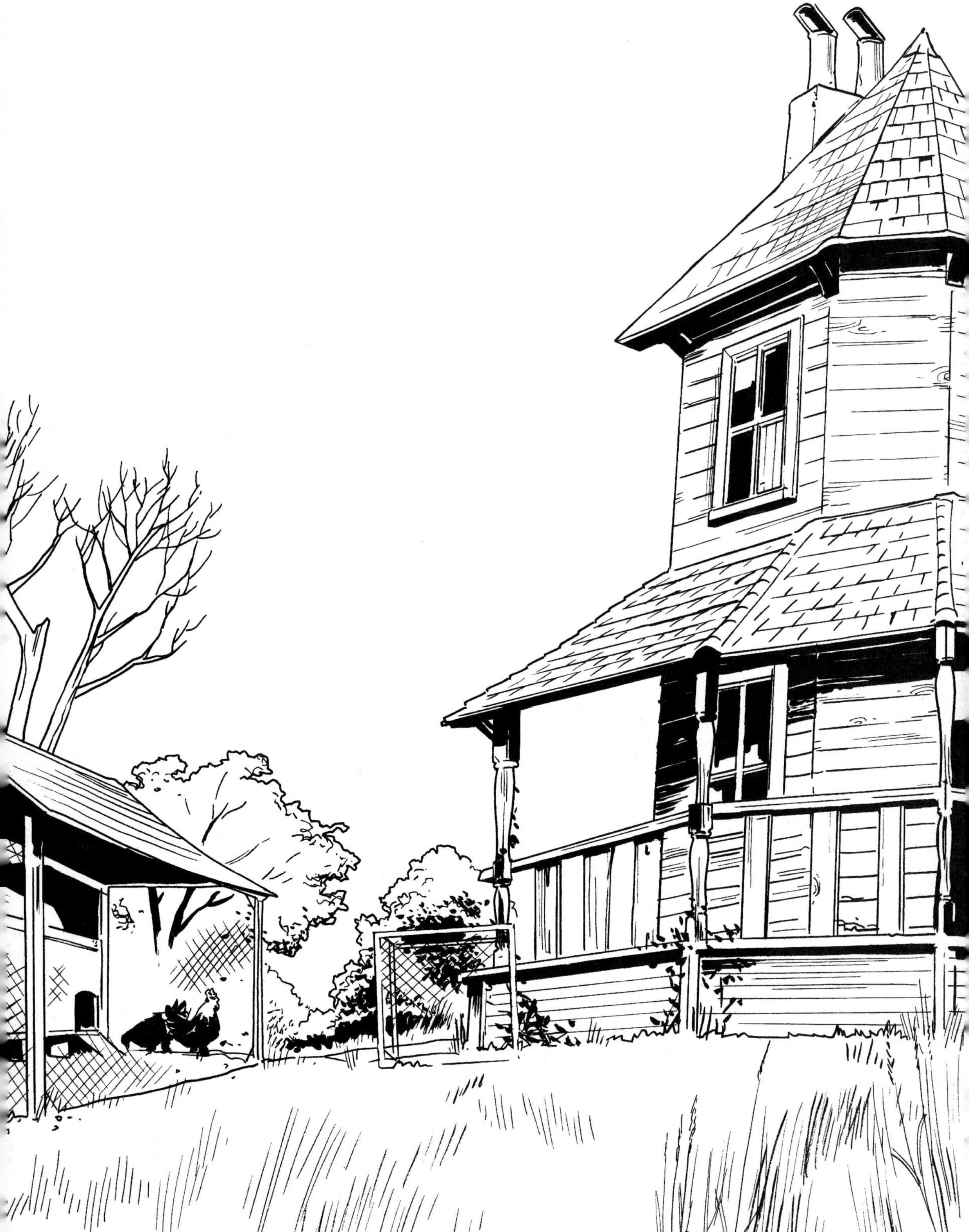

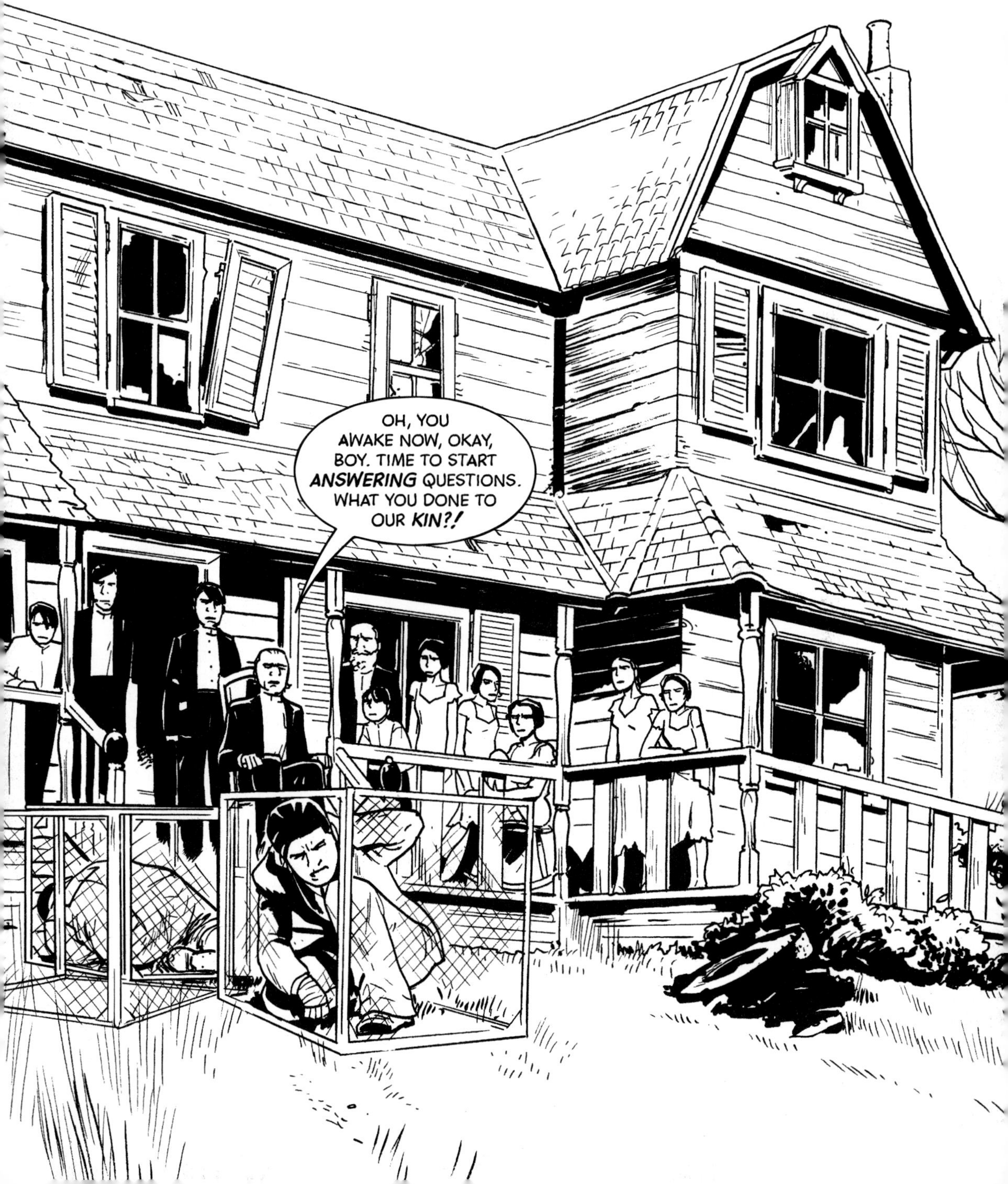
OH, YOU AWAKE NOW, OKAY, BOY. TIME TO START ***ANSWERING*** QUESTIONS. WHAT YOU DONE TO OUR ***KIN?!***

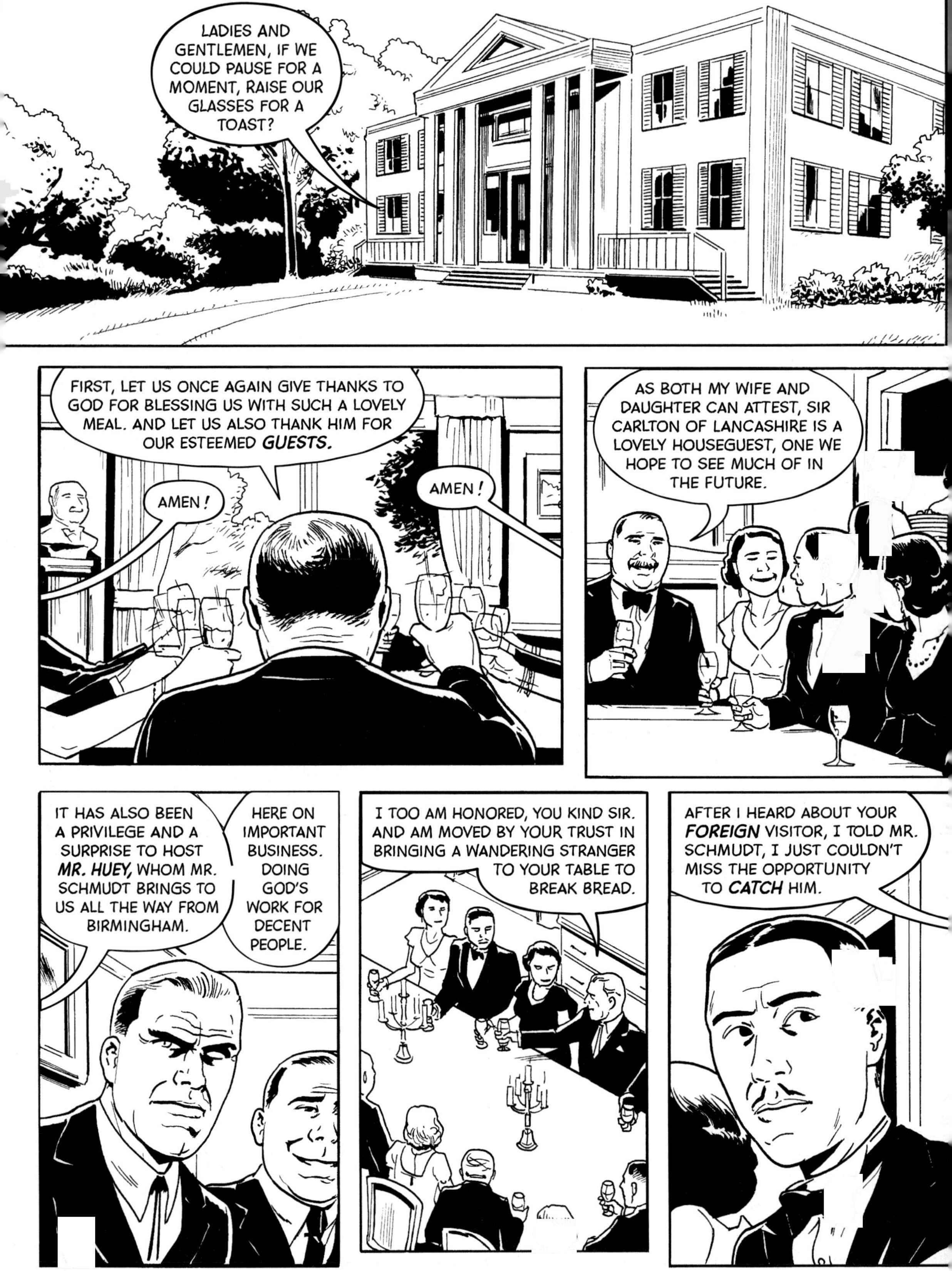
LADIES AND GENTLEMEN, IF WE COULD PAUSE FOR A MOMENT, RAISE OUR GLASSES FOR A TOAST?
FIRST, LET US ONCE AGAIN GIVE THANKS TO GOD FOR BLESSING US WITH SUCH A LOVELY MEAL. AND LET US ALSO THANK HIM FOR OUR ESTEEMED ***GUESTS.***
AMEN!
AMEN!
AS BOTH MY WIFE AND DAUGHTER CAN ATTEST, SIR CARLTON OF LANCASHIRE IS A LOVELY HOUSEGUEST, ONE WE HOPE TO SEE MUCH OF IN THE FUTURE.
IT HAS ALSO BEEN A PRIVILEGE AND A SURPRISE TO HOST ***MR. HUEY,*** WHOM MR. SCHMUDT BRINGS TO US ALL THE WAY FROM BIRMINGHAM.
HERE ON IMPORTANT BUSINESS. DOING GOD'S WORK FOR DECENT PEOPLE.
I TOO AM HONORED, YOU KIND SIR. AND AM MOVED BY YOUR TRUST IN BRINGING A WANDERING STRANGER TO YOUR TABLE TO BREAK BREAD.
AFTER I HEARD ABOUT YOUR ***FOREIGN*** VISITOR, I TOLD MR. SCHMUDT, I JUST COULDN'T MISS THE OPPORTUNITY TO ***CATCH*** HIM.

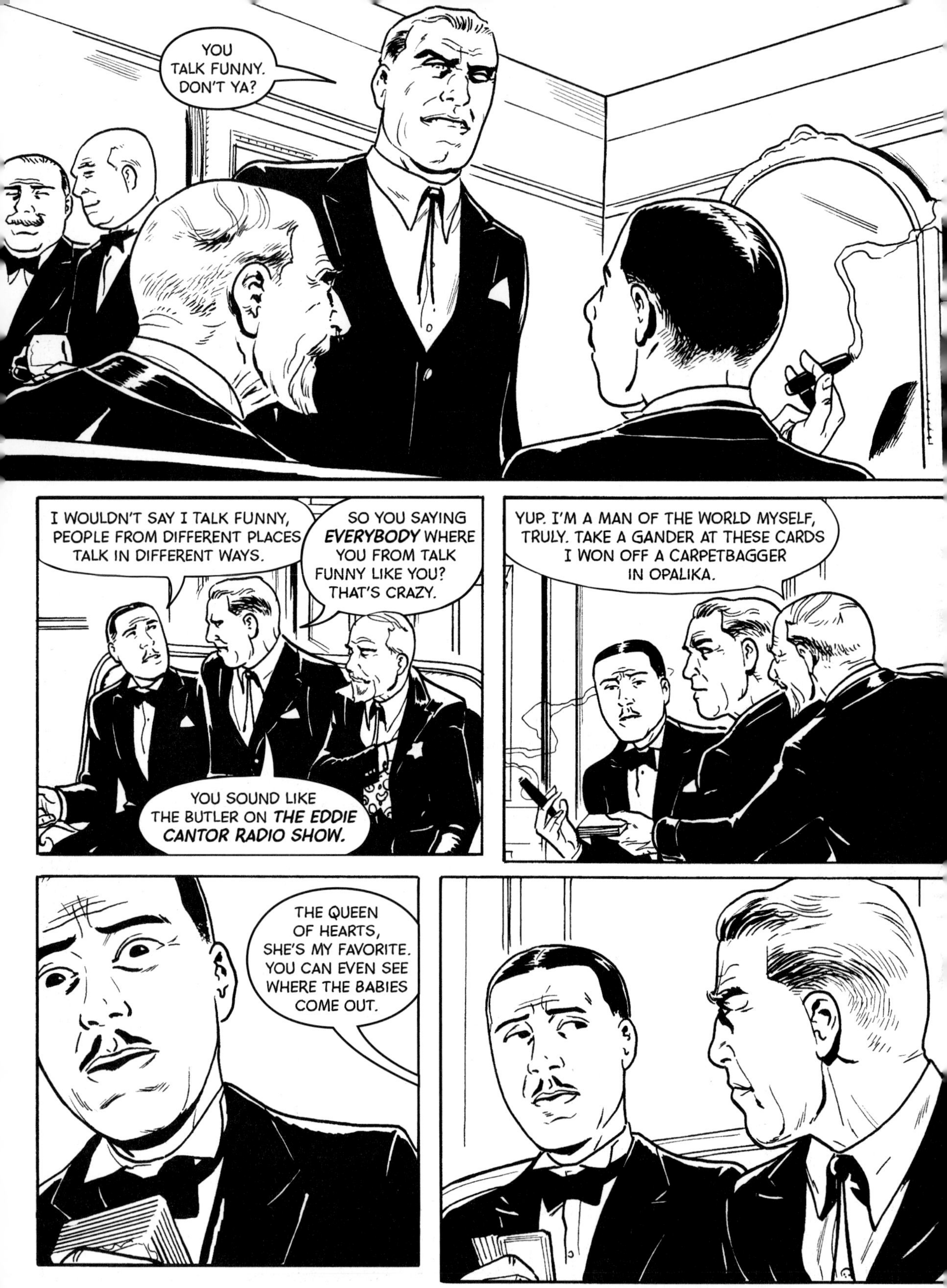
YOU TALK FUNNY. DON'T YA?
I WOULDN'T SAY I TALK FUNNY, PEOPLE FROM DIFFERENT PLACES TALK IN DIFFERENT WAYS.
SO YOU SAYING *EVERYBODY* WHERE YOU FROM TALK FUNNY LIKE YOU? THAT'S CRAZY.
YOU SOUND LIKE THE BUTLER ON *THE EDDIE CANTOR RADIO SHOW.*
YUP. I'M A MAN OF THE WORLD MYSELF, TRULY. TAKE A GANDER AT THESE CARDS I WON OFF A CARPETBAGGER IN OPALIKA.
THE QUEEN OF HEARTS, SHE'S MY FAVORITE. YOU CAN EVEN SEE WHERE THE BABIES COME OUT.

75

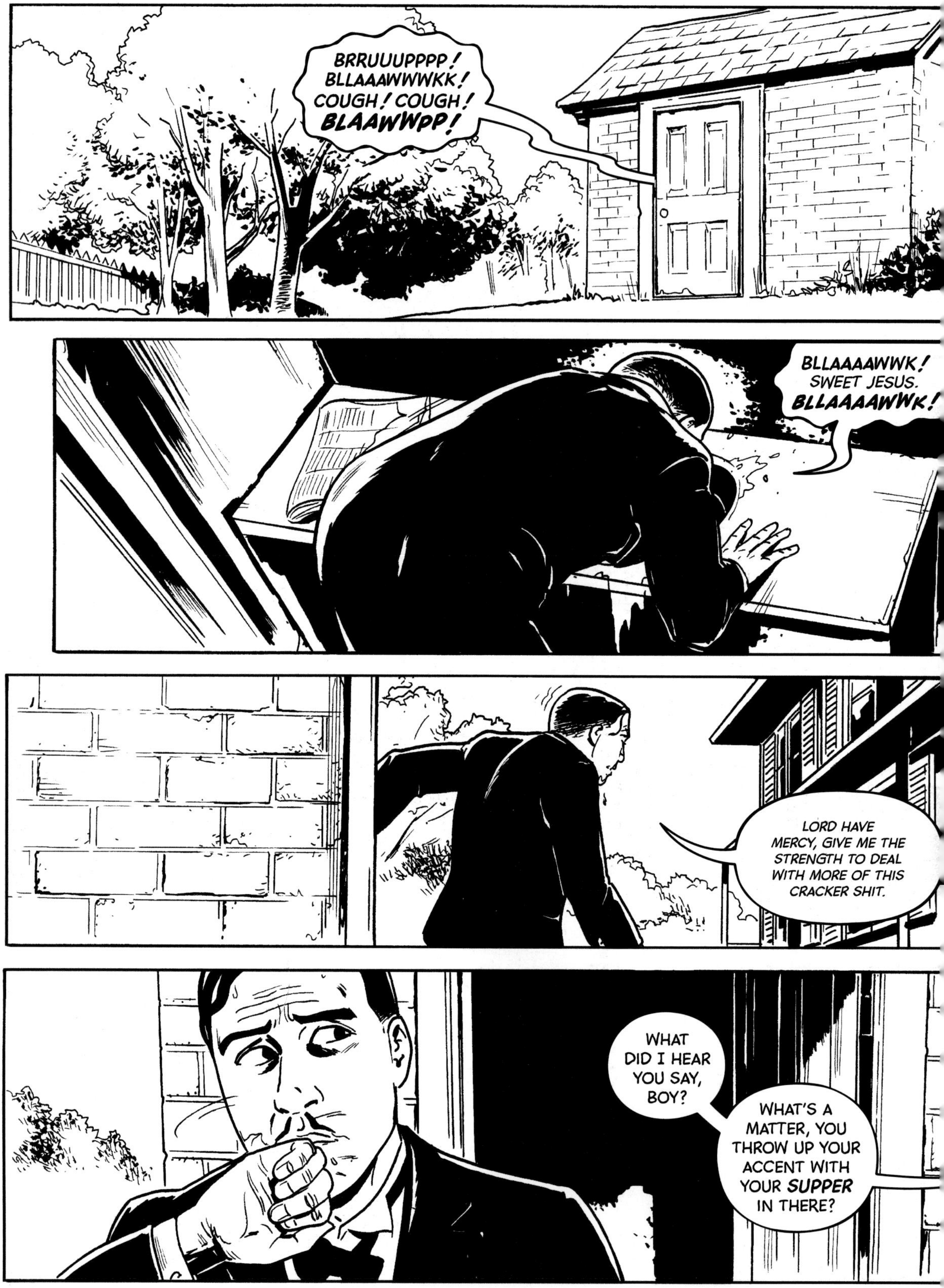
BRRUUUPPPP! BLLAAAWWWKK! COUGH! COUGH! BLAAWWPP!
BLLAAAAWWK! SWEET JESUS. BLLAAAAWWK!
LORD HAVE MERCY, GIVE ME THE STRENGTH TO DEAL WITH MORE OF THIS CRACKER SHIT.
WHAT DID I HEAR YOU SAY, BOY?
WHAT'S A MATTER, YOU THROW UP YOUR ACCENT WITH YOUR SUPPER IN THERE?

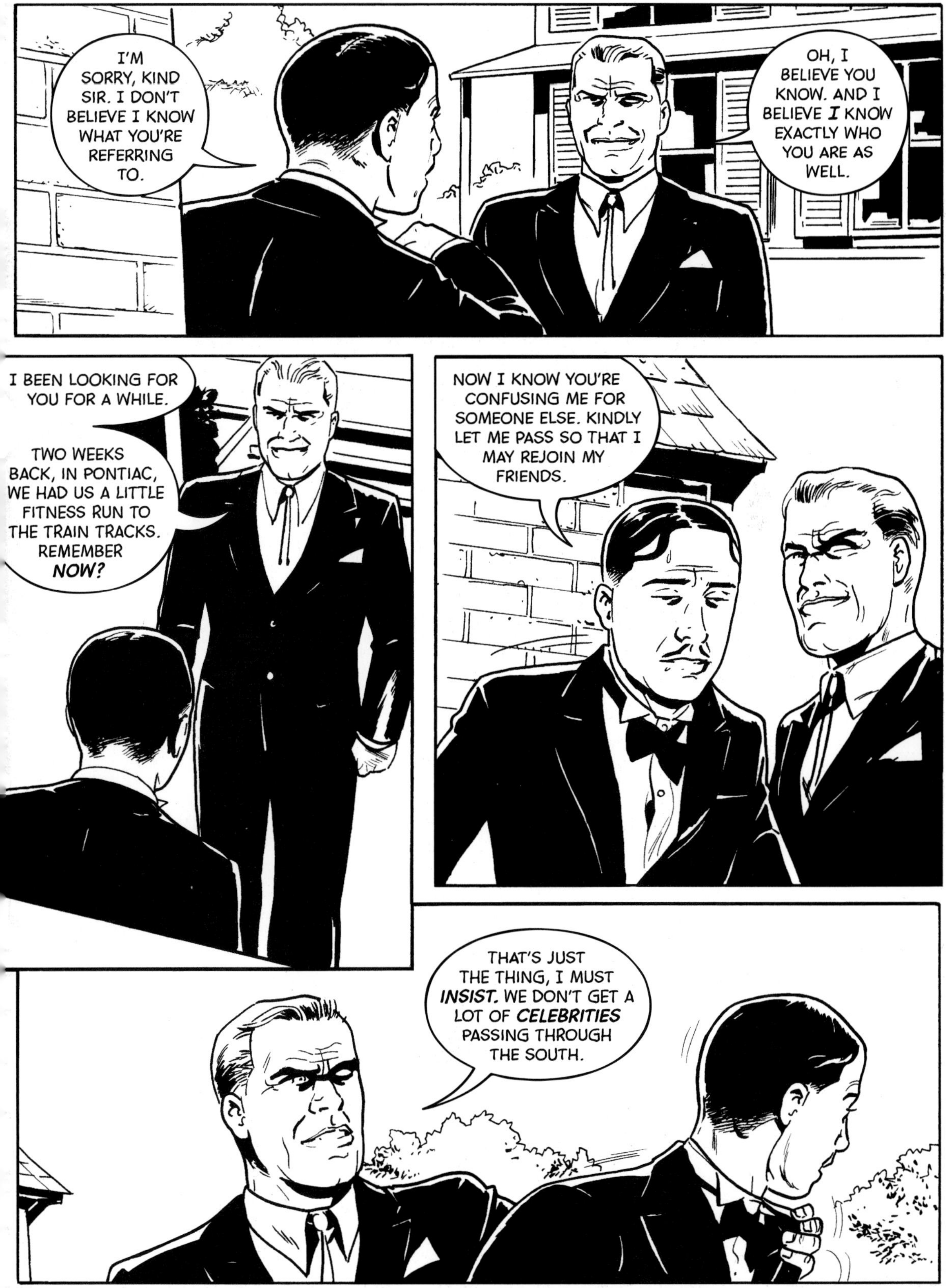

I'M SORRY, KIND SIR. I DON'T BELIEVE I KNOW WHAT YOU'RE REFERRING TO.
OH, I BELIEVE YOU KNOW. AND I BELIEVE *I* KNOW EXACTLY WHO YOU ARE AS WELL.
I BEEN LOOKING FOR YOU FOR A WHILE.
TWO WEEKS BACK, IN PONTIAC, WE HAD US A LITTLE FITNESS RUN TO THE TRAIN TRACKS. REMEMBER ***NOW?***
NOW I KNOW YOU'RE CONFUSING ME FOR SOMEONE ELSE. KINDLY LET ME PASS SO THAT I MAY REJOIN MY FRIENDS.
THAT'S JUST THE THING, I MUST ***INSIST.*** WE DON'T GET A LOT OF ***CELEBRITIES*** PASSING THROUGH THE SOUTH.

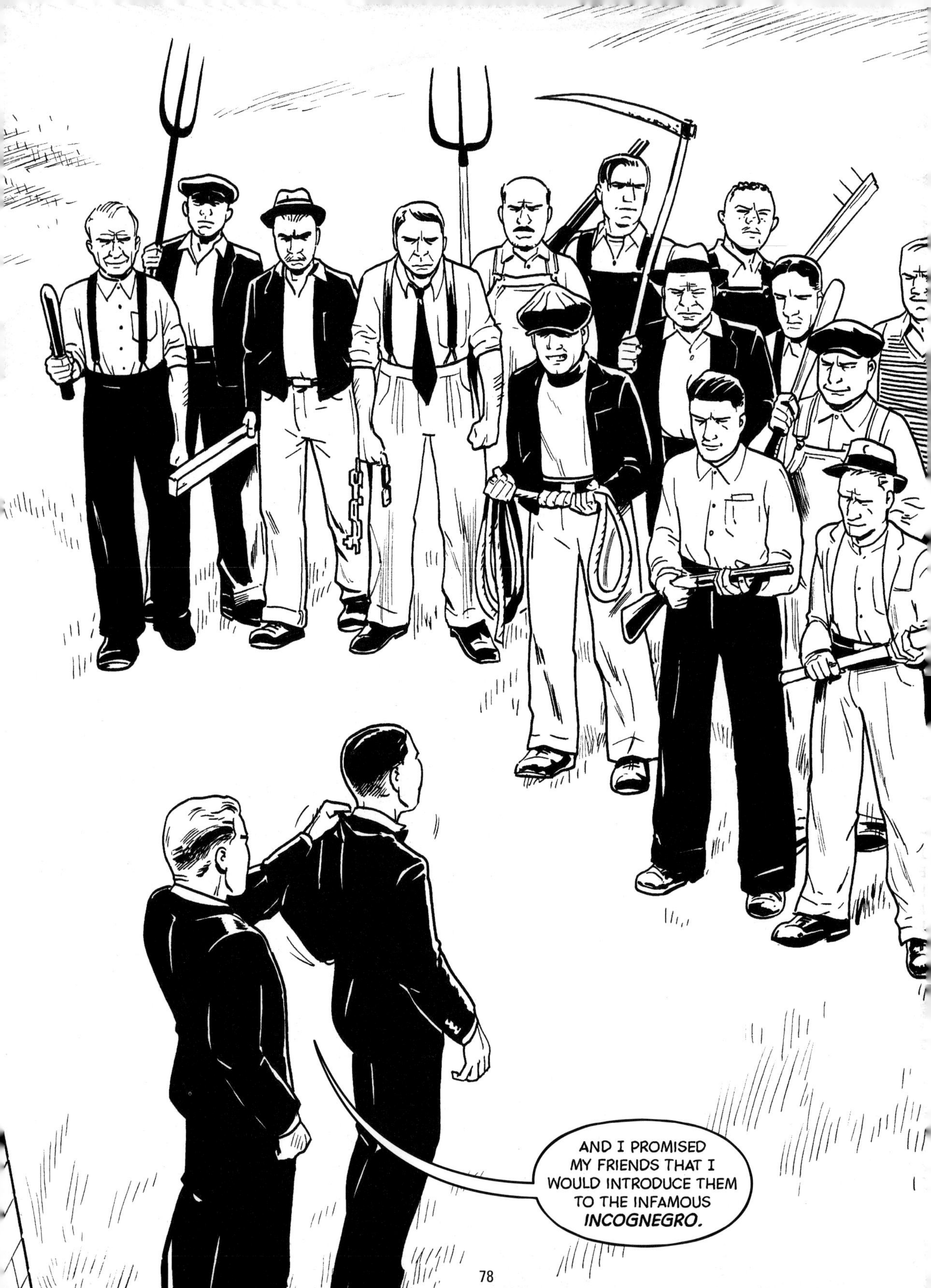
AND I PROMISED MY FRIENDS THAT I WOULD INTRODUCE THEM TO THE INFAMOUS *INCOGNEGRO.*

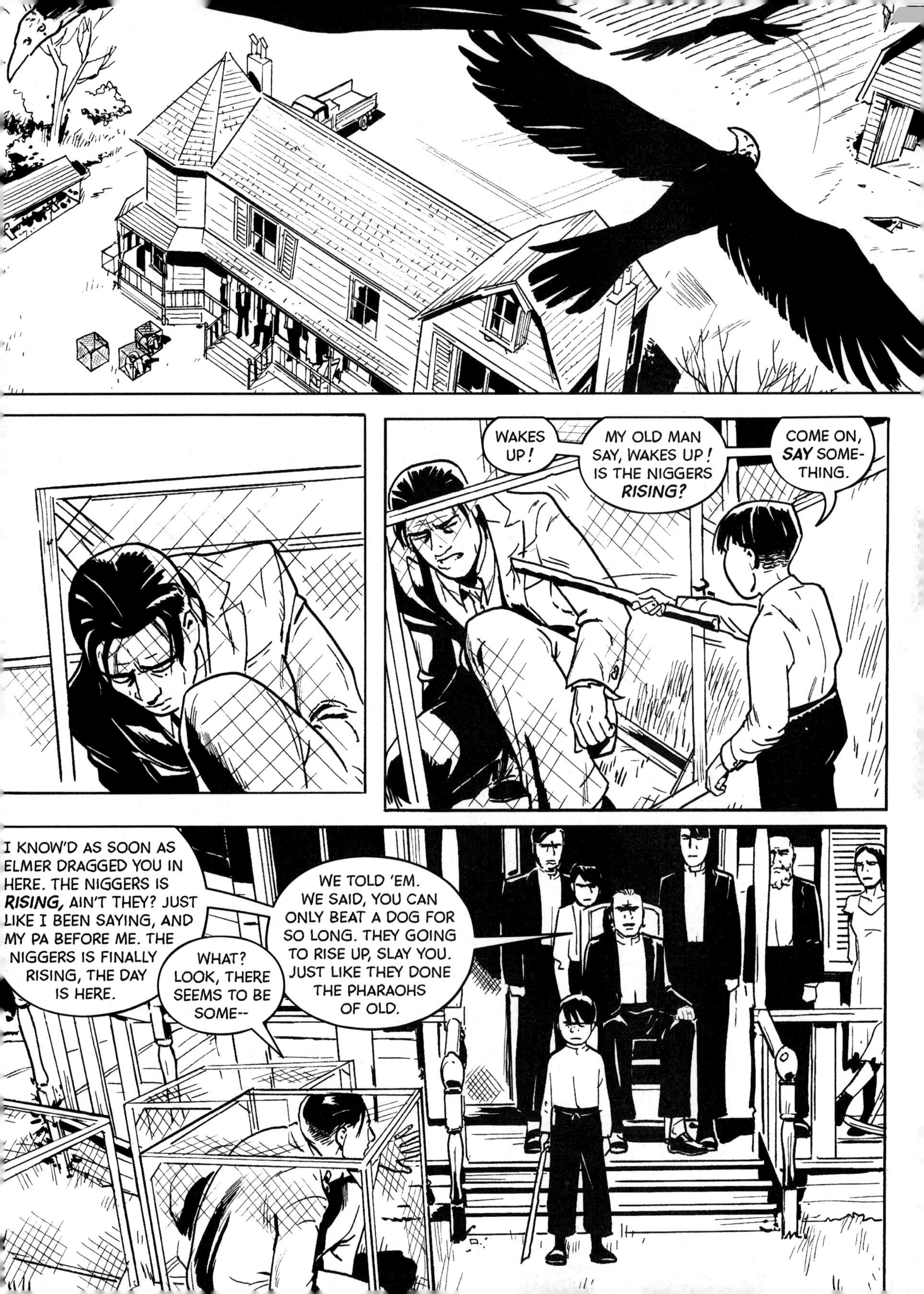

WAKES UP!
MY OLD MAN SAY, WAKES UP! IS THE NIGGERS RISING?
COME ON, SAY SOMETHING.
I KNOW'D AS SOON AS ELMER DRAGGED YOU IN HERE. THE NIGGERS IS RISING, AIN'T THEY? JUST LIKE I BEEN SAYING, AND MY PA BEFORE ME. THE NIGGERS IS FINALLY RISING, THE DAY IS HERE.
WHAT? LOOK, THERE SEEMS TO BE SOME--
WE TOLD 'EM. WE SAID, YOU CAN ONLY BEAT A DOG FOR SO LONG. THEY GOING TO RISE UP, SLAY YOU. JUST LIKE THEY DONE THE PHARAOHS OF OLD.

81

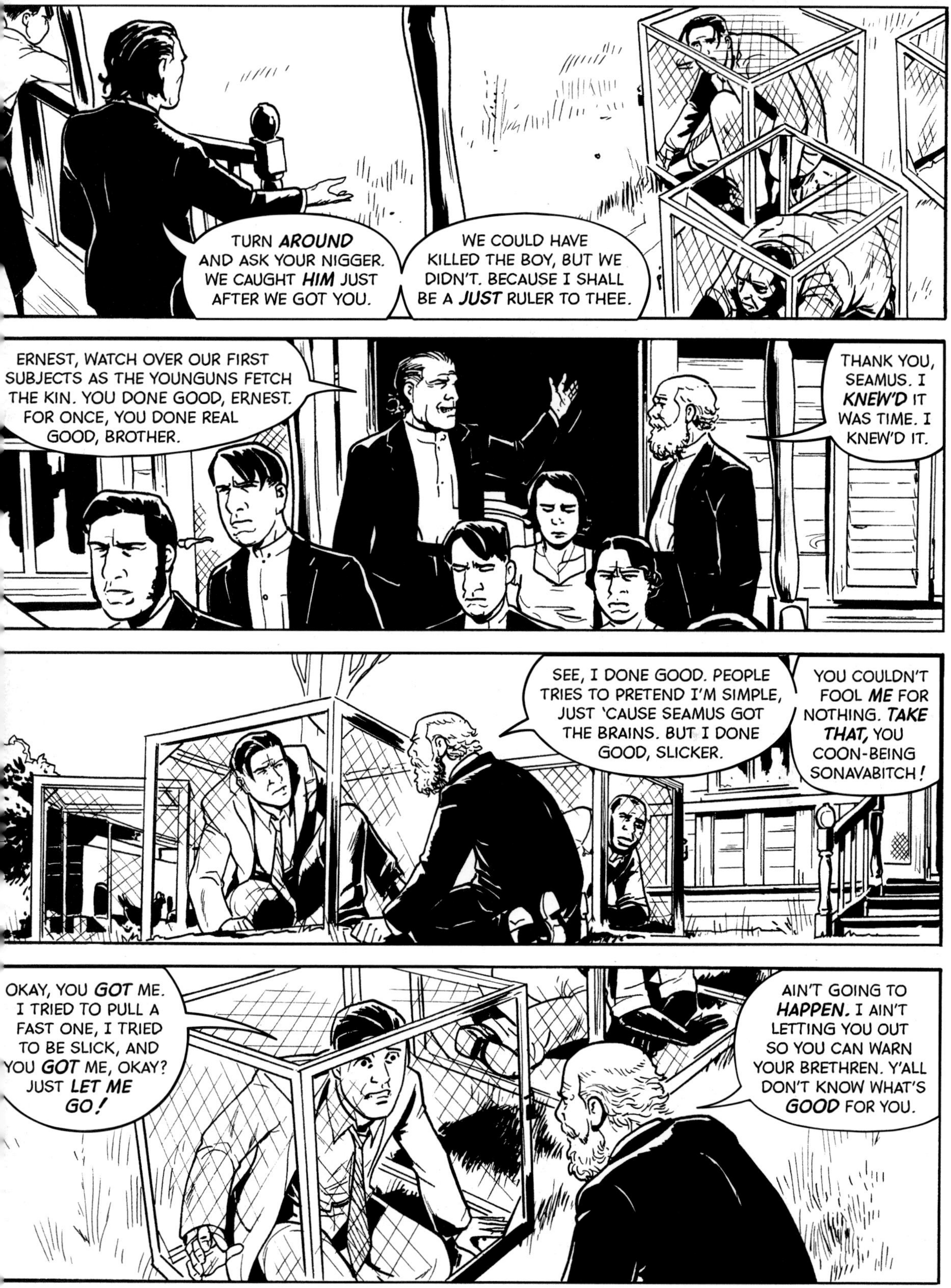
TURN *AROUND* AND ASK YOUR NIGGER. WE CAUGHT *HIM* JUST AFTER WE GOT YOU.
WE COULD HAVE KILLED THE BOY, BUT WE DIDN'T. BECAUSE I SHALL BE A *JUST* RULER TO THEE.
ERNEST, WATCH OVER OUR FIRST SUBJECTS AS THE YOUNGUNS FETCH THE KIN. YOU DONE GOOD, ERNEST. FOR ONCE, YOU DONE REAL GOOD, BROTHER.
THANK YOU, SEAMUS. I *KNEW'D* IT WAS TIME. I KNEW'D IT.
SEE, I DONE GOOD. PEOPLE TRIES TO PRETEND I'M SIMPLE, JUST 'CAUSE SEAMUS GOT THE BRAINS. BUT I DONE GOOD, SLICKER.
YOU COULDN'T FOOL *ME* FOR NOTHING. *TAKE THAT,* YOU COON-BEING SONAVABITCH!
OKAY, YOU *GOT* ME. I TRIED TO PULL A FAST ONE, I TRIED TO BE SLICK, AND YOU *GOT* ME, OKAY? JUST *LET ME GO!*
AIN'T GOING TO *HAPPEN.* I AIN'T LETTING YOU OUT SO YOU CAN WARN YOUR BRETHREN. Y'ALL DON'T KNOW WHAT'S *GOOD* FOR YOU.

85

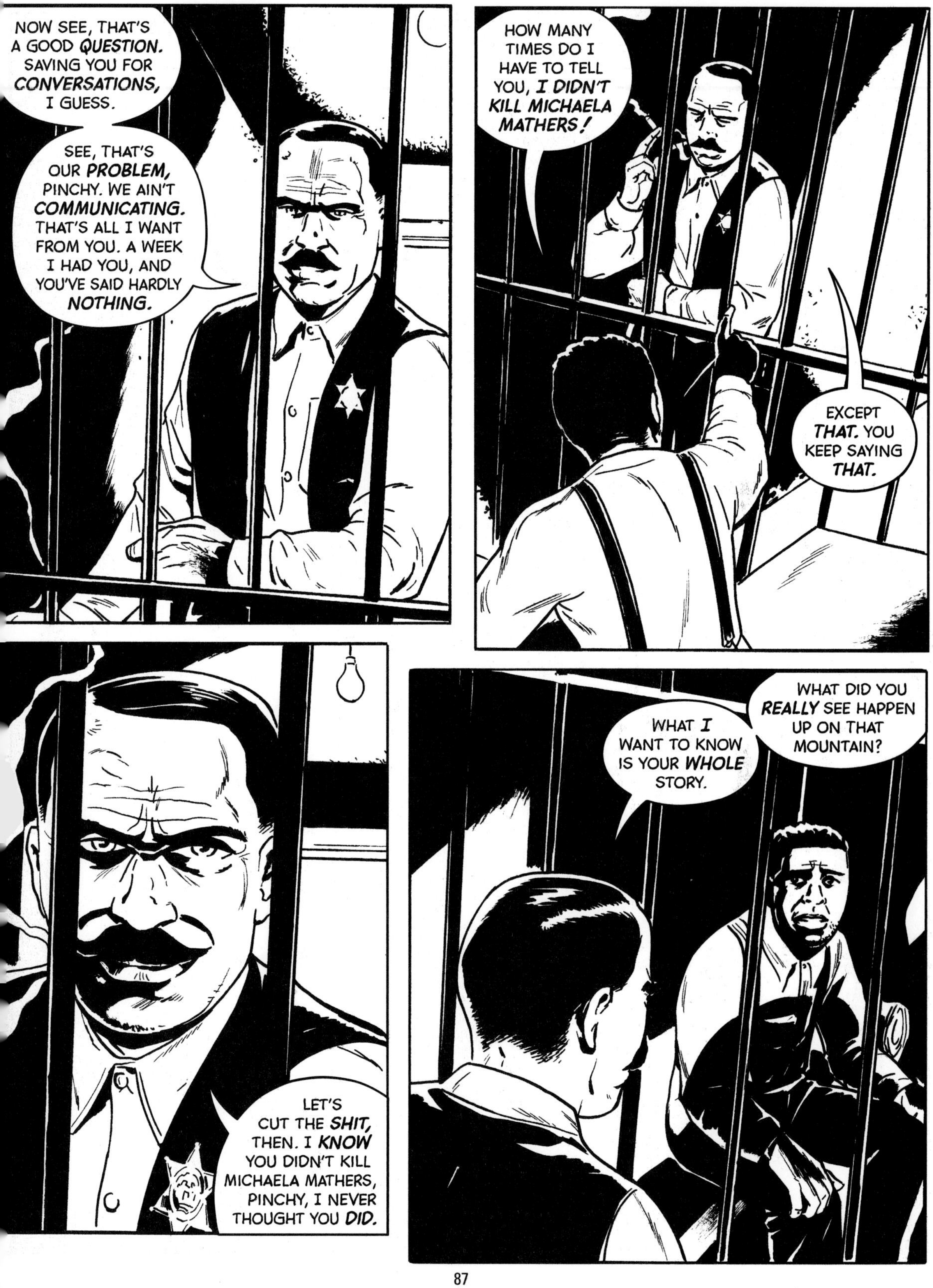
NOW SEE, THAT'S A GOOD QUESTION. SAVING YOU FOR CONVERSATIONS, I GUESS.
SEE, THAT'S OUR PROBLEM, PINCHY. WE AIN'T COMMUNICATING. THAT'S ALL I WANT FROM YOU. A WEEK I HAD YOU, AND YOU'VE SAID HARDLY NOTHING.
HOW MANY TIMES DO I HAVE TO TELL YOU, I DIDN'T KILL MICHAELA MATHERS!
EXCEPT THAT. YOU KEEP SAYING THAT.
LET'S CUT THE SHIT, THEN. I KNOW YOU DIDN'T KILL MICHAELA MATHERS, PINCHY, I NEVER THOUGHT YOU DID.
WHAT I WANT TO KNOW IS YOUR WHOLE STORY.
WHAT DID YOU REALLY SEE HAPPEN UP ON THAT MOUNTAIN?

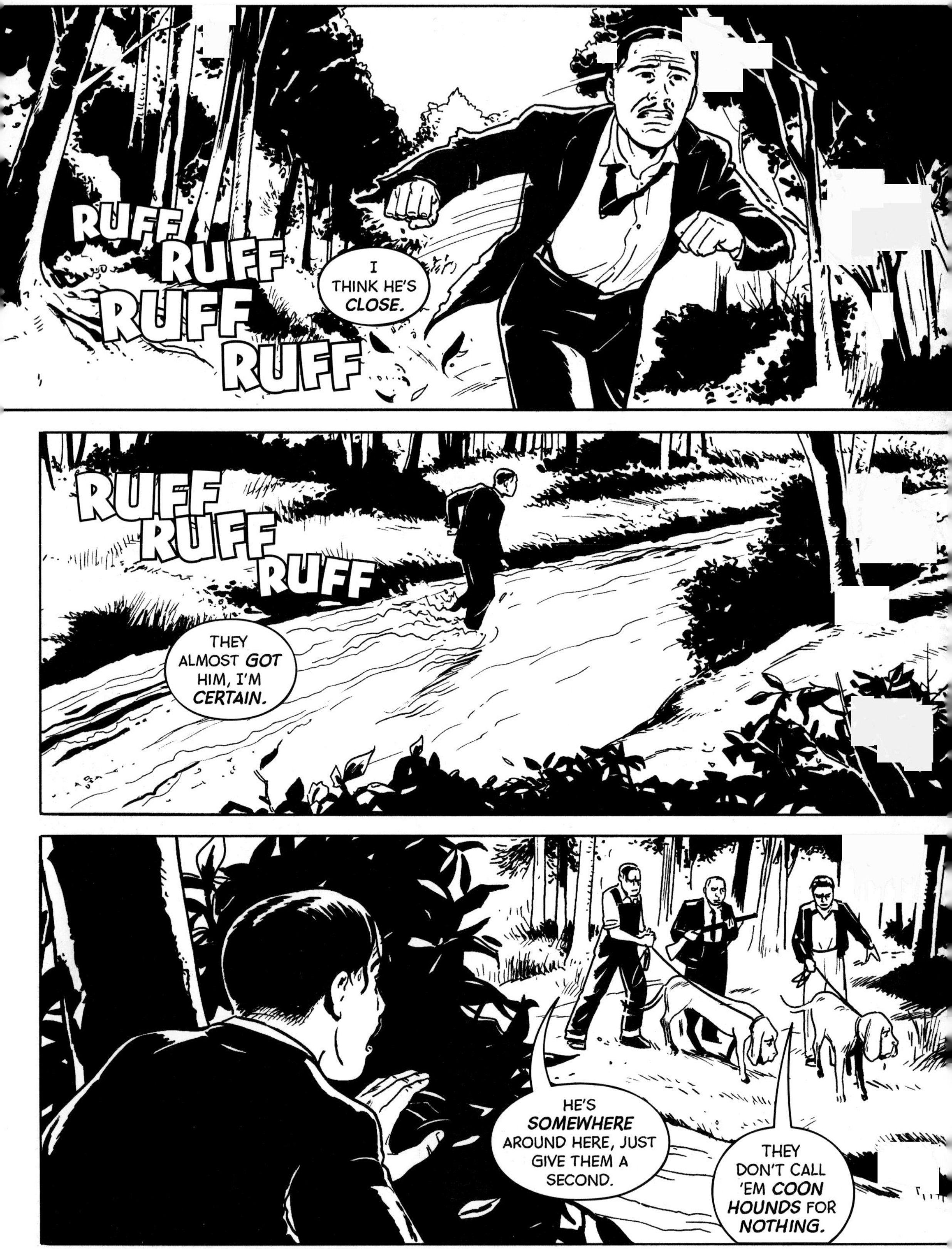
RUFF RUFF RUFF RUFF
I THINK HE'S CLOSE.
RUFF RUFF RUFF
THEY ALMOST GOT HIM, I'M CERTAIN.
HE'S SOMEWHERE AROUND HERE, JUST GIVE THEM A SECOND.
THEY DON'T CALL 'EM COON HOUNDS FOR NOTHING.

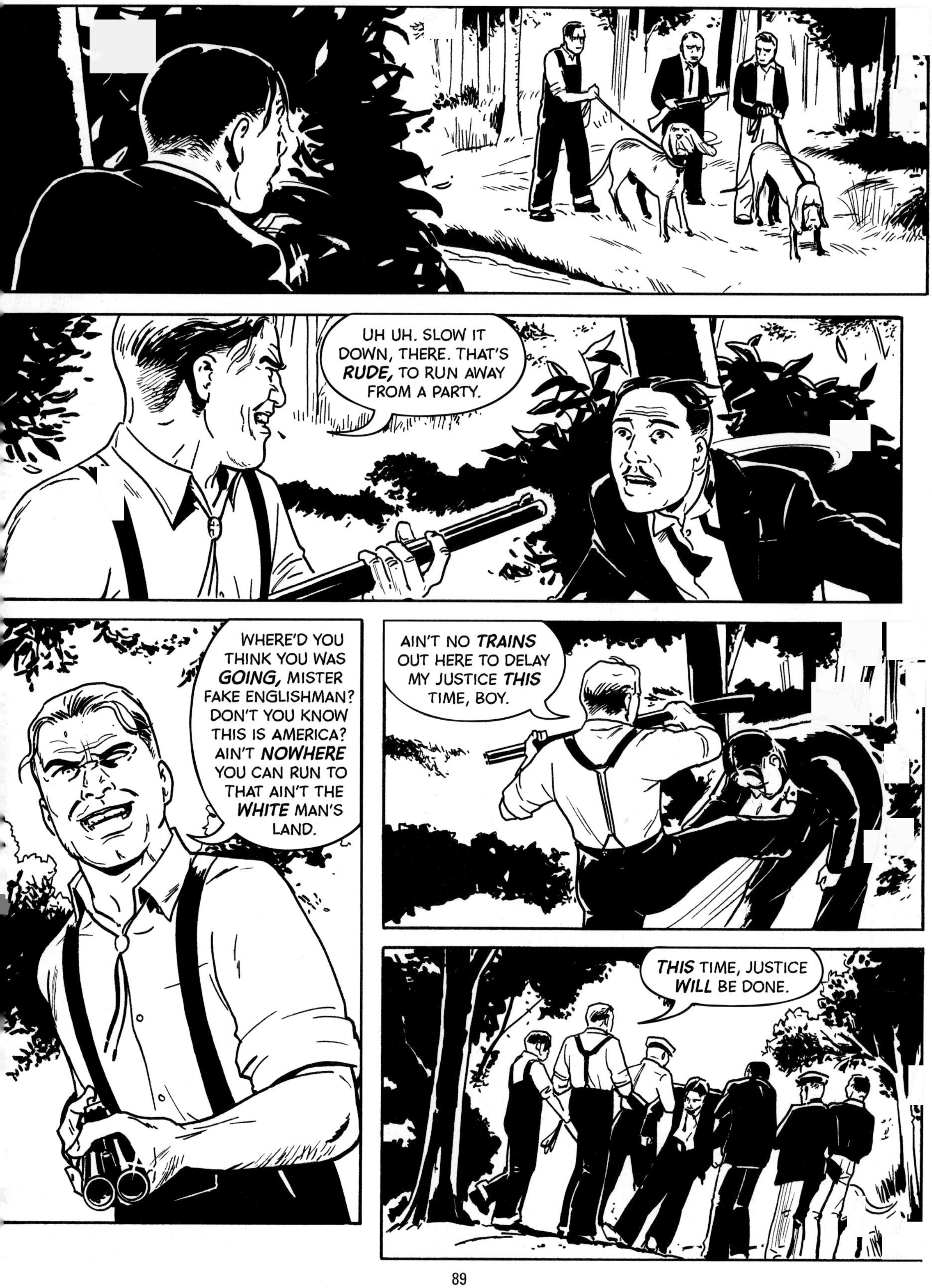
UH UH. SLOW IT DOWN, THERE. THAT'S *RUDE,* TO RUN AWAY FROM A PARTY.
WHERE'D YOU THINK YOU WAS *GOING,* MISTER FAKE ENGLISHMAN? DON'T YOU KNOW THIS IS AMERICA? AIN'T *NOWHERE* YOU CAN RUN TO THAT AIN'T THE *WHITE* MAN'S LAND.
AIN'T NO *TRAINS* OUT HERE TO DELAY MY JUSTICE *THIS* TIME, BOY.
*THIS* TIME, JUSTICE *WILL* BE DONE.

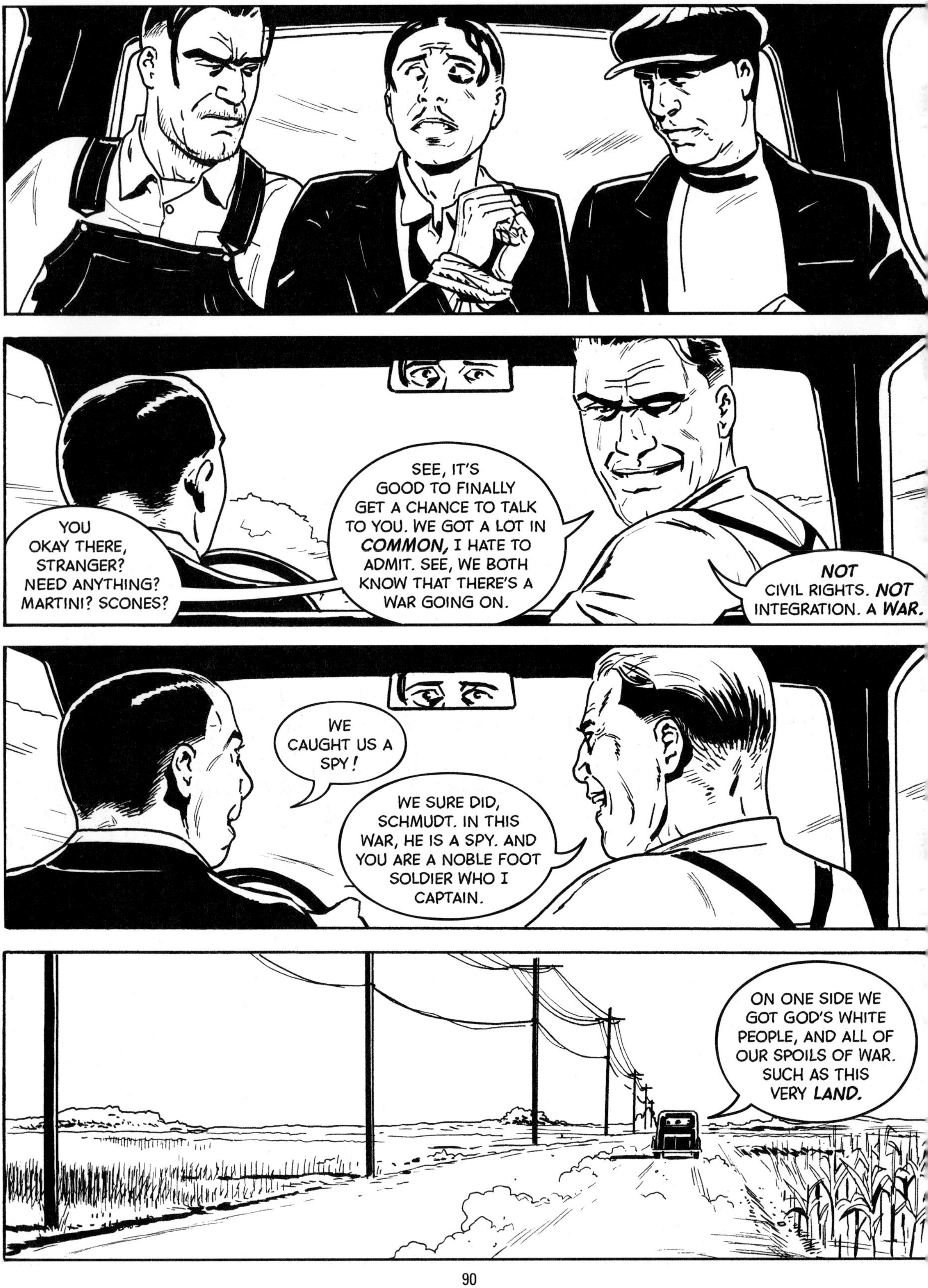
YOU OKAY THERE, STRANGER? NEED ANYTHING? MARTINI? SCONES?
SEE, IT'S GOOD TO FINALLY GET A CHANCE TO TALK TO YOU. WE GOT A LOT IN COMMON, I HATE TO ADMIT. SEE, WE BOTH KNOW THAT THERE'S A WAR GOING ON.
NOT CIVIL RIGHTS. NOT INTEGRATION. A WAR.
WE CAUGHT US A SPY!
WE SURE DID, SCHMUDT. IN THIS WAR, HE IS A SPY. AND YOU ARE A NOBLE FOOT SOLDIER WHO I CAPTAIN.
ON ONE SIDE WE GOT GOD'S WHITE PEOPLE, AND ALL OF OUR SPOILS OF WAR. SUCH AS THIS VERY LAND.

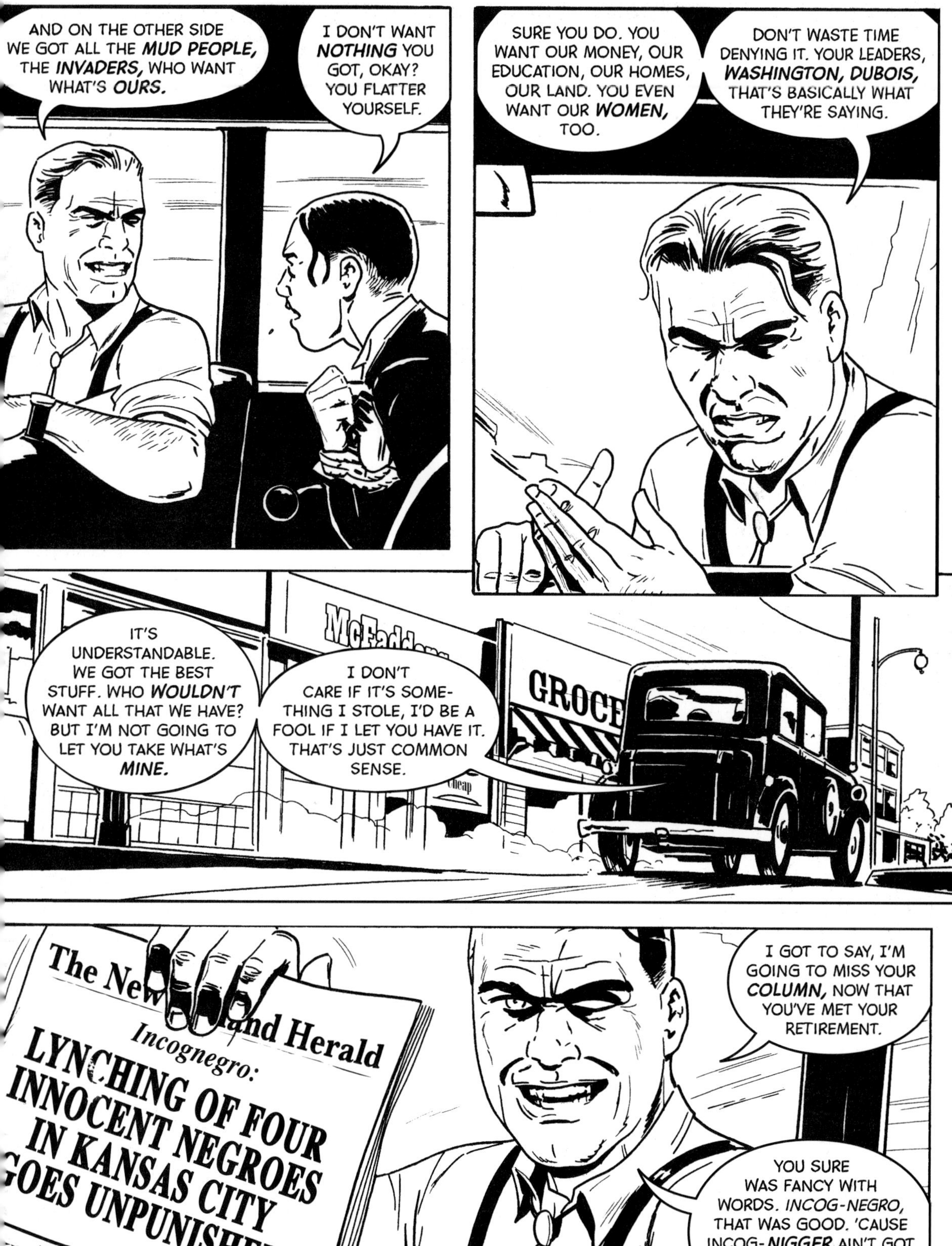

AND ON THE OTHER SIDE WE GOT ALL THE *MUD PEOPLE,* THE *INVADERS,* WHO WANT WHAT'S *OURS.*
I DON'T WANT *NOTHING* YOU GOT, OKAY? YOU FLATTER YOURSELF.
SURE YOU DO. YOU WANT OUR MONEY, OUR EDUCATION, OUR HOMES, OUR LAND. YOU EVEN WANT OUR *WOMEN,* TOO.
DON'T WASTE TIME DENYING IT. YOUR LEADERS, *WASHINGTON, DUBOIS,* THAT'S BASICALLY WHAT THEY'RE SAYING.
McFadden
GROCE
Cheap
IT'S UNDERSTANDABLE. WE GOT THE BEST STUFF. WHO *WOULDN'T* WANT ALL THAT WE HAVE? BUT I'M NOT GOING TO LET YOU TAKE WHAT'S *MINE.*
I DON'T CARE IF IT'S SOME-THING I STOLE, I'D BE A FOOL IF I LET YOU HAVE IT. THAT'S JUST COMMON SENSE.
The New
land Herald
Incognegro:
LYNCHING OF FOUR INNOCENT NEGROES IN KANSAS CITY GOES UNPUNISHED
I GOT TO SAY, I'M GOING TO MISS YOUR *COLUMN,* NOW THAT YOU'VE MET YOUR RETIREMENT.
YOU SURE WAS FANCY WITH WORDS. *INCOG-NEGRO,* THAT WAS GOOD. 'CAUSE INCOG-*NIGGER* AIN'T GOT NO KIND OF *RING* TO IT.

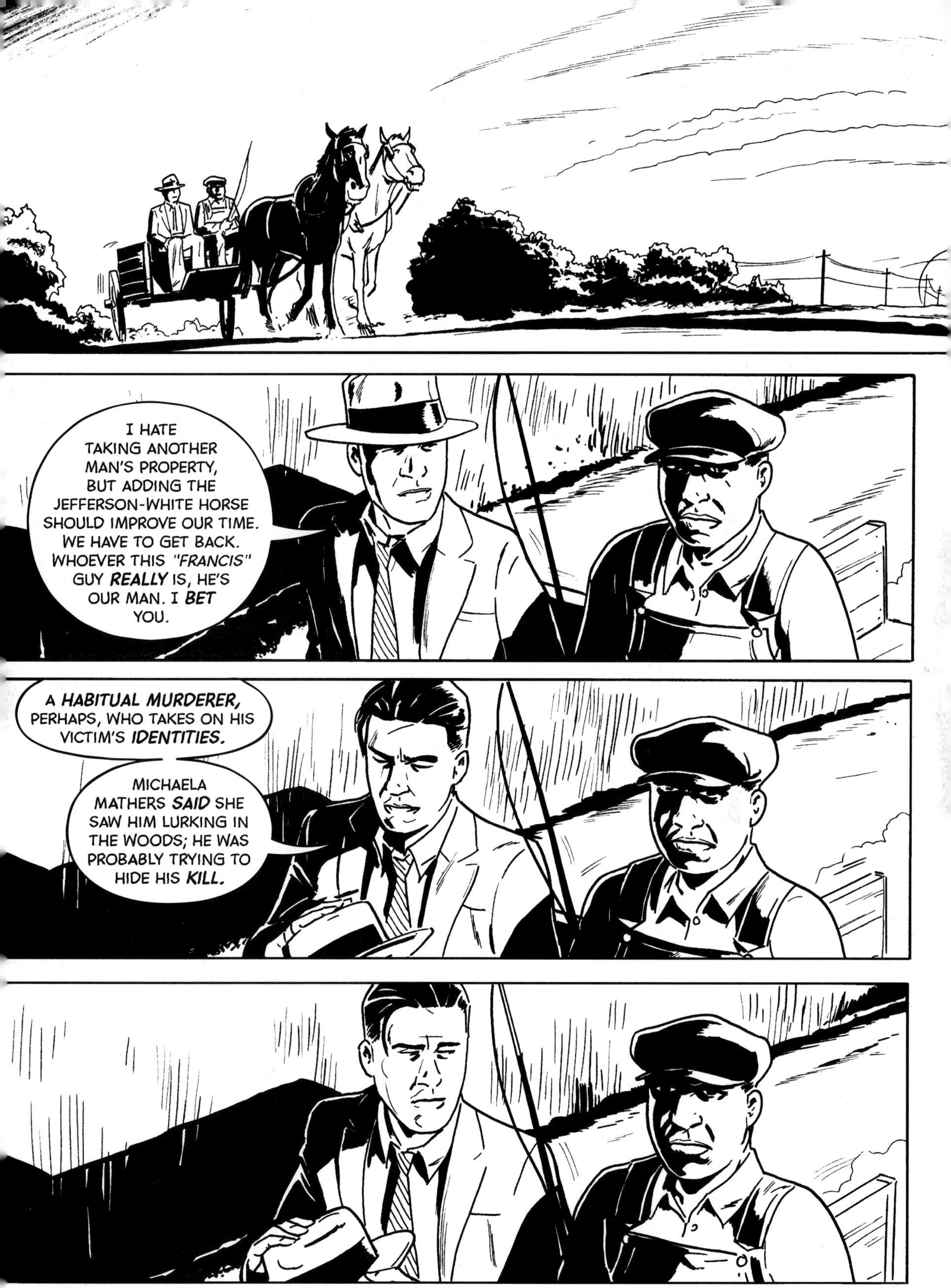
I HATE TAKING ANOTHER MAN'S PROPERTY, BUT ADDING THE JEFFERSON-WHITE HORSE SHOULD IMPROVE OUR TIME. WE HAVE TO GET BACK. WHOEVER THIS "FRANCIS" GUY REALLY IS, HE'S OUR MAN. I BET YOU.
A HABITUAL MURDERER, PERHAPS, WHO TAKES ON HIS VICTIM'S IDENTITIES.
MICHAELA MATHERS SAID SHE SAW HIM LURKING IN THE WOODS; HE WAS PROBABLY TRYING TO HIDE HIS KILL.

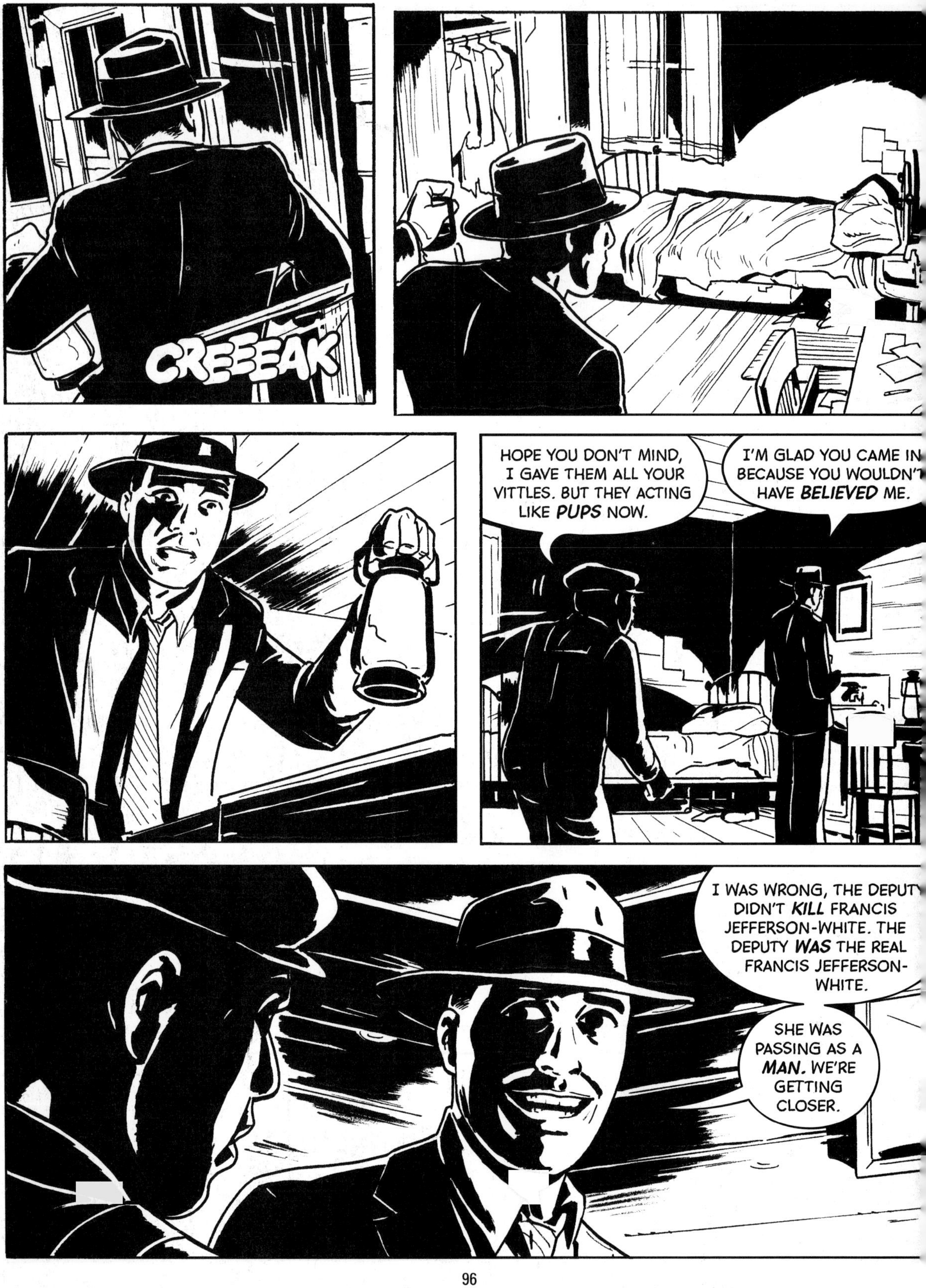
CREEEAK
HOPE YOU DON'T MIND, I GAVE THEM ALL YOUR VITTLES. BUT THEY ACTING LIKE PUPS NOW.
I'M GLAD YOU CAME IN BECAUSE YOU WOULDN'T HAVE BELIEVED ME.
I WAS WRONG, THE DEPUTY DIDN'T KILL FRANCIS JEFFERSON-WHITE. THE DEPUTY WAS THE REAL FRANCIS JEFFERSON-WHITE.
SHE WAS PASSING AS A MAN. WE'RE GETTING CLOSER.

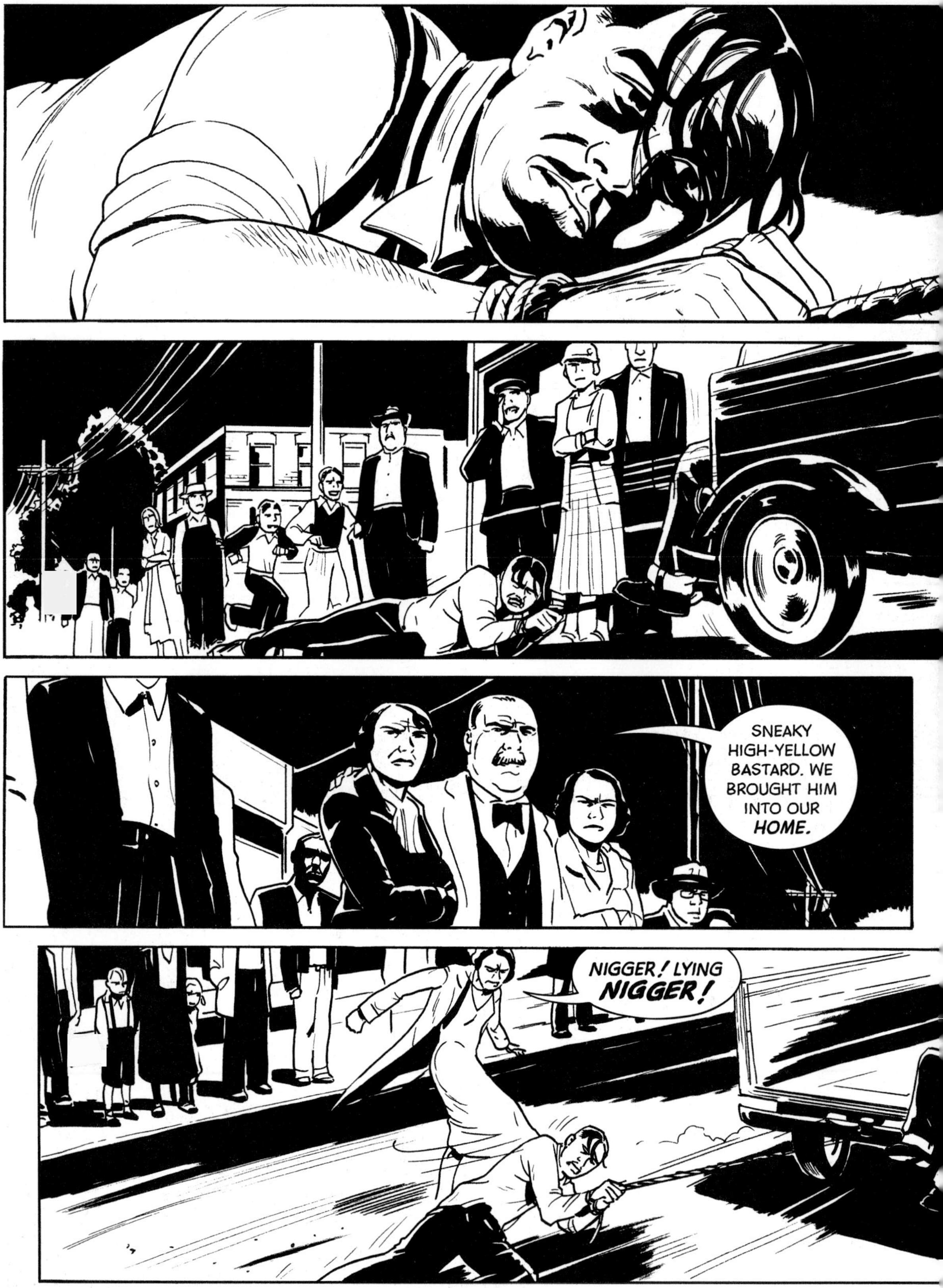
SNEAKY HIGH-YELLOW BASTARD. WE BROUGHT HIM INTO OUR HOME.
NIGGER! LYING NIGGER!

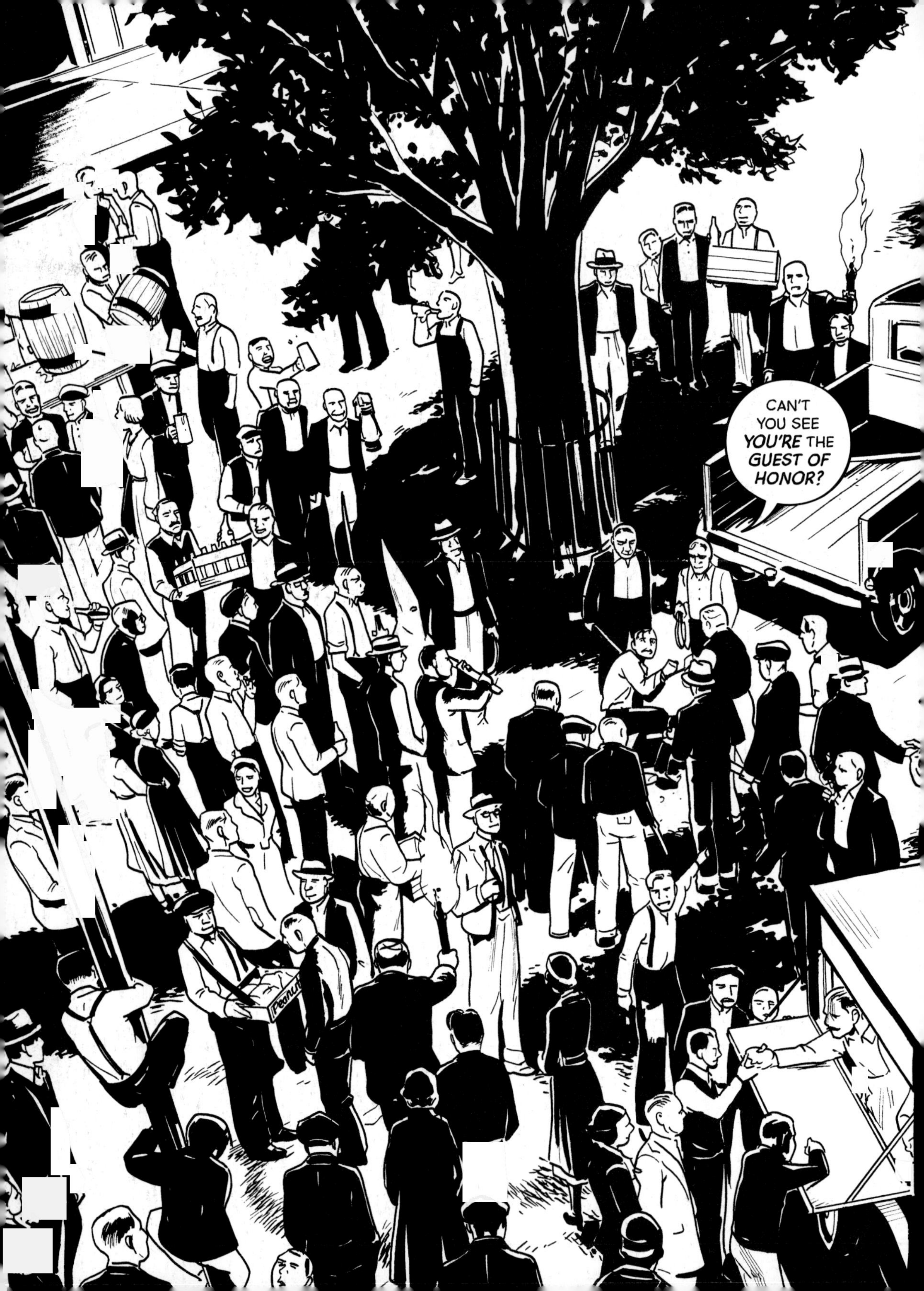
CAN'T YOU SEE *YOU'RE* THE *GUEST OF HONOR?*
Peanuts

# PART III

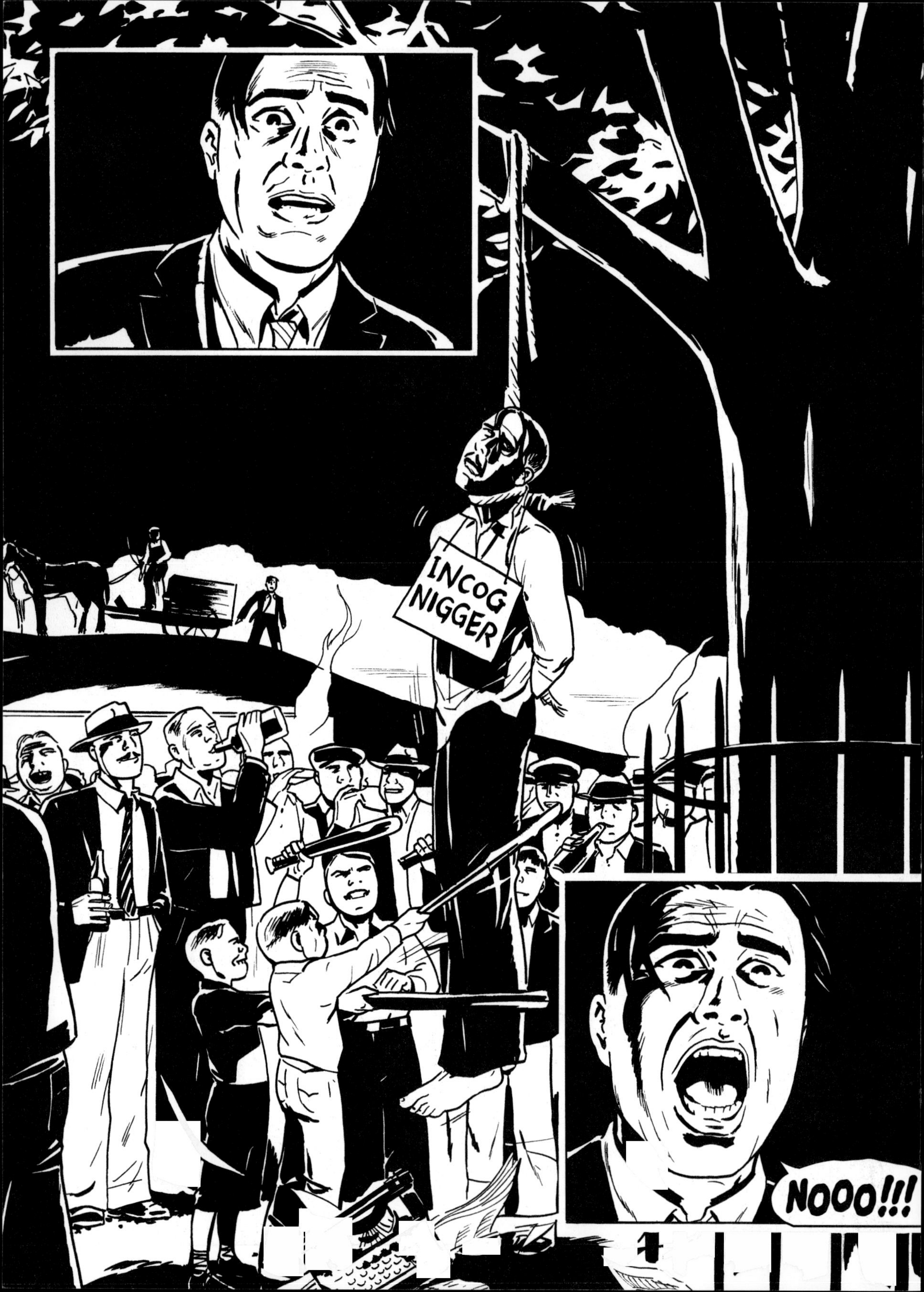
INCOG NIGGER
NOOO!!!

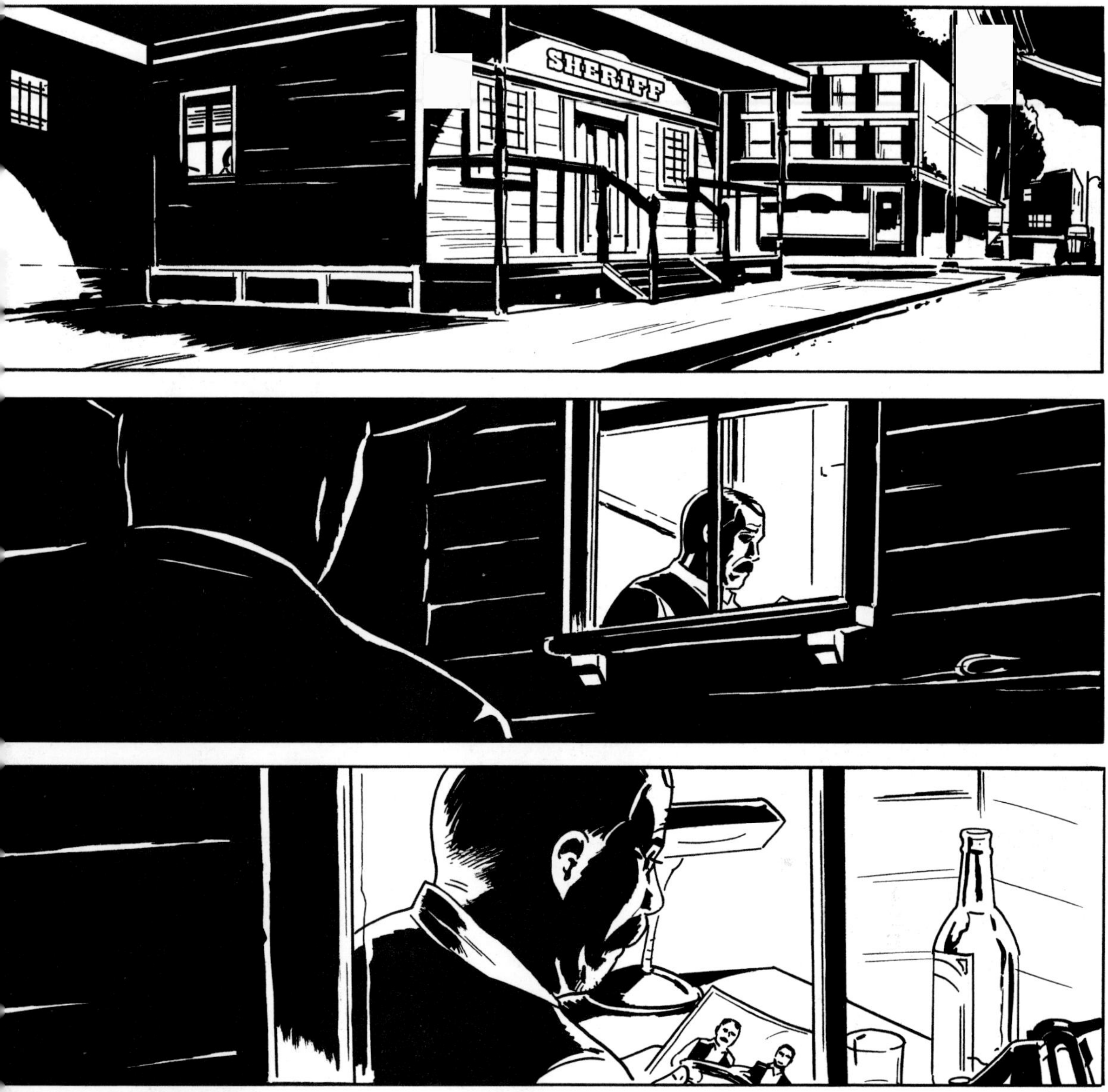
SHERIFF

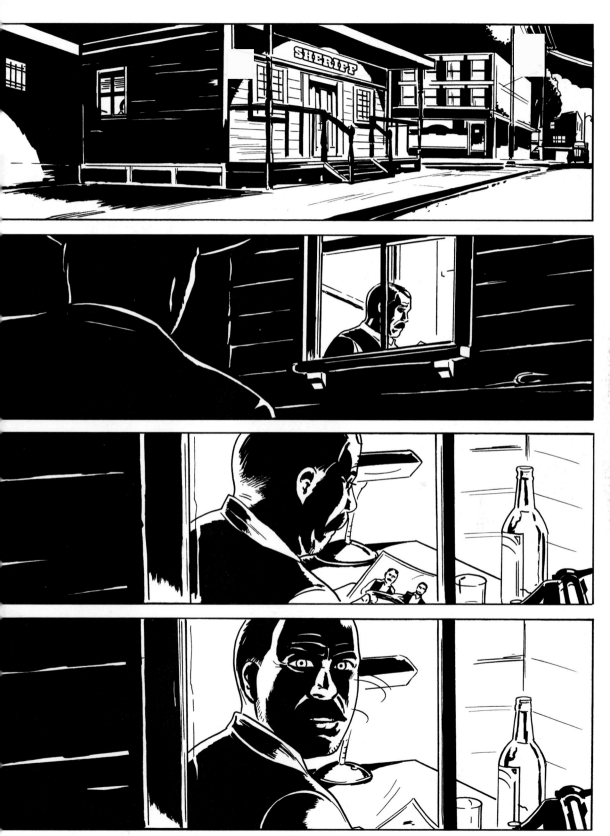

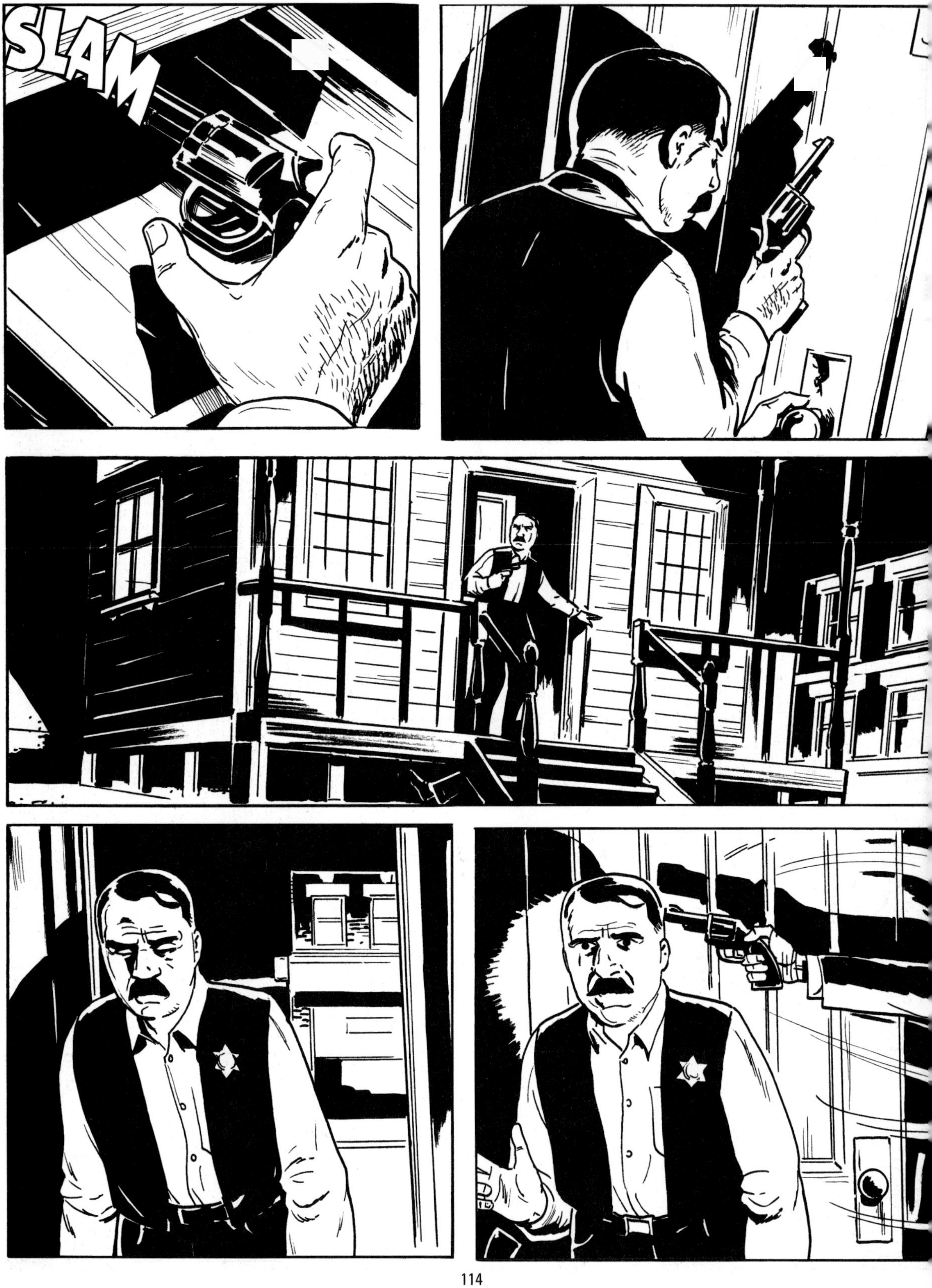
SLAM

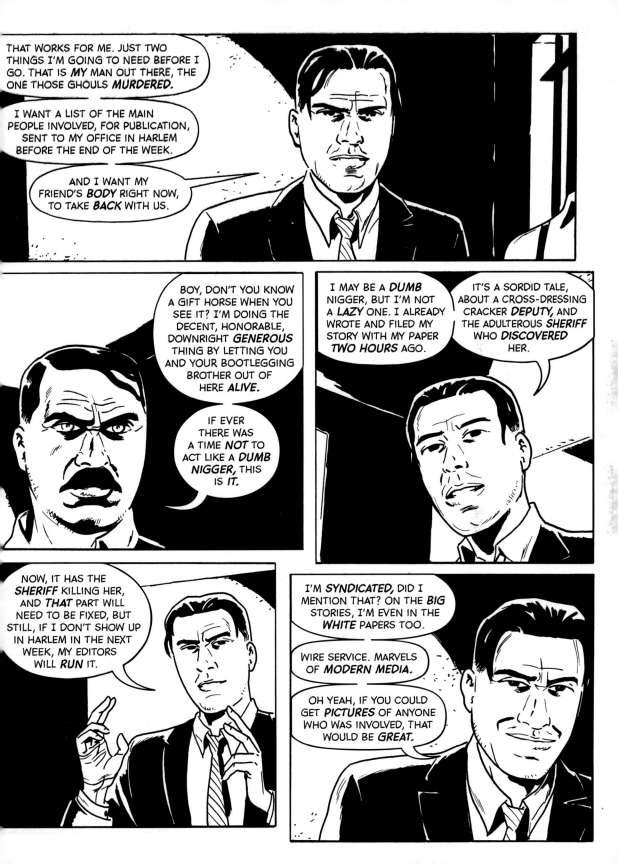

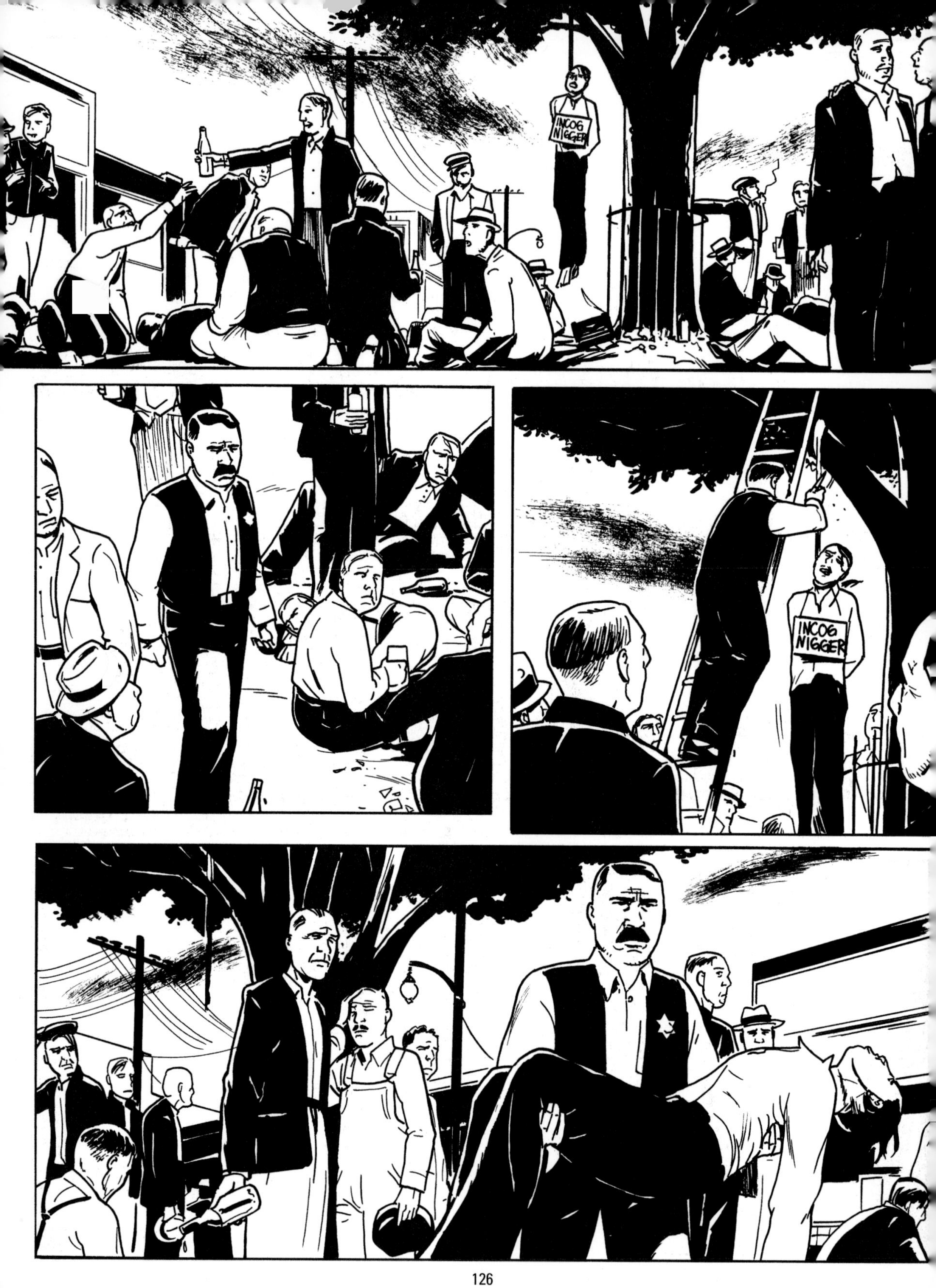
INCOG NIGGER
INCOG NIGGER

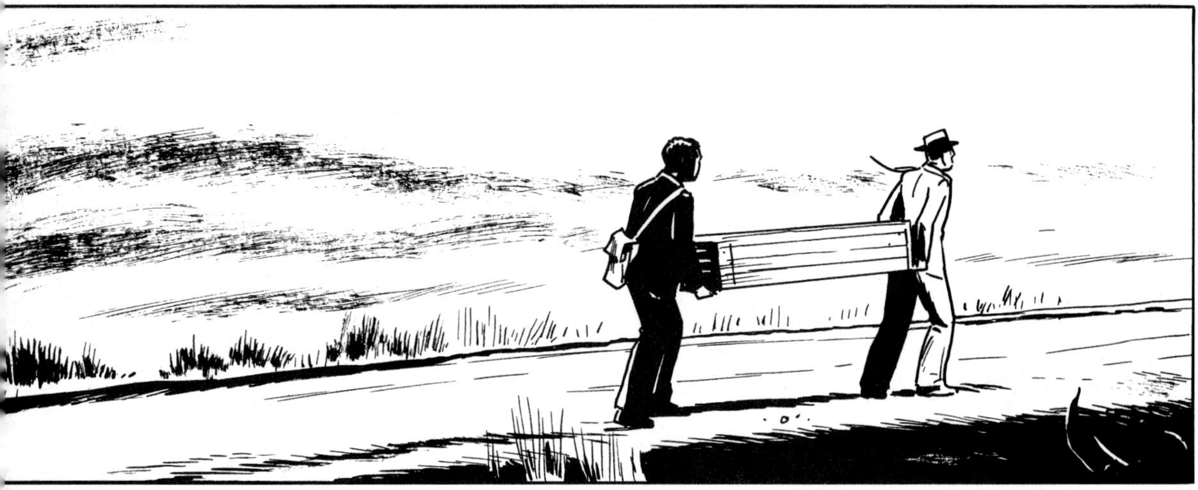

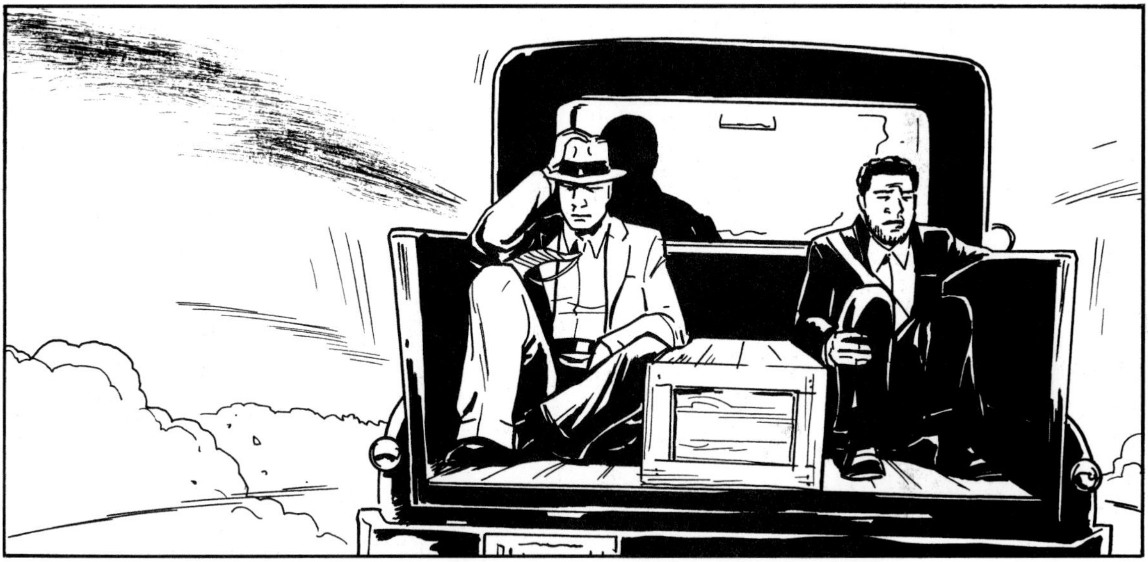

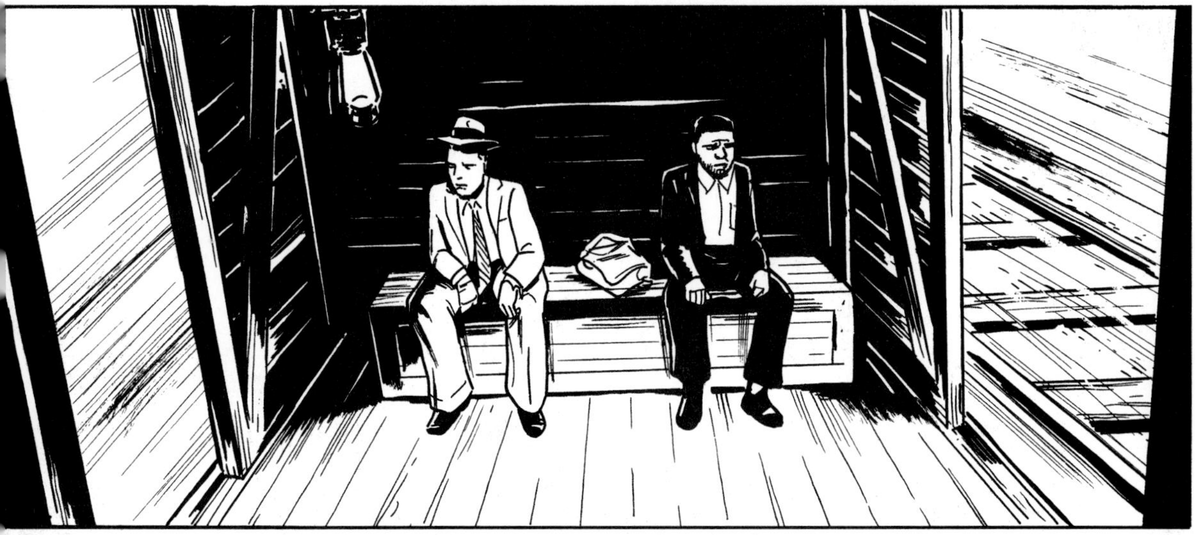

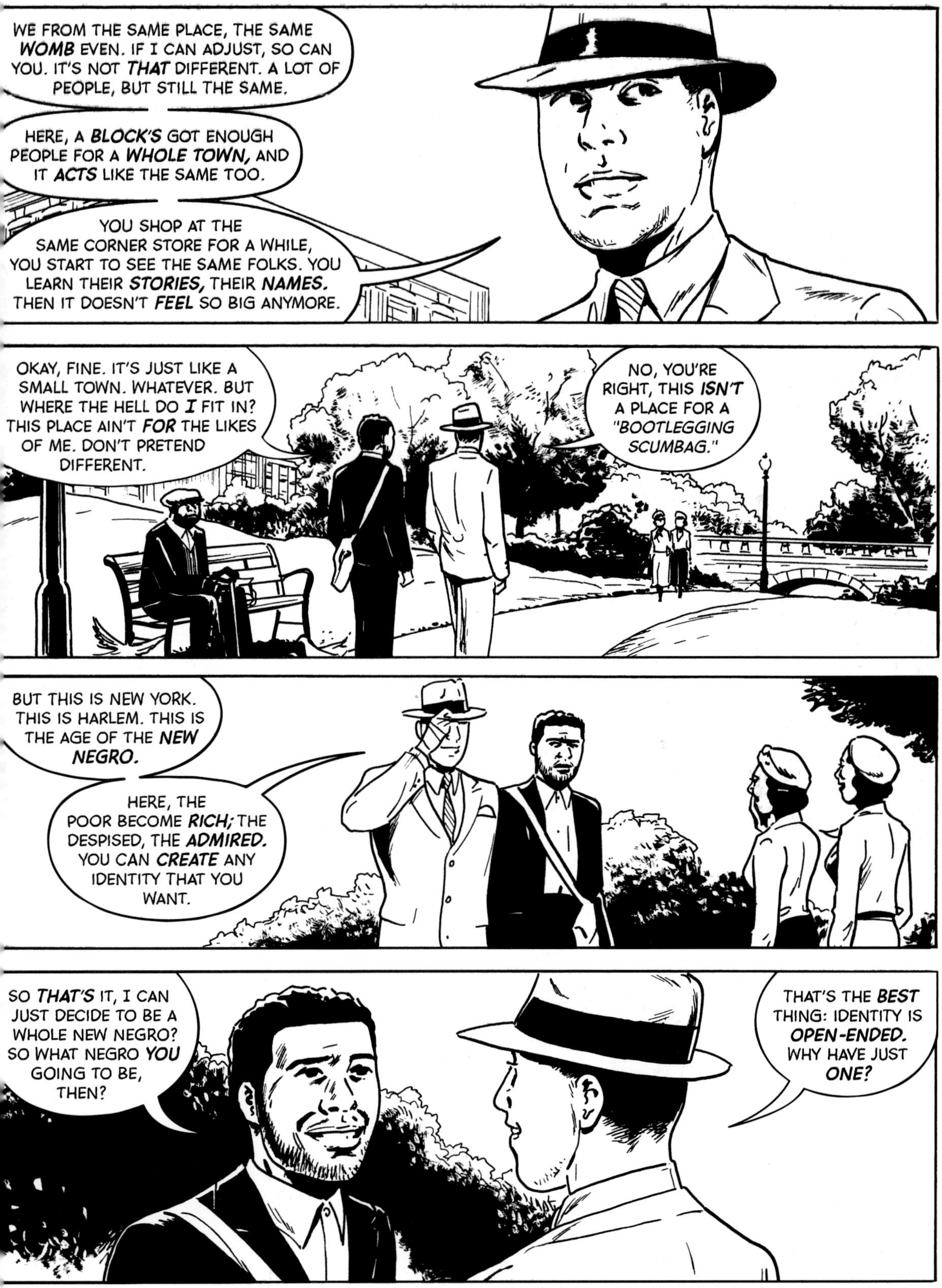
WE FROM THE SAME PLACE, THE SAME WOMB EVEN. IF I CAN ADJUST, SO CAN YOU. IT'S NOT THAT DIFFERENT. A LOT OF PEOPLE, BUT STILL THE SAME.
HERE, A BLOCK'S GOT ENOUGH PEOPLE FOR A WHOLE TOWN, AND IT ACTS LIKE THE SAME TOO.
YOU SHOP AT THE SAME CORNER STORE FOR A WHILE, YOU START TO SEE THE SAME FOLKS. YOU LEARN THEIR STORIES, THEIR NAMES. THEN IT DOESN'T FEEL SO BIG ANYMORE.
OKAY, FINE. IT'S JUST LIKE A SMALL TOWN. WHATEVER. BUT WHERE THE HELL DO I FIT IN? THIS PLACE AIN'T FOR THE LIKES OF ME. DON'T PRETEND DIFFERENT.
NO, YOU'RE RIGHT, THIS ISN'T A PLACE FOR A "BOOTLEGGING SCUMBAG."
BUT THIS IS NEW YORK. THIS IS HARLEM. THIS IS THE AGE OF THE NEW NEGRO.
HERE, THE POOR BECOME RICH; THE DESPISED, THE ADMIRED. YOU CAN CREATE ANY IDENTITY THAT YOU WANT.
SO THAT'S IT, I CAN JUST DECIDE TO BE A WHOLE NEW NEGRO? SO WHAT NEGRO YOU GOING TO BE, THEN?
THAT'S THE BEST THING: IDENTITY IS OPEN-ENDED. WHY HAVE JUST ONE?

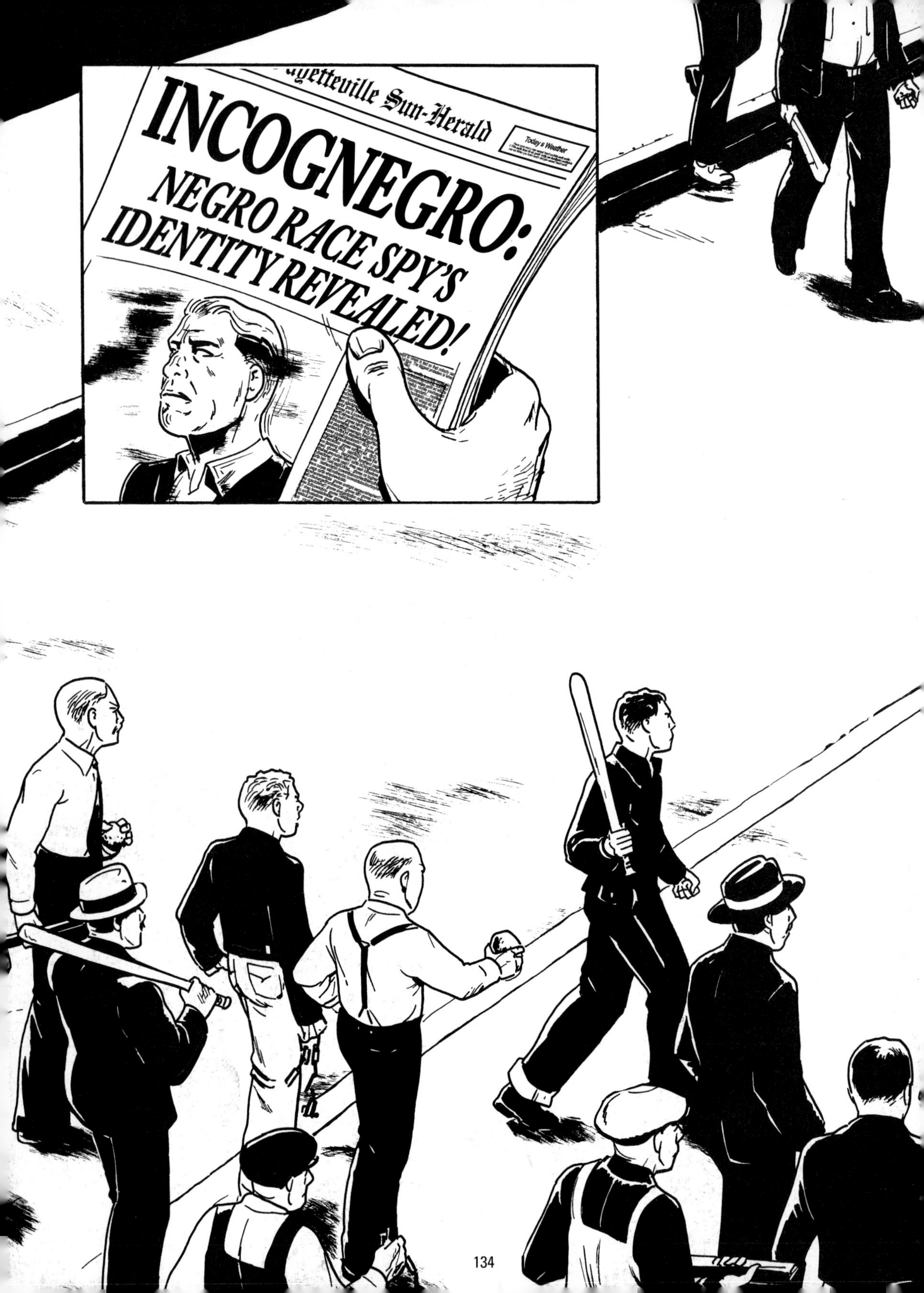
ayetteville Sun-Herald
Today's Weather
INCOGNEGRO:
NEGRO RACE SPY'S
IDENTITY REVEALED!

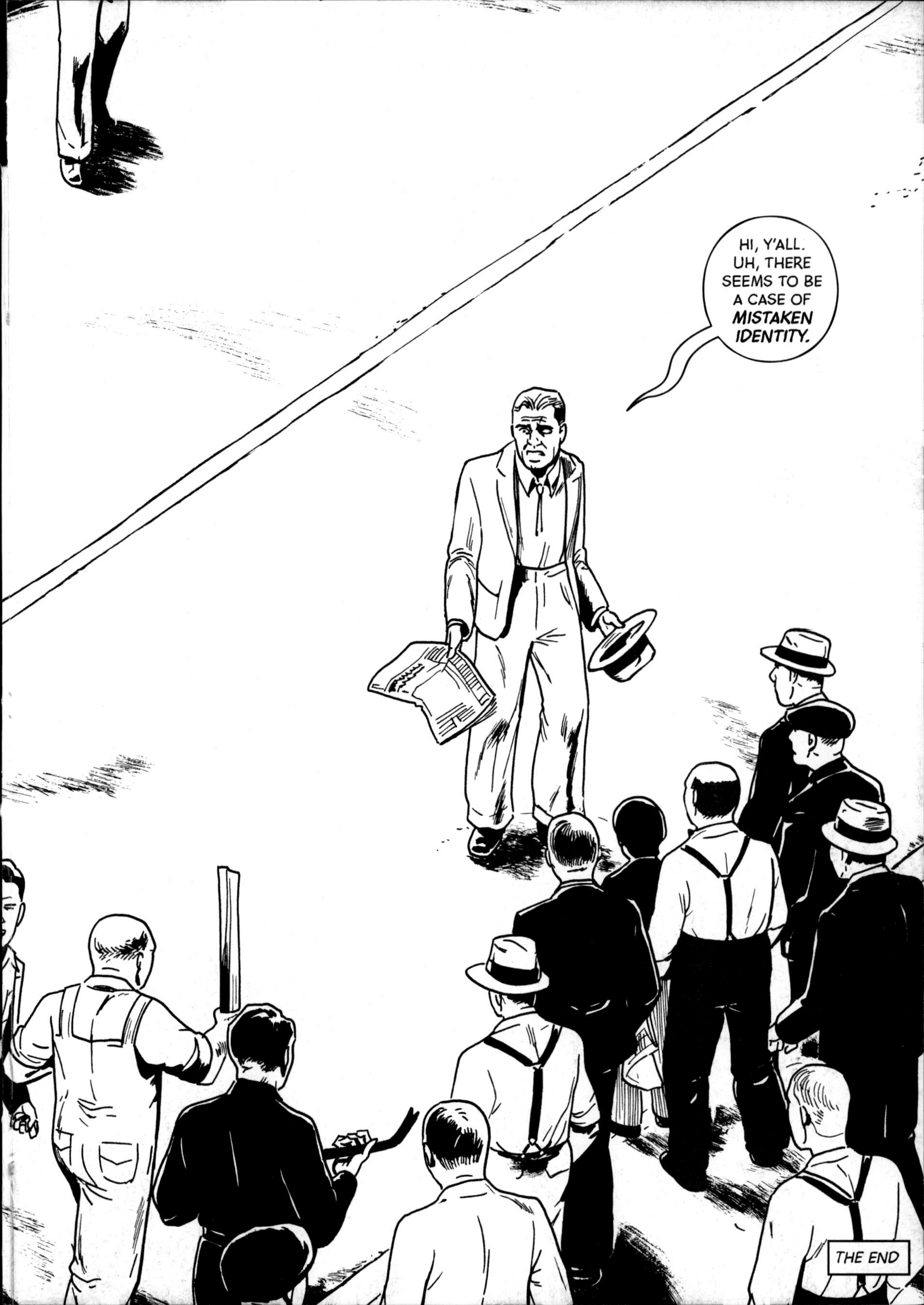
HI, Y'ALL. UH, THERE SEEMS TO BE A CASE OF *MISTAKEN IDENTITY.*
THE END

**Mat Johnson** is the award-winning author of the novels *Drop* and *Hunting in Harlem*, the nonfiction book *The Great Negro Plot*, and Vertigo's graphic novel *Hellblazer: Papa Midnite*. Mat is the recipient of the Hurston-Wright Legacy Award for fiction and the USA James Baldwin Fellowship for Literature. He is a writing professor at the University of Houston's Creative Writing Program and lives in the loop of Houston, Texas with his family.

**Warren Pleece** started drawing on his Dad's jazz records in the late '60s, before progressing through a greyish, '70s education to art college in the '80s. Inspired by old black & white films and fueled by the ridiculousness of Thatcher's Britain, he started the magazine *Velocity* with his brother, Gary, before moving on to work for Dark Horse and DC/Vertigo in the comics mainstream. He has worked on many titles for DC, including *True Faith*, *Hellblazer* and *Deadenders*, but still gets a kick out of drawing over priceless Blue Note album sleeves. He lives in Brighton, on the south coast of England, with his wife and two sons.